The Four Horsemen

The Winds of Theopolitical Change

Curtis Liebl

ISBN: 979-8-9914759-0-7

All Scripture is taken from the New American Standard Bible (NASB) unless otherwise noted.

This book references The Exhaustive Concordance of the Bible, generally known as Strong's Concordance, it is a Bible concordance, constructed under the direction of American theologian James Strong. This source an index of every word in the New American Standard Bible (NASB).

Each original-language word (Hebrew or Greek) is given an entry number in the dictionary of those original language words listed in the back of the concordance. These have become known as the "Strong's numbers".

This allows the user of the concordance to look up the meaning of the original language word in the associated dictionary in the back, thereby showing how the original language word was translated into the English word

Acknowledgment

For the many hours spent putting thoughts into script, no author truly writes from a vacuum. We are all the product of countless experiences and years of learning, during which many people touch our lives.

I want to thank my mother and my very first teacher, whose dedication and faith laid the foundation for my walk with Jesus/Yeshua. Both of my parents left this world way too young; we will be together again. To all the teachers in my life and especially my pastors growing up, Reinhold and Lydia Sass, who were faithful to pass on their great faith and biblical insights.

I want to thank my family, my wife Becki, our six children, and five grandchildren; you know what you mean to me. I love you!

An undying appreciation for the biblical prophets of old whose messages wcrc often ignored and overlooked. Their lives have inspired countless believers to live their own lives of faith and to never give up.

Finally, to My Lord and Savior, Yeshua, the True Messiah, who is the reason I live and whose return I anxiously await. To Yahweh God, Father of all, Creator of the universe, thank you for believing in humanity through all of our brokenness.

To quote the words of that old Sunday School song, "I have decided to follow Jesus, and if none go with me, still I will follow, no turning back, no turning back!"

CONTENTS

Acknowledgment iii

About the Author ix

Preface... xi

Introduction xv

Chapter 1 – The Four Winds of Heaven 1

    Winds Versus Spirits.. 10

    The Patrol... 14

    The Bronze Mountains 19

    Out of the North 20

    The Mount of Assembly 24

    Yahweh Sabaoth.. 30

    The "Sons of God" 34

        The Mesopotamian Context... 37

Chapter 2 – The Four Horns and the Four Craftsmen.............. 38

    The Scatterers... 39

    The Strategists.. 42

    Appointed Times.. 46

Chapter 3 – Four Horsemen 54

    The White Horse 56

The Red Horse 59

The Black Horse.. 63

The Pale or Ashen Horse 66

Chapter 4 - The First City Builders............................. 71

The Great Flood 75

The Table of Nations - The Sixteen Grandsons of Noah 77

The Seven Sons of Japheth 79

The Four Sons of Ham 82

The Five Sons of Shem 84

Seventy Nations and The Seventy Sons of God.................... 86

Yahweh's Portion... 90

Chapter 5 – The Rebellion of Nimrod 95

The First Rebellion.. 97

The Great Rebellion 104

Babel – National Rebellion 112

Chapter 6 - Post-flood Cities and Kingdoms 117

Babel – The Prototype City.. 120

Babylon's Origins 127

Early Jerusalem, The Foundation Stone 130

Joshua, Son of Nun 141

The Jerusalem of Joshua 146

The Jerusalem of King David 149

The Adversary Stood Up.................................... 152

Solomon Builds the Temple in Jerusalem........................ 155

Babylon Rising.. 161

Jerusalem Falls 176

Not All is Lost! 177

Chapter 7 – Daniel's Image of the Beast – 605 BCE............. 180

The Medes and Persians – 539 BCE 187

Cyrus, The Great 193

Zerubbabel Rebuilds - 536 BCE 198

Prophetic Cycles 199

A Final Analysis of the Restoration of Jerusalem.............. 211

Chapter 8 – The Horn of Greece, Alexander the Great - 334 BCE
.... 215

The Horn Wars.. 220

The Conspicuous Horn Between the Eyes.......................224

Greece Divided – 323 BCE.............................. 227

Antiochus VI Epiphanes (or Epimanes?).......................... 229

The Syrian Wars.. 231

The New Culture vs the Old Ways 233

The Abomination (which brings) Desolation – 168 BCE.. 236

The Maccabean Revolt.. 238

The Oppressor Analysis 241

The Yasha 249

Chapter 9 – The Great Roman Empire – 146 BCE................ 253

The 400 Silent Years... 255

Israel Under Roman Rule.. 258

Yeshua, the Messiah - 2 BCE to 32 CE 260

The Fig Tree Parable... 265

The Fig Tree Prophecy.. 267

The Roman Oppressor 268

Not One Stone Left Upon Another! 270

Titus and the Oppressor model 271

Chapter 10 – The Four Apocalyptic Horsemen – 70 CE 276

The War Horse 279

The Horse of Chaos... 280

The Dark Horse 283

The Death Horse 285

Wild Beasts of the Earth 287

Gain-of-Function Research 289

The Pale Horse in 70 CE.. 293

Chapter 11 – The Culmination of the Metal Empires 297

Two Women, Two Cities, and Two Destinies 303

Jezebel, the Seductress 309

The Greater Disruptor 321

"News Flash, Stop the Press!" 322

The Book with Seven Seals 326

Chapter 12 - The Final Ride of the Four Horsemen, the Assembling of the Nations 330

The Countermove, Marxism 333

The First Seal is Broken 339

The Rise of the Nation of Israel 345

What About China, You Ask? 347

The Global Shift of 1917 349

The Second Seal is Broken 352

The Third Seal is Broken 355

It All Came Crashing Down 356

The Fourth Seal is Broken 360

Technologies of the Global Shift 363

The Fifth Seal is Broken 366

The Sixth Seal 376

In Summary 380

References 383

About the Author

Curtis Liebl has been speaking to audiences for over forty-five years. He is a passionate Bible teacher whose work has taken him to seven countries on three continents. He has served in Christian ministry as senior Pastor and founder of River of Life Ministries, a non-denominational Christian church. Today, he is retired from pastoring and now serves as an author and speaker at large.

Curtis has a passion for helping foster an awareness of God's work in the world through what he has called Theopolitics. From the beginning of time, God's plan was a Theocracy, where Yahweh, as the Righteous King, would command a kingdom of peace and prosperity alongside humankind. He originated this reality in the context of a Heavenly Father who is creating a royal dynasty to be inherited by His true sons and daughters. His world is the real world, and everything else is…well…just an illusion.

Page Blank Intentionally

Preface

In order to unpack the mystery of the Four Horsemen, We must first be willing to invest in learning some important context. That context includes a historical framework, an understanding of certain Hebraic or biblical patterns, and a biblical worldview as understood by those closest to Yahweh/God, e.g. Moses, the prophets, and the apostles of Yeshua, and of course Yeshua Himself. It is from this lens that we can see into the spiritual realm and gain a true understanding.

It has taken me years to discover these biblical patterns, but this book will take you through that learning process in a concise and relatively easy manner. In each successive chapter I will build one concept upon another. There may be times when certain ideas or explanations won't immediately make sense, but I assure you, if you continue reading, you will find the answer, and discover some amazing insights that will transform the way you learn about Yahweh and His realm.

One such experience is found in Exodus, contained in the story of Moses. It was during a time when the children of Israel were camped out at the base of Mt Sinai, where the presence of Yahweh was hovering over the mountain top in a thick dark cloud of lighting and thunder. Moses was given the unique invitation to climb the mountain and meet with God. It was at this moment that Moses makes a most interesting request,

*"Now therefore, I pray You, if I have found favor in Your sight, **let me know Your ways that I may know You**, so that I may find favor in Your sight."*

Exodus 33:13 (emphasis added)

Moses was in a position to ask anything from Yahweh. He could have asked about the many mysteries of the universe or insights into the future, but he didn't, instead he asked, "Let me know Your ways, that I might know You." There is a huge tell in this request. You see this is very personal, Moses wanted to know the mind of Yahweh, how He thinks, the way He purposes and plans for His creation. Yahweh would later return this intimacy with this statement,

"If there is a prophet among you, I, the LORD, shall make Myself known to him in a vision.
*I shall speak with him in a dream. **Not so, with My servant Moses,** he is faithful in all My household; **With him I speak mouth to mouth, even openly, and not in dark sayings, and he beholds the form of the LORD**."*

Numbers 12:6-8 (emphasis added)

Consequently, the writings of Moses, Genesis through Deuteronomy, contain the richest of seeds. We will explore what this new understanding reveals, and why it is important to us.

To know Yahweh starts with the way He communicates with us, the language He gave to mankind. I believe the very first language was Hebrew. It is a rich multi-layered language comprised of letters, pictures, and numbers. The Hebrew language itself contains hidden layers of understanding, as captured in the saying, a picture is worth a thousand words. I will explain some of these ideas in this book.

The second way is found in understanding Hebraic patterns. This is the way Yahweh reveals truths to us. Each pattern starts in seed form, then the pattern is repeated over and over again, growing over time. It ultimately produces the fruit of understanding, known as wisdom. This is why Yeshua gave us a parable about a farmer who goes out and sows seed, the seeds are the Words of God, according to the parable. This seed must fall on the good ground of our hearts and grow to produce good fruit. If you can recognize the seed, you can find the pattern and discover the truth hidden in it. Genesis is a book of seeds from which all the patterns come from. I know that is a huge statement, but you will discover more as you read this book.

Some of the seeds we will talk about in this book are found in the first cities and civilizations. Studying these will reveal their purposes, and who is behind their developments. You might remember that Yahweh interrupted the growth of civilization with a great flood, and personally came down to observe the workings of the city of Babel after the flood.

We will discover the introduction of ancient entities and their incursion into our world. You will see how Yahweh must manage our world and the unseen realm at the same time. This was a part of the biblical worldview of most, if not all of, the writers that contributed to the Bible as we know it.

For example, there is a reason why Genesis starts with the development of the city of Babel and the book of Revelation ends with the destruction of Babylon. Genesis starts with the guarded city of Shalem (ancient Jerusalem) and ends in Revelation with the exaltation of the Holy City of Jerusalem. These two themes run throughout the entire Bible. This is the true Tale of Two Cities.

You will be introduced to the Four Horsemen, the Four Horns, and the Four Craftsmen, placing them all in the context of two realms, the seen and the unseen. Their expressed purpose is to patrol the earth and manage the geopolitics of civilizations over the course of time, guiding humanity to an ultimate outcome: the establishment of the Kingdom of Yahweh on earth. How will this happen and are there signs we can observe that revealed when and where these incursions took place, and will take place in the future?

We will learn from an examination of history and the Bible, including extra-biblical writings, that rebellion is not unique to the human race, and Yahweh has ways of quashing these types of revolts. He has a vast supernatural army of heavenly hosts who engage in righteous campaigns. He has an appointed council of advisors that are seated in His presence to help make decisions that impact our world.

Finally, this is not a work of fiction. These ideas are seeds of truth found in the Bible, which are Yahweh's words to us, and they are also seen through the framework of history (His-story). He communicated these truths over the course of time, through prophets, and ultimately through Yeshua, and continues to reveal them to us through His many ways.

Introduction

A good historian will eventually ask the question, "What shapes our world?"

Although the answer to that question may be complicated, I discovered that when we distill down historical events, what emerges are four major forces at work that are constantly bringing about change. We will discuss these ominous forces as the focus of this book.

The British Statesman Sir Winston Churchill wrote, "Those who fail to learn from history are doomed to repeat it."[1]

We often look at history as a linear progression of people and events, national powers that exist for a time and then mysteriously disappear or fade into the past. Yet history is more cyclical than linear. Patterns begin to appear over years, decades, or even centuries. The world map constantly changes, and great leaders rise and fall, but the story seems vaguely similar in the passing of each great civilization.

There are various but similar patterns observed over time. For example, when a society has become weakened by famine or pestilence, Empirical forces will often seek to invade and conquer new territories.

A quote from an article by History.com talks about the devastation that took place because of the Black Plague of the Middle Ages.

"Even before the 'death ships' pulled into port at Messina, many

Europeans had heard rumors about a 'Great Pestilence' that was carving a deadly path across the trade routes of the Near and Far East. Indeed, in the early 1340s, the disease had struck China, India, Persia, Syria, and Egypt."[2]

By the end of what was known as the Decade of Plague, one-third of the population of Europe was wiped out. We saw the beginning of the Hundred Years War (1337-1453) between France and England and the disastrous Byzantine Civil War (1341-1347), resulting in shifts of political power in Europe, Africa, and China. These changes ultimately weakened the Roman Papal control over Europe, giving way to freedom of Christian thought and expression. This movement formed modern Protestantism and eventually a new era called the Age of Enlightenment.

Another example is how religious wars fuel the subjugation of neighboring cities, states, and even regions. The arrival of Islam in the 7th century led to the rise of the Ottoman Empire, which held power over the Middle East for centuries. During this time, there were many wars fought over Jerusalem and the Jewish homeland, but the strong arm of the Ottomans remained firm. The Jewish people would not return to their land for more than 1200 years, not until after WWI in 1917 CE.

The question to ask is, was there a reason the nation of Israel was prevented from rising again until these latter days? Does this suggest that supernatural forces were at work preventing their return, and was the realignment of the nations used to accomplish that outcome? We will shed light on the answers to these questions in the chapters to come.

Some of our bloodiest wars have been fought because of deeply held religious ideologies. War and conflict bring change; some changes improve the human condition, while others cause oppression and hardship. What can we learn from these patterns?

In an address made by British Prime Minister Harold Macmillan to the Parliament of South Africa on February 3, 1960, in Cape Town, Macmillan states the following:

"The wind of change is blowing through this continent. Whether we like it or not, this growth of national consciousness is a political fact."[3]

Mr. Macmillan uses the metaphor of wind to describe these types of changes. Although scientifically, we can define the properties of winds, they are still perceived as unseen forces that shape our natural world. The power of wind changes the world's climate. Forces of wind, such as hurricanes and tornados, can decimate populations. They can bring with them scorching heat or bitter cold.

Are there supernatural forces, just like the winds, responsible for shaping the landscape of human history…or even about to change our future?

Did you know that the bible talks about the Four Winds of Heaven, Four Horns, Four Craftsmen, and the Four Horsemen? In the pages that follow, we will explore the meaning of these biblical figures, these supernatural off-world forces that have existed from the beginning of civilization.

Chapter 1 – The Four Winds of Heaven

"I will bring upon Elam the four winds from the four ends of heaven, and will scatter them to all these winds; And there will be no nation."

Jeremiah 49:36

An ancient story tells of a "divine wind" that twice saved Japan from Kublai Khan's Mongol fleets. So powerful was the legend that centuries later, thousands of World War II pilots known as kamikazes would sign up to protect Japan again by crashing their planes in suicide missions.

During the 13th century, in 1274 and 1281 AD, led by Kublai Khan, grandson of Genghis Khan, the Mongols attempted two major invasions of Japan. On both occasions, however, a massive typhoon (tropical cyclone) obliterated the Mongol fleet, forcing the attackers to abandon their plans and fortuitously saved Japan from foreign conquest. The Japanese believed the typhoons had been sent by the gods to protect them from their enemies and called them Kamikaze, meaning "divine wind."[4]

To be clear, I am not suggesting that the tragedies of WWII in the Pacific were some form of divine judgment, but rather that their belief in a supernatural force moving through the wind motivated the Japanese in their cause.

The nature of wind itself makes it a powerful force. It is often described as coming from four cardinal directions, north, south, east, and west, hence four winds. Powerful jet streams usher in our seasons and change global climates. Wind can be a devastating force; like in the story of the kamikaze, it can decimate areas of the world with brief and swift strikes. Could this be why God chose winds to describe the forces that He uses to affect change?

The parallel here is that the kamikaze winds in Japan not only disrupted the battle scene but also changed the outcome of the war twice. The loss incurred by the Mongols prevented a major shift in the geopolitics in that region of the world. These changes in geopolitics can be understood as "the winds of change."

The biblical passage in Jeremiah suggests that four supernatural winds destroyed Elam, and they were no longer a nation. The scriptures are filled with similar references to heaven shaping the nations of the world. We will be exploring this topic as we move forward.

What is geopolitics in simple terms?

Ge·o·pol·i·tics (jē'ō-pŏl'ĭ-tĭks), noun; A combination of geographic and political factors relating to or influencing a nation or region.

The word geopolitics was originally coined by the Swedish political scientist Rudolf Kjellén about the turn of the 20th century, and its use spread throughout Europe in the period between World Wars I and II (1918–39) and came into worldwide use during the latter.[5]

This term is used to describe how our world changes and what factors are behind these changes. History and the Bible are filled with references to the rise and fall of cities and empires. Some of these regime changes are actually critical to God's plans.

For example, the fall of Babylon in 539 BC shifted regional power from the Babylonians to the Medo-Persian King, Cyrus the Great. It was Cyrus who would make a decree that would release the Jewish exiles to return to their homeland exactly 70 years from their original Babylonian captivity, fulfilling the prophecy given by Jeremiah,

> *"This whole land will be a desolation and a horror, and these nations will serve the king of Babylon **seventy years**."*
>
> *Jeremiah 25:11* (emphasis added)

At the end of seventy years, it would become necessary for the chains of Babylonian oppression to be broken off of the Jewish exiles so they could return to their land and begin rebuilding. How would this happen, and what action would be required to change their seemingly hopeless situation?

A biblical prophecy in Isaiah 44:28 declares that this same Cyrus would do God's bidding and release the exiled Jews to return and rebuild their cities. The interesting fact is that this prophecy was given one hundred years before Cyrus was born.

> *"It is I who says of Cyrus, 'He is My shepherd! And he will perform all My desire.' and he declares of Jerusalem, 'She will be built,' And of the temple, 'Your foundation will be laid.'"*
>
> *"Thus says the LORD to Cyrus His anointed, whom I have taken by the right hand, To subdue nations before him and to lose the loins of kings; to open doors before him so that gates will not be shut."*
>
> *Isaiah 44:28; 45:1*

As stated, these two prophecies were given to Isaiah over one hundred years before Cyrus was born and decades before Israel was besieged and exiled. At the time, these words would fall on deaf ears, but the prophecy would most certainly come true. Yahweh wanted to remove any doubt as to who was shaping these events.

For many years I explained this type of prophecy as - God knows all things, so He looked into the future and dictated these events back to the prophets as He saw them unfold. So, then I could stop thinking about it, right?!…so I thought. Eventually I began to discover there are too many scriptural and historical clues that tell us a different story. The Bible reveals that there are spiritual forces at work behind the scenes and that well-orchestrated strategies often create these changes.

In another example, we have a glimpse behind the veil in the book of Daniel, where an angelic messenger is prevented from coming to Daniel because he was doing battle with the "prince" of the kingdom of Persia. It was revealed this was not a human prince but a supernatural principality holding power over that region. It reads,

> *"Then he said to me, "Do not be afraid, Daniel, for from the first day that you set your heart on understanding this and on humbling yourself before your God, your words were heard, and I have come in response to your words. But **the prince of the kingdom of Persia was withstanding me for twenty-one days;** then behold, Michael, one of the chief princes, came to help me, for I had been left there with the kings of Persia."*

Daniel 10:12-13 (emphasis added)

A territorial principality was fighting with the angel Gabriel while trying to advance the (human) kings of Persia. This type of altering of historical events can be considered the effects of the winds of change, but these winds are not as benign as a jet stream or storm system; they seem to have a distinct personality and purpose. The force of just one of these supernatural gale storms will reshape a region like the swift-moving sands in a desert, what was familiar can become quickly unrecognizable. They move with intelligence, like a well-trained militia, disarming any opposing obstacles.

When the veil of the physical world is pulled back, we see a cosmic battleground, an interplay of good and evil forces. These beings are not human, but they are created spirit beings. In a biblical worldview, we reduce them to angels and demons, but that doesn't completely describe the multiple variations of beings created by Yahweh, and I might add, likely formed eons before the creation of man.

There are several types of angels created for different purposes. The Hebrew word for angel is *malak,* which simply means "messenger" (Strong's H4397). Interestingly, it is the same Hebrew consonant root *m-l-k* from which the word *melek or* "king" is derived. I believe this informs us that angels are not just couriers of information. They are powerful beings that are given various levels of dominion, as we would understand a human king to have.

Just like the title of king is not the name of a species, "angel" is not a name, but a description attached to a specific spirit-world being who is given authority. These messengers would be better compared to a foreign ambassador. An ambassador is someone sent by a government and given authority to represent that country's interests in the host region. Angels are sent from their heavenly domain by the authority of Yahweh into the earthly realm. His earthly embassy is located in the territory known as Israel, in the city of Jerusalem. Many angelic visions have occurred in or near the Holyland, although they also are observed wherever God's people are.

Among the different classes of messengers, one of the more powerful angels is the Watcher Class. In the bible, Watcher Class angels or holy ones as they are called in some places, are mentioned in the book of Daniel.

> *" 'I was looking in the visions in my mind as I lay on my bed, and behold, **an angelic watcher, a holy one**, descended from heaven...' "*
>
> *"In that the king saw **an angelic watcher, a holy one**, descending from heaven and saying, 'Chop down the tree and destroy it'... "*
>
> *Daniel 4:13, 23* (emphasis added)

There is an interesting connection between angelic watchers and cities, as seen by examining the original language. The Hebrew word for both watcher and city is *ir*; the root consonants are *a-y-r* (Strong's H5894) and is the same root consonant for both words. It is seen in this passage in Isaiah,

> *"Prepare for his sons a place of slaughter*
> *Because of the iniquity of their fathers.*
> *They must not arise and take possession of the earth*
> ***And fill the face of the world with cities*** *[watchers]. "*
>
> *Isaiah 14:21* (emphasis added)

The "they" in this passage refers to sons of the fallen ones, who are "their fathers." The elusive subject of Isaiah 14:4-20 is Lucifer, star of the morning, son of the dawn. I will explain more about this in chapter five, "The First Rebellion."

The fact that the word for "cities" here is the same word as "watchers," tells us there is a connection between the two ideas. According to this passage then, is the world going to be filled with more cities or more watchers, or both? We must look deeper into this link.

When the Old Testament was translated into the Greek language, the Septuagint, translators chose the Greek word *egrḗgoroi* for "watcher," meaning "wakeful," and "those who are awake or guard" for these angelic beings. One explanation may be that a heavenly watcher is an angel, sent to protect or watch over a city.

To support this claim, the Genesis story of Lot, Abraham's nephew, tells us two angels came to the cities of Sodom and Gomorrah to bring judgment upon them because of their sins. We find here these Watchers did more than just watch; they were not only sent with a message of divine judgment but were also responsible for raining down the destructive fire and brimstone.

> *"When morning dawned, the angels urged Lot, saying, 'Up, take your wife and your two daughters who are here, or you will be swept away in the punishment of the city.'"*
>
> *"'Hurry, escape there [Zoar], **for I cannot do anything until you arrive there.**'"*
>
> *Genesis 19:15, 22* (emphasis and brackets added)

The apocryphal Books of Enoch (2nd–1st centuries BC) refer to both good and bad Watchers, with a primary focus on the rebellious ones. "In the Books of Enoch, the first Book of Enoch devotes much of its attention to the fall of the watchers. The second Book of Enoch addresses the watchers who are in the fifth heaven where the fall took place. The third Book of Enoch gives attention to the unfallen watchers."[6]

"In the Book of Enoch, the watchers are angels dispatched to Earth to watch over the humans. They soon begin to lust for human women and, at the prodding of their leader, Samyaza, defect to illicitly instruct humanity and procreate among them. The offspring of these unions are the Nephilim, savage giants who pillage the earth and endanger humanity."[7]

We will discuss more about the fallen angels of the book of Enoch and their connection to Genesis 6 in another section of this book titled "The Great Rebellion."

According to the book of Enoch, the fallen angels produced offspring from their unholy union with human women. These offspring are known as Nephilim or giants. Upon their death, these spirits are left to wander the earth realm and become those whom we call demons and evil or unclean spirits.

In summary, we have seen how these four winds are supernatural beings with intelligence and purpose. Whether these are four in number, or four legions is unclear. They have a role in the cosmic struggle of good and evil over which Yahweh is in control. He appears to delegate these tasks to other heavenly beings. There is an opposing spirit force made up of fallen angels and their hybrid offspring called the Nephilim, who make up the demonic forces of evil.

All of this sounds like a work of fiction to the average reader. Even mainstream Christian churches have sanitized this message from their bible discussions and sermons. The so called era of enlightenment elicited the removal of any reference to these spiritual realities of the Bible. The truth of the matter is that this spiritual world was a major part of the biblical worldview of those who wrote the Bible. We need to rediscover the world where Yahweh lives, where true reality exists.

Winds Versus Spirits

*"Now I lifted up my eyes again and looked, and behold, **four chariots were coming forth** from between the two mountains, and the mountains were bronze mountains. With the **first chariot were red horses**, with **the second chariot black horses**, with **the third chariot white horses**, and with **the fourth chariot strong dappled horses**. Then I spoke and said to the angel who was speaking with me, "What are these, my lord?"*

*The angel replied to me, **'These are the four spirits of heaven, going forth after standing before the Lord of all the earth.'"***

Zechariah 6:1-5 (emphasis added)

It is clear from this passage that the four spirits ARE the four horsemen and vice versa; they are heavenly beings described as having military-like distinction. Policing terms are used to explain their movements, like standing or riding on patrol and coming in or going out, in the sense of missions. What was their heavenly mission? Some questions to ask here are: what is the explanation for their enlistment, and how does that connect to the timing of biblical events?

In an earlier example, we learned that it was critical in 539 BC that Cyrus, King of Persia, would be willing to release God's people back to Jerusalem to rebuild the city and the temple. A prophet of that day, Zechariah, was told that the four spirits of heaven would be used to help accomplish this. They were created for this purpose and enlisted into the service of God, whom I will refer to by His name, Yahweh.

We find more clarity in a word-study of wind and spirit. The same Hebrew word used for both "wind" and "spirit," it is *ruach*. The

Strong's definition, H7307, *ruach* means "breath, wind, or spirit," all three of these words are interchangeable. For example, this same word for wind, *ruach,* is used for the Holy Spirit – *Ruach* (Spirit) *HaKodesh* (The Holy).

The idea formed around these words would be compared to a man breathing or blowing. Breath is a force that originates from within a man and extends out from himself, carrying some biological essence (think of the odor of breath) with it. The Holy Spirit is the essence of God (spirit) that proceeds from God (breath) into the world, just like the wind. This could actually be called "Divine Wind," by definition.

Yeshua/Jesus gave us a picture of this in John 20:22,

> *"And when He had said this* (to his disciples)*, He breathed on them and said to them, 'Receive the Holy Spirit.'"*

> (Parenthesis added)

And on Shavuot (The Day of Pentecost) in Acts 2:1-4, it says,

> *"When the day of Pentecost had come, they were all together in one place. And suddenly there came from heaven a noise like a violent **rushing wind**, and it filled the whole house where they were sitting... And they were all **filled with the Holy Spirit**."*

> *Acts 2:1-4* (emphasis added)

Yeshua was showing his disciples, when He breathed on them, that what they were about to experience on that Feast Day was His presence blowing into that upper room. They had no doubt who was in the wind and that it was the Spirit of Yeshua filling them. Yeshua offers us this insight in His priestly prayer for us in John 17.

*"The glory which You have given Me I have given to them, that they may be one, just as We are one; **I in them and You in Me**, that they may be perfected in unity."*

John 17:22-23 (emphasis added)

The joining of spirits is an essential part of Yeshua's ministry and mission. The upgrade from the Old Covenant to the New Covenant includes that Yahweh's Law could now be written in our hearts and minds as opposed to just a Torah Scroll for us to read. There is also included with the New Covenant, a change in nature, the constant presence of a new nature imparted to the believer.

*"Moreover, **I will give you a new heart and put a new spirit within you,** and I will remove the heart of stone from your flesh and give you a heart of flesh. I will put My Spirit within you and cause you to walk in My statutes, and you will be careful to observe My ordinances."*

Ezekiel 36:26-27 (emphasis added)

We are never meant to walk this path alone. Yeshua promises to be with us, close to us, deeply within us. It is because of His abiding presence we can overcome this world and rise above the darkness.

In a dark twist, the enemies of Yahweh, the adversaries of old, try to inhabit the human heart. In a cheap imitation, these evil spirits do not influence men for good but blacken the soul and pollute the mind. The battleground is truly in the heart of man, and we all know the struggle is real. We will see this demonic influence as we study the warrior kings of ancient (and modern) empires. They will refer to these spirits as "their gods," they will claim to have achieved divine or demi-god status, like the Sumerian Kings or Egyptian Pharaohs, the rulers of Greece, or the Ceasars of Rome; these renowned men were perceived to possess a divine right to rule over all other men.

As the entire world is swirling with spiritual interplay. Yahweh's army marches forward offering protection for the believer yet delivering harsh consequences for the rebellious. Leading the charge are the four spirits of heaven, who are synonymous with the four winds. These will not allow the enemy to advance too far or take unfair advantage of Yahweh's people. We will see they are also referred to as The Four Horsemen who patrol the earth!

The Patrol

*"I saw at night, and **behold, a man was riding on a red horse**, and he was standing among the myrtle trees which were in the ravine, with red, sorrel, and white horses behind him. Then I said, **"My lord, what are these?"** And the angel who was speaking with me said to me, "I will show you what these are." And the man who was standing among the myrtle trees answered and said, **"These are those whom the LORD has sent to patrol the earth."***

Zechariah 1:8-10 (emphasis added)

This patrol is sent by Yahweh, God (or The Divine Council, more on that later) to carry out their mission in the world. They are tasked with keeping regional powers at bay and effecting change when needed. The idea of patrolling is applied here as a military or policing term. Patrols are sent to guard or protect, gather intelligence, and report back to a commander. Patrols can be given specific missions which focus on a critical outcome. They are also reactionary by nature and will respond to situations that are in line with performing their duties.

When the US Military is operating on foreign soil, they use Special Forces like the Navy SEAL teams to carry out covert missions. These are elite soldiers who are well-trained in full <u>SE</u>a, <u>A</u>ir, and <u>L</u>and tactics, or S.E.A.L.s. They are deployed to engage in direct raids or assaults on enemy targets and conduct reconnaissance missions to report on enemy activity. These strategic forces are essential to the United States retaining a global military advantage and bringing down those opposed to our system of justice.

If mere humans can recruit and train such elite military forces that can effectively change the balance of power in regions of the world, how much more can Yahweh create His supernatural Horsemen who ride with similar precision and purpose? In contrast, these heavenly hosts are sent into the world on righteous missions to keep at bay enemy assaults, enforce order and balance in a region, and assist in planned strategies, even to bring judgment against a disobedient generation of the nation of Israel.

"I have commanded My consecrated ones, I have even called My mighty warriors, My proudly exulting ones, To execute My anger."

Isaiah 13:3

At first glance, it seems that Yahweh is calling the armies of Babylon "His consecrated ones," in this oracle concerning Babylon. In verse 5 of the same chapter of Isaiah, He calls them "His instruments of indignation."

It becomes clear in this passage that the armies of Babylon are being used to bring judgment upon the disobedient nation of Israel. Still, I believe it also reveals the supernatural forces that are at work guiding these earthly armies of Babylon.

The phrase "My mighty warriors" is also used by King David to describe the elite fighting men in his army (2 Samuel 23:8-38).

The Hebrew word for mighty warriors in this passage is *gibborim,* meaning "champions, heroes, or valiant warriors."

The question to ask is, who are Yahweh's valiant warriors?

The answer is His patrol, His elite military forces, the Four Horsemen that carry out His commands. I believe the Horsemen and the heavenly armies marched alongside Babylon's troops to influence the outcome of the war.

A king protects his subjects, an honorable judge renders a finding of the facts, and a righteous military polices their kingdom to uphold law and order. Yahweh is no different in the governance of the world He created. What happens when His creation foolishly rebels against their benevolent Creator or when the rebellious ones join together to subvert Yahweh's authority and subjugate His creation for their nefarious plans? Yahweh intervenes!

"The earth is the LORD'S, and all it contains, the world, and those who dwell in it. For He has founded it upon the seas and established it upon the rivers."

Psalms 24:1-2

We must always remember whose world this is. Individuality and free will are rights given to us by God, but they are not without limits or consequences. For example, we cannot use our privilege of free will to infringe on someone else's right to exist or selfishly use the resources given to us and not consider the needs of others.

When Yahweh had an opportunity to talk to his people from Mount Sinai, He could have said any number of things to His audience. He chose to give them the ten most important statements He could think of - the Ten Commandments. They form the foundation of laws and principles that, when applied, will bring order, and guide the world to peace.

Divine Law determines right and wrong behavior, and it establishes a system of justice. This system can only operate when there is a judge to determine a finding of the facts. It also requires enforcement of the consequences of good or bad behavior. This is the basic concept of righteousness, a system built on what is right in The Creator's eyes. To put it plainly, rebellion against HIS system needs to be quashed for righteousness to endure.

The righteousness of the King and Judge of the world requires divine enforcement. The Horsemen were formed to be this elite force whose mission is to protect the territory and people of the King but also to enforce the consequences of disobedience.

To protect against whom or what one might ask? This is the point at which we must expand our understanding to realize that there are enemies to righteousness. These enemies are not just humans exhibiting bad behavior, the true enemies have existed before the world, as we know it, was created. In the beginning, as revealed in the book of Genesis, there was an adversary that suddenly appeared in the Garden of Eden and seduced Eve and Adam to rebel against their Creator. We are all familiar with the story, but we need to consider the truth that this enemy is supernatural, evil, and pre-existent to man.

> *"You are of your father the devil, and you want to do the desires of your father. **He was a murderer from the beginning and does not stand in the truth because there is no truth in him.** Whenever he speaks a lie, he speaks from his own nature, for he is a liar and the father of lies."*
>
> *John 8:44* (emphasis added)

The Devil, or Satan, does not work alone. For his rebellion to succeed, he needed to create an army of his own. Just as he did in the Garden, he recruits other beings created by Yahweh to join his coup d'état.

*"Then another sign appeared in heaven: and behold, a great red dragon having seven heads and ten horns, and on his heads were seven diadems. And **his tail swept away a third of the stars of heaven and threw them to the earth**."*

Revelation 12:3-4 (emphasis added)

As we discussed earlier, there are Watcher Class angels who stay awake day and night watching over humankind. This concept has led to an ancient idea that the stars that shine in the night skies are representative of these heavenly Watchers, or possibly a star may be home to a watcher. When the Dragon swept away a third of the stars, it is a reference to a supernatural rebellion where Satan recruits a third of the angels to defect to his side. I believe this is only one example of this type of tactic. We will discuss evidence of other supernatural adversarial entities at work in the world in the chapters to come.

The Bronze Mountains

Coming back to The Four Horsemen, let's look at where they came from. The passage at the head of this section states they came from "behind the Myrtle trees" and from "between two bronze mountains." The symbology used to describe the horsemen's entrance is key. The Myrtle Tree is a dense evergreen with leaves that adorn the branches year-round. It's a small tree or shrub, ideally used as camouflage.

The picture here is that these horsemen are hidden out of plain sight, and their actions are covert. They are not seen or understood by the natural world.

They come from between two bronze mountains; it is my opinion that these two mountains represent two established realms: the earthly realm and the heavenly one. The horsemen ride between the realms on their inter-dimensional missions.

They are multi-directional; they can come from or go to the north, south, east, or west. This geographical positioning is necessary in a three-dimensional world. They metaphorically ride on the winds or as divine winds.

Out of the North

When we discuss weather patterns, we are all familiar with the type of weather conditions proceeding from a given direction. For example, if you live in the Midwest states of North America, you will know that colder air and more harsh conditions come with the North winds, whereas warmer and more mild conditions originate from southerly breezes. So, too, there seems to be a correlation between purpose and the direction of these four winds of heaven.

The sun rises in the east, bringing with it the dawn of a new day, and it sets in the west, marking the end of the day. Likewise, east winds usher in new seasons, signaling something is about to change. It may be the onset of a period of judgment or consequence.

"You contended with them by banishing them, by driving them away. With His fierce wind, He has expelled them **on the day of the east wind.***"*

Isaiah 27:8 (emphasis added)

Or, in another place,

"An east wind will come, the wind of the LORD coming up from the wilderness; *and his fountain will become dry, and his spring will be dried up; It will plunder his treasury of every precious article. Samaria will be held guilty, for she has rebelled against her God."*

Hosea 13:15-16 (emphasis added)

The west wind marks the end of a season or a cessation of a period of harsh discipline.

*"**So the LORD shifted the wind to a very strong west wind**
which took up the locusts and drove them into the Red Sea; not
one locust was left in all the territory of Egypt."*

Exodus 10:19 (emphasis added)

Again,

*"So they will fear the name of the LORD from **the west***

And His glory from the rising of the sun,

For He will come like a rushing stream

Which the wind of the LORD drives."

Isaiah 59:19 (emphasis added)

The idea here is they will fear the LORD when He accomplishes or completes His acts of judgment upon the disobedient, and the "wind of the Lord" will drive home the point.

These passages could simply be interpreted as natural winds, but with Yahweh, nothing is simply natural. The natural is frequently used to be understood as an explanation of something spiritual or supernatural. This is why words like ruach, for wind, also mean spirit, it expressly merges two or more ideas.

Directionally, the north represents that which is above or up, as in the phrase we use in the Midwest, "up-north." It often symbolically refers to heaven or Yahweh's realm.

"Now men do not see the light which is bright in the skies;

But the wind has passed and cleared them.

Out of the north comes golden splendor;

21

Around God is awesome majesty."

Job 37:21-22 (emphasis added)

Or,

"…'And I will sit on the mount of assembly
In the recesses of the north. *I will ascend above the heights of*
the clouds;

I will make myself like the Most High.'"

Isaiah 14:13-14 (emphasis added)

Whereas *the east* signals to us that something is rising, *the north* tells us where or who it's coming from.

"As I looked, behold, **a storm wind was coming from the**
north*, a great cloud with fire flashing forth continually and a*
bright light around it, and in its midst something like glowing
metal in the midst of the fire. Within it there were figures
resembling four living beings."

Ezekiel 1:4-5 (emphasis added)

In this heavenly vision, Ezekiel was seeing Yahweh coming to him from the north (the realm above), riding on a great storm. The vision was incredible, full of awe-striking detail, revealing four Living Beings powering an other-worldly vehicle of some sort, with wheels in the middle of wheels, emitting lightning bolts and fire as they went, and they were able to move swiftly in all directions simply at will. They emerged from another dimension into our physical world and then returned to their spiritual domain. They came from the symbolic north.

The southern breeze seemingly brings more mild conditions, just like a southern weather pattern. A warm breeze from the south signals that the storm is over, and things will return to normal.

> *"And when you see **a south wind blowing**, you say, 'It will be a hot day,' and it turns out that way. You hypocrites! **You know how to analyze the appearance of the earth and the sky, but why do you not analyze this present time?"***
>
> *Luke 12:55-56* (emphasis added)

In summary, the direction of a spiritual wind gives us a message. East winds signal something is coming, and West winds tell us that something is leaving. North winds, which often bring storms, tell us where the event is coming from; it reveals the heavenly realm. South winds represent a calming or peaceful change back to our earthly norm.

We need to turn our attention to the question of who commands these Patrols. How are these decisions made that affect the entire world and the fate of mankind? For answers to these questions, we must look at what the bible reveals about this subject. It starts with a courtroom and the hidden place it convenes.

The Mount of Assembly

The Bible has much to say about Mountains. They are important from a theological standpoint. Many events occur on mountains, making them points of intrigue, for example, Mount Sinai, Mount Moriah, Mount Zion, the Mount of Olives, Mount Carmel, and the Mount of Transfiguration to name a few. All these mountains have had significant biblical events happen on them, and they are, therefore, important to Yahweh. Other writers have expounded on the importance of mountains. One good source is the author Derek P. Gilbert, in his book titled "The Great Inception."

"Mountains have always been key in this drama. People have known since our earliest days that mountains are sacred, the abode of the gods. Why? Is it the mystery inherent in locations that are remote and inaccessible? Is it the awe inspired by their size and beauty? Is it simply that primitive humans noticed that mountains were tall and closer to heaven than where they lived?

No. Mountains are sacred because the original location of the divine council was on a mountain. The original home of humankind was also on that mountain. After rebellion broke out, the Fallen chose other mountains to call their own. And all of history is a chronicle of the long war that broke out on the original cosmic mountain."[8]

The elevation of mountains has held a symbolic importance in our visibly dimensional world. From the second day of creation, we see the expanse was created separating the waters above separated from the waters below. There are winged creatures that fly in the open sky, called heavens. One example is the reptilian fifth-day creatures created from the waters yet made to fly. Other creatures designed for flight would include our many species of birds and insects, even man has taken to the skies.

This great expanse inserted between and around the earth and the stars is a physical picture of the spirit realm where spirit creatures move on the metaphoric winds (ruach). The earthly winged creatures are not only airborne, but they symbolically represent spirit beings, a natural picture teaching us a spiritual reality. The scripture gives us details of spiritual winged beings in heaven like the cherubim and seraphim, or the four living creatures around the Throne of Yahweh, having six wings (Rev 4:8). Our natural sky proclaims to us that there is another place that exists above our world, invisible like the air, but inhabited by creatures that are not bound to this earth or even this realm.

A mountain projects into this expanse and its peak reaches into the heavens (the sky); it represents a place where man and God can meet, where these two dimensions intersect. I believe this is why mountains are important to God, they symbolically represent the place where these two realms or dimensions intersect.

Yahweh has manifested himself in some physical form on several mountains. I have also included the mountains that Yeshua (Yahweh in the flesh) made famous. The most obvious from the list above would be Mount Sinai.

> *"Now Mount Sinai was all in smoke because the LORD descended upon it in fire; and its smoke ascended like the smoke of a furnace, and the whole mountain quaked violently."*   *Exodus 19:18*

Sinai was a temporary location, and Yahweh's presence would

eventually be enshrined in the Temple built on Mount Moriah or the Temple Mount. Solomon declares at the dedication of the Temple in Jerusalem,

> *"Now therefore arise, O LORD God, to Your resting place,*
> *You and the ark of Your might;"*

> *2 Chronicles 6:41*

…But Yahweh declares that a house cannot hold him.

> *"Thus says the LORD, 'Heaven is My throne, and the earth is*
> *My footstool. Where then is a house you could build for Me?*
> *And where is a place that I may rest.'"*

> *Isaiah 66:1*

We can follow this thinking down the path to a more symbolic type of mountain, the Mount of Assembly. There is a heavenly or Divine Council seated on the Mount of Assembly. Judgements or decisions are made there, that are carried out on earth. Isaiah 14 refers to this Mount of Assembly,

> *"But you said in your heart, 'I will ascend to heaven; I will*
> *raise my throne above the stars of God,*
> *And I will sit on **the mount of assembly** in the recesses of the*
> *north."*

> *Isaiah 14:13* (emphasis added)

The Divine Counsel seems to function as God's court where decisions are made concerning the affairs of men. It can also be understood in the context of a royal court, where the King and his advisors deliberate, perhaps similar to King Arthur's Knights of the

Round Table. Daniel gives us a glimpse into Yahweh's court.

"I kept looking until thrones were set up, and the Ancient of
Days took His seat;
His vesture was like white snow and the hair of His head like
pure wool. His throne was ablaze with flames, its wheels were a
burning fire. "A river of fire was flowing and coming out from
before Him;
Thousands upon thousands were attending Him, and myriads
upon myriads were standing before Him;
The court sat, and the books were opened.*"**

Daniel 7:9-10 (emphasis added)

In this grand courtroom there is a great throne upon which the Ancient of Days sits. There is life in this courtroom, which also doubles as a throne room, complete with a river of fire flowing through it, and it is attended by myriads upon myriads of other-realm beings. But it is a functional high court in every aspect, records are kept, and decisions are made on issues throughout the realms.

As in heaven, so on earth, is a concept seen when Yahweh spoke to Moses about building the Tabernacle according to the pattern that was shown to him on the mountain, suggesting there is a heavenly building that should be mirrored on earth. Another picture from the Mount Sinai experience illustrates that Yahweh's instruction for a Council of Seventy Elders in Israel was also a mirror of a heavenly reality. When Moses was invited to meet with Yahweh on top of Mount Sinai, he didn't go alone.

"Then Moses went up with Aaron, Nadab and Abihu, and

seventy of the elders of Israel, and they saw the God of Israel; *and under His feet there appeared to be a pavement of sapphire,* *as clear as the sky itself. Yet He did not stretch out His hand* *against the nobles of the sons of Israel;* **and they saw God, and** **they ate and drank**.*"*

Exodus 24:9-11 (emphasis added)

I believe what we see here is a foreshadowing of the Divine Council. First, all of this takes place on the mountain of Yahweh's choosing, a reflection of a spiritual or heavenly mountain where His Divine Council was presently seated. It is clear that the group on the Mountain were observing a heavenly vision as they saw a pavement of sapphire, the same sapphire seen in Ezekiel 10:1 describing Yahweh's Throne.

Secondly, the priests, Aaron, and his sons, Nadab and Abihu, were invited up the mountain, along with the seventy elders of Israel. In Rabbinical thought, these seventy elders represented the seventy nations that were divided among the seventy sons of God at the Tower of Babel event (Duet. 32:8-9). Although these seventy elders of Israel were not actively on Yahweh's Council, they were a foreshadowing of the future destiny of Yahweh's earthly children.

Thirdly, they ate and drank a meal together. Important meetings take place around the dinner table. I'm reminded of the Last Supper with Yeshua and his disciples when the covenant was declared and celebrated. Yeshua said He would not drink the cup of the covenant with them again until they met Him in the heavenly kingdom. He had this meeting around the dinner table.

This brings us to another Throne scene in the book of Revelation, chapter 4.

*"Immediately I was in the Spirit; and behold, a throne was standing in heaven, and **One sitting on the throne**. And He who was sitting was like a jasper stone and a sardius in appearance; and there was a rainbow around the throne, like an emerald in appearance. **Around the throne were twenty-four thrones; and upon the thrones I saw twenty-four elders sitting**, clothed in white garments, and golden crowns on their heads."*

Revelation 4:2-4 (emphasis added)

This is still another example of a council of thrones and seated elders serving in Yahweh's presence in the Throne room. If I could speculate, I suggest that the twenty-four elders could be comprised of representatives from the Twelve Tribes of Israel and The Twelve Apostles of the Lamb, but there could be another explanation. What we do know is that the decision making process is shared in a council of appointed ones.

Yeshua says this to His disciples,

*"You are those who have stood by Me in My trials; and just as My Father has granted Me a kingdom, I grant you that you may eat and drink at My table in My kingdom, **and you will sit on thrones judging the twelve tribes of Israel**."*

Luke 22:28-30 (emphasis added)

Who are these advisors to the Great King, the legal counsel before the Great Judge of the world?

Well, we at least know who they answer to: the Commander in Chief, Yahweh Sabaoth.

Yahweh Sabaoth

Yahweh Sabaoth is one of Yahweh's (God's) names in the Bible. It occurs more than 270 times in the Old Testament. It combines God's personal name, Yahweh, with the Hebrew word, Sabaoth, meaning "host" or "multitude," often rendered LORD of Hosts.

Sabaoth is a military term and has a military connotation, revealing that Yahweh is the commander of armies.

> ***"I have commanded My consecrated ones****, I have even called My mighty warriors,*
>
> *My proudly exulting ones, To execute My anger."*

> *Isaiah 13:3* (emphasis added)

> ***"The LORD of hosts*** *[Yahweh Sabaoth] is mustering the army for battle. They are coming from a far country, From the farthest horizons, The LORD and His instruments of indignation, to destroy the whole land."*

> *Isaiah 13:4-5* (emphasis and brackets added)

One of Yahweh's greatest earthly generals was King David. As a young man, David knew who fought with him. In his epic battle with the giant Goliath, he declares,

> *"You come to me with a sword, a spear, and a javelin, but I come to you in the name of **the LORD of hosts, the God of the armies of Israel**, whom you have taunted."*

> *1 Samuel 17:45* (emphasis added)

Yahweh's army not only fights alongside the armies of men but there is a heavenly army of much greater numbers than any human army at His disposal. In a rare glimpse, the prophet Elisha, after being surrounded by the Aramean army, prays that the eyes of his servant, Gehazi, might be opened to see the armies of heaven.

*"Now when the attendant of the man of God had risen early and gone out, behold, an army with horses and chariots was circling the city. And his servant said to him, "Alas, my master! What shall we do?" So he answered, "**Do not fear, for those who are with us are more than those who are with them**." Then Elisha prayed and said, "O LORD, I pray, open his eyes that he may see." And the LORD opened the servant's eyes and he saw; **and behold, the mountain was full of horses and chariots of fire** all around Elisha."*

2 Kings 6:15-17 (emphasis added)

Another term used in the Bible is the "hosts of heaven," this refers to warrior angels who are numbered as *"a thousand thousands"* and *"ten thousand times ten thousand."* (Daniel 7:10 KJV)

*"Therefore, hear the word of the LORD. I saw the LORD sitting on His throne, and all the **host of heaven** standing by Him on His right and on His left."*

1 Kings 22:19 (emphasis added)

If we take that last number literally, ten thousand times ten thousand, we arrive at a 100 million-strong angelic army.

Isaiah specifically identifies the LORD of Hosts as our Redeemer. *"Our Redeemer, the LORD of hosts* [Yahweh Sabaoth] *is His name, the Holy One of Israel."* (Isaiah 47:4, see also 44:6; 54:5) Yeshua our

Messiah (Jesus Christ) is our Redeemer. He is the personification of Yahweh Sabaoth, the Lord of Hosts.

The Hebrew name Yeshua means "Yahweh is salvation" (Matthew 1:21). It is interesting to note that the name of the prophet Isaiah, in Hebrew, is *Yeshayahu*. It is a compound of two root words: *Yasha* (the root word for Yeshua), which means "deliverance or salvation," and *Yah* or *Yahu*, a shortened version of Yahweh. Isaiah's name means "Salvation of Yahweh." Much of the Old Testament prophecy about who Yeshua Messiah is and what he would do is written by the prophet Isaiah, who reveals to us the "Salvation of Yahweh."

> *"Behold, **God is my salvation [Yeshua (Jesus)],***
> *I will trust and not be afraid;*
> *For the LORD GOD is my strength and song,*
> *And **He has become my salvation [Yeshua]**.*
> *Therefore you will joyously draw water*
> *From the springs of salvation [Yeshua}.*
> *And in that day you will say,*
> *Give thanks to the LORD, **call on His name**.*
> *Make known His deeds among the peoples;*
> *Make them remember that **His name is exalted**."*

> *Isaiah 12:2-4* (emphasis and brackets added)

Isaiah reveals the name of the Messiah to us and who He is; He (God) has become our Yeshua.

When Yeshua came to earth to redeem us, He repeatedly demonstrated His power over the forces of the Adversary (Satan). He freed those possessed of demons. (Mark 1:34; Luke 8:26-39)

He raised the dead to life, showing His power over death. (John 11:1-44; Luke 7:11-17; Matthew 9:18-26)

He healed lepers and the blind. (Matthew 8:1-4; 9:27-31; 11:5)

As the Lord of Hosts, Yeshua even ruled over the forces of nature, commanding a violent wind-driven storm to cease when it threatened to swallow the little boat carrying Him and His disciples. Instantly, the wind stopped blowing, and the waves were calm. (Mark 4:35-41)

Just before the cross, Yeshua told His disciples, *"Be of good cheer, I have overcome the world"* (John 16:33). And following His death, before going back to heaven, He told them, *"All authority has been given to Me in heaven and on earth"* (Matthew 28:18). By His death for us on the cross, Yeshua destroyed the devil's power over us and delivered us from the bondage of sin. (Hebrews 2:14, 15)

Because of His powerful victory over sin on our behalf, the name of Yeshua is above every name, *"At the name of Yeshua every knee should bow, of those in heaven, and of those on earth, and of those under the earth, and that every tongue should confess that Yeshua Messiah is Lord."* (Philippians 2:10. 11)

Finally, we will see Yeshua Messiah riding back to earth on a white war horse with all authority, leading the armies of heaven as King of Kings and LORD of LORDS. He is their commander, the LORD of Hosts. (Revelation 19:11-16)

The "Sons of God"

Yahweh's throne room is in the heavens but extends into the earthly realm. As we have discussed, it manifests most often on Mountains. The scriptures inform us that Yahweh is not alone. It is clear from the Bible that there are none like Him in power and majesty, and He alone has the power to create from nothing. He is referred to as the El-Elyon or The Most High God (El). There are other created beings around Him. These are referred to as the "sons of God."

In Yahweh's own words, He declares to Job that the sons of God were present when the world was being created before man was formed,

> *"Where were you when I laid the foundation of the earth? ... When the morning stars sang together **And all the sons of God shouted for joy?"***

Job 38:4-7 (emphasis added)

First, we have the angels, created beings that are present to serve God in His interactions with mankind. It is apparent that there is a hierarchy in God's realm. We have references to archangels, like Michael and Gabriel, for example. The archangels seem to have a higher rank than some other angelic beings. There are also Cherubim, Seraphim, and Watcher Class angels. Are there other created beings in heaven?

The book of Revelation mentions four living creatures in the Throne Room. They are intelligent and speak with great insight. As mentioned, there is a Council of twenty-four Elders (Rev. 4:4,7-8), but this Book of Revelation reference is not the first mention of a Divine Council.

> *"God* (Elohim-singular) *takes His stand in His own congregation; He judges in the midst of the rulers* (Elohim-plural). *"*
>
> *Psalms 82:1* (parentheses added)

And continuing in verse 6,

> *"I said,* **"You are gods** (Elohim), *And all of you are sons of the Most High. "*
>
> *Psalms 82:6* (emphasis added)

Here, we are introduced to Yahweh's congregation. The Hebrew word for congregation is *edah,* translated as "congregation" or "assembly," it is derived from the root word *yaad,* which means "to appoint". The idea here is that Yahweh sits as The Judge in the midst of an appointed assembly.

In verse 6, we see this assembly referred to as the sons of the Most High. In verse 1, they are called rulers. The Hebrew word for "rulers" here is *Elohim or "gods, "* we can refer to them as the "small g" gods or lesser gods who are mentioned elsewhere in the Bible. I know this stretches the theology most of us have been taught in the Christian church, but this understanding does not change the nature of God Himself. It just informs us that there are other created beings called the sons of God in the heavenly realm. They are spiritual beings that exist in an other-dimensional or spiritual realm.

God declares to these sons, "You are Elohim," and that He alone is the Most High. The word Elohim in Hebrew can be used in singular form or plural, depending on the context, even though Elohim also has El as a singular form. For example, in English, we have the word fish. It can refer to one fish or a school of fish depending on the context it is used in. In this passage, we have God (Elohim-singular) in the midst of other Elohim (plural). These other Elohim are referred to as the "sons of God."

Plural Elohim does not mean polytheism. Dr. Michael Heiser explains it this way,

"Many scholars believe that Psalm 82 and other passages demonstrate that the religion of ancient Israel began as a polytheistic system and then evolved into monotheism. I reject that idea, along with any other explanations that seek to hide the plain reading of the text. In all such cases, the thinking is misguided. The problem is rooted in a mistaken notion of what exactly the word Elohim means. Since Elohim is so often translated God, we look at the Hebrew word the same way we look at capitalized G-o-d. When we see the word God, we instinctively think of a divine being with a unique set of attributes—omnipresence, omnipotence, sovereignty, and so on. But this is not how a biblical writer thought about the term. Biblical authors did not assign a specific set of attributes to the word Elohim. That is evident when we observe how they used the word." [9]

We should also consider sources outside the Bible for context. The ancient world drew on a common understanding of the spirit realm, which has been lost in our modern worldview.

The Mesopotamian Context

The Bible is not the only source of the idea of a Divine Council or a Royal Court. Most ancient cultures have stories of a pantheon of gods that ruled over mankind. These ancient stories start with a creator god who was replaced by his offspring. According to the many writings recovered from archaeological digs, the ancient Sumerian and Akkadian cultures write of detailed interactions with their gods.

The Eridu Genesis or the Epic of Gilgamesh, for example, reveal such stories, except with a twist. Each civilization inserted its own deities and elevated them above all others. As I stated before, as a believer in biblical truth, we reject the notion of a polytheistic (many co-equal Gods) view and see this as a deception of the Adversary.

I won't explore these concepts here; there is a great body of work out there on this subject. I simply want to inform the reader that the idea of a Divine Council is infused into most, if not all, ancient writings. This idea was also a commonly accepted concept by the writers of the Bible.

Again, to be clear, I am not suggesting that these stories reveal hidden truths supporting some type of polytheism. They simply inform us of the possibility that other "created" beings existed prior to the creation of mankind, and these have become the source of ancient mythology. I am convinced there is a kernel of truth that can be extracted from such history.

As a final thought, to quote Derek Gilbert, "If this worldview is incorrect, then the apostle Paul was either lying or badly misinformed when he repeatedly warned us against principalities, powers, thrones, dominions, rulers, and the elemental spirits of the world."[10]

Chapter 2 – The Four Horns and the Four Craftsmen

*"Then I lifted up my eyes and looked, and behold, there were **four horns**. So I said to the angel who was speaking with me, "What are these?" And he answered me, "These are the horns which have scattered Judah, Israel, and Jerusalem." Then the LORD showed me **four craftsmen**. I said, "What are these coming to do?" And he said, "These are the horns which have scattered Judah so that no man lifts up his head; but these craftsmen have come to terrify them, to throw down the horns of the nations who have lifted up their horns against the land of Judah in order to scatter it.""*

Zechariah 1:18-21 (emphasis added)

In Zechariah's account, these horns were used to scatter the nation of Israel when they were driven out of their Land into exile. They were present as the Babylonian army pushed its way into the entire world, conquering nations as it went. The horns were also pushing the Persian forces to overthrow Babylon, only after Babylon had served its purpose.

The most common biblical references to horns are illustrated as goats, rams, or bulls' horns. Have you ever met a goat? They tend to be strong-willed and push at everything around them. Symbolically, the "pushing of horns" is used to describe a forced change of events or the unnatural movement of people. They are referenced as four horns to illustrate scattering into the four cardinal directions or coming from a specific direction. The bible calls this scattering.

The Scatterers

*"Therefore its name was called Babel, because there the LORD confused the language of the whole earth; and from there **the LORD scattered them abroad over the face of the whole earth**."*

Genesis 11:9 (emphasis added)

Scattering is a method seen repeatedly in Yahweh's plans. Scattering can come in the form of judgment but almost always has secondary purposes. In this example, the people were scattered to stop them from accomplishing an unwanted outcome for humanity. Still, by doing so, this pushing by the supernatural Horns created the Table of Nations. Like a farmer scattering seeds, separation brings multiplication, but it's not always seen that way at first. It isn't until the crop is harvested that we see the wisdom in scattering the seed. In another place, it says,

*"Then the LORD your God will restore you from captivity, and have compassion on you, **and will gather you again from all the peoples where the LORD your God has scattered you**."*

Deuteronomy 30:3 (emphasis added)

When scattering has become affective for God's purposes, He will then regather. The important point here is that scattering is needed, effective, and is done on purpose and for a purpose.

To accomplish these goals Yahweh uses four horns, also referred to as the "horns of the nations." Many times, there are human agents involved with these horns. These horns attach themselves to warrior-kings and their armies. For example, the land of Judah was scattered by the King of Babylon, Nebuchadnezzar; it is clear that he was guided to this end. In the book of Daniel, Yahweh reveals some future geo-political changes coming into the world.

> *"In the third year of the reign of Belshazzar the king a vision appeared to me, Daniel, subsequent to the one which appeared to me previously. I looked in the vision, and while I was looking I was **in the citadel of Susa, which is in the province of Elam**; and I looked in the vision and I myself was beside the Ulai Canal. Then I lifted my eyes and looked, and **behold, a ram which had two horns** was standing in front of the canal. Now the two horns were long, but one was longer than the other, with the longer one coming up last. **I saw the ram butting westward, northward, and southward**, and no other beasts could stand before him nor was there anyone to rescue from his power, but he did as he pleased and magnified himself."*

Daniel 8:1-4 (emphasis added)

The two horns mentioned here are the kings of Medea and Persia, Cyrus the Great, and the longer horn, Darius the Great. The story begins while the King of Babylon is in power. Daniel was in Susa of Elam. Susa served as the capital of Elam and the Achaemenid or Medio-Persian Empire.

If you look closely at the details, Daniel receives this vision while in the capital city of the empire that would soon overthrow Babylon. Cyrus (the Great) is depicted here as one of the two horns. Notice these horns only pushed three of the four directions. The Medio-Persian Empire mainly existed in the eastern Mesopotamia region and mainly spread north, south, and west, as predicted by the prophecy.

A key element to this "horn" imagery is that, at first glance, the horns seem to represent human warrior-kings. However, further examination reveals they are territorial authorities or principalities working through human agents.

This is revealed in Gabriel's message to Daniel where he references the prince of the kingdom of Persia, and the kings of Persia, separately.

*"But the **prince of the kingdom of Persia** was withstanding me for twenty-one days; then behold, Michael, one of the chief princes, came to help me, for I had been left there with **the kings of Persia**."*

Daniel 10:13 (emphasis added)

To give it a finer point, I believe these horns of Zechariah refer to the supernatural principalities behind these kings.

The takeaway is that God used these horns to change world politics. It wasn't the first time and won't be the last. There is another force at work here, a counterforce. To prevent the horns from pushing too far or too hard. The Four Craftsmen achieve this balancing counterforce.

The Strategists

*"Then the LORD showed me four craftsmen. I said, "What are these coming to do?" ...**these craftsmen have come to terrify them, to throw down the horns of the nations** who have lifted up their horns against the land of Judah in order to scatter it."*

Zechariah 1:20-21 (emphasis added)

A craftsman, in this context, is a strategist. A quick definition - Strategists are adept at generating and translating concepts and ideas into effective strategies to achieve desired outcomes. They tend to be both conceptual and structured thinkers, curious and open-minded while also being reliable and pragmatic. Their work can be found in a close examination of scripture; the following passages should open our minds,

*"**This is the plan devised against the whole earth**; and this is the hand that is stretched out against all the nations. **For the LORD of hosts has planned, and who can frustrate it?** And as for His stretched-out hand, who can turn it back?"*

Isaiah 14:26-27 (emphasis added)

The Bible gives us a crow's nest view of such a planning session.

*"Micaiah said, "Therefore, hear the word of the LORD. I saw the LORD sitting on His throne and all the host of heaven standing by Him on His right and on His left. The LORD said, 'Who will entice Ahab to go up and fall at Ramoth-gilead?' And one said this while another said that. **Then a spirit came forward and stood before the LORD and said, 'I will entice him.'** The LORD said to him, 'How?'*

And he said, 'I will go out and be a deceiving spirit in the mouth of all his prophets.' Then He said, **'You are to entice him and also prevail. Go and do so.'** *Now therefore, behold, the LORD has put a deceiving spirit in the mouth of all these your prophets; and the LORD has proclaimed disaster against you."*

1 Kings 22:19-23 (emphasis added)

In a rare opportunity, we observe a divine strategy to change the balance of power among the kings of Israel. The wicked king, Ahab, was killed in battle, and another took his place. Who orchestrated the outcome of that battle? Was a heavenly rider sent to carry out Yahweh's plan?

"Now a certain man drew his bow at random and struck the king of Israel in a joint of the armor."

1 Kings 22:34

As the battle ensued, the King of Israel was targeted by the captains of the chariots of Aram. In what seems to be an amazing coincidence, a random arrow flies and strikes the King between the plates of his armor, critically wounding him. Taking out this wicked leader brought needed change to the people of Israel. It allowed a new political power to rise and guide God's nation in a different direction, a desired outcome.

I do have a few questions. How did that random arrow strike in the precise location on Ahab's armor and inflict a deadly blow? What force or forces were guiding that outcome? Now, we can chalk this up to coincidence, but I don't believe that is the answer here.

The story revealed a plan devised by Strategists/Craftsmen, then a

Horn pushed them into battle, and a Horseman riding the "winds of change" successfully altered the politics of the region.

A Babylonian king named Nebuchadnezzar tried to take all the glory for himself, believing that it was by his own great power and wisdom he built his kingdom. He was warned in a dream from God that his pride was dangerous and judgement was looming. In the dream, he was shown a great tree in the midst of the earth.

"The tree grew large and became strong.
And its height reached to the sky,
And it was visible to the end of the whole earth.
It's foliage was beautiful, and its fruit abundant,
And in it was food for all.
The beasts of the field found shade under it,
And the birds of the sky dwelt in its branches,
And all living creatures fed themselves from it.
I was looking in the visions in my mind as I lay on my bed, and
behold, an angelic watcher, a holy one, descended from heaven. He
shouted out and spoke as follows:
Chop down the tree and cut off its branches,
Strip off its foliage and scatter its fruit."

Daniel 4:11-14

He was sentenced to seven years of divine punishment. He lost his mind and was left to roam the outdoors day and night, crawling on the ground and eating grass for food like an animal. After the appointed time, he regained his senses and said,

"But at the end of that period, I, Nebuchadnezzar, raised my eyes

toward heaven, and my reason returned to me, and I blessed the
Most High and praised and honored Him who lives forever;
For His dominion is an everlasting dominion,
And His kingdom endures from generation to generation.
'All the inhabitants of the earth are accounted as nothing,
But He does according to His will in the host of heaven
And among the inhabitants of earth;
And no one can ward off His hand
Or say to Him, 'What have You done?'"

Daniel 4:34-35

This was a unique punishment that led to Nebuchadnezzar's revelation of The Almighty. Could it possibly have been the work of the Craftsmen who devised that effective plan? It seems so.

Appointed Times

The Horns have the task of scattering, resulting in weakening or dividing centers of power in a region. They move the players around the board in the four cardinal directions. I see them as the movers and the shakers.

As Winston Churchill was working to form the United Nations after WWII, he famously said, "Never let a good crisis go to waste." This is the exact type of statement that applies to "movers and shakers," the idea is to seize the opportunity to bring about change when a crisis arises.

A more nefarious objective would be to create a crisis in order to bring about the desired change. Is it possible that this strategy was first used by God, albeit for righteous purposes? This would be a job for the Craftsmen/Strategists.

The Craftsmen devise plans for desired outcomes, affecting the rise or fall of regional authorities. In my analysis, these are off-world entities that work through human agents to accomplish God's will on earth.

To successfully strategize, you need to see all the pieces, observe events, and consider all factors. You need to have eyes on the ground, surveying each situation.

"And I saw between the throne (with the four living creatures) and the elders a Lamb standing, as if slain, having seven horns and **seven eyes, which are the seven Spirits of God, sent out into all the earth."** *Revelation 5:6 (emphasis added)*

*"But these seven will be glad when they see the plumb line in the hand of Zerubbabel—**these are the eyes of the LORD which range to and fro throughout the earth.**"*

Zechariah 4:10 (emphasis added)

And finally,

*"For the ways of a man are before **the eyes of the LORD**, and He watches all his paths."*

Proverbs 5:21 (emphasis added)

Not that we need to challenge the idea that Yahweh sees all things, but the Seven Spirits perform the role of observation in the realm of men. Consider it tactical reconnaissance. These Seven Eyes are connected to Yeshua, the Lamb of God, also known as the Commander of the Hosts. *"These seven were glad to see the plumbline in Zerubbabel's hand,"* is a reference to the rebuilding of the temple after the Babylonian exile. This was a key component in establishing the right conditions for Yeshua Messiah to come to earth.

*"Behold, I am going to send My messenger, and he will clear the way before Me. **And the Lord, whom you seek, will suddenly come to His temple**; and the messenger of the covenant, in whom you delight, behold, He is coming," says the LORD of hosts."*

Malachi 3:1 (emphasis added)

This prophecy emphasizes the need to keep a timeline. When you live outside of time, as Yahweh does, you will need players who operate inside of time or in real-time from our perspective. You need to make appointments or create appointed times. In Gen 1:14, we see that Yahweh created the celestial bodies for time keeping.

"Then God said, "Let there be lights in the expanse of the heavens to separate the day from the night, and let them be for signs and for seasons and for days and years;"

Genesis 1:14

The rotation of the planets around the sun and the moon around the Earth gives us our days, weeks, months, and years. The earth's orbital travel in proximity to the sun gives us our seasons. Even the stars are placed in the heavens with precision, giving us the *mazzaroth* (Hebrew word) or constellations.

The rotation of the celestial bodies serves as a heavenly timepiece. Imagine if an interdimensional being wishes to enter our four-dimensional realm (time being the fourth dimension) at a specific hour, day, month, or year. They would simply need to know the position of the stars and planets for the specified time of entry. If NASA can turn back the position of stars and planets to a historical date and study the skies, how much smarter is Yahweh, who created them as His cosmic clock?

Yahweh celebrates these cycles in His Torah, and we are told to observe them. The 24 hour rotation cyclical each day is separated by the distinction of nighttime and daytime.

According to Genesis, Yahweh's day starts at sundown and goes until the next sundown, *"there was evening and there was morning, the third day."* (Gen 1:13). The progression starts with the evening and moves to the morning, taking us back to the next evening.

This is critical when trying to determine when a specific holy day begins or even when the seventh day of the week begins.

The concept of understanding how the day starts reveals to us a spiritual reality. The day starts in the evening time when the world is becoming dark. Eventually, the sun rises and sets, only for the world to return to darkness. This is how Yahweh created the world. It began in darkness or chaos; He alone created the light and caused it to shine into the obscurity of that darkness, bringing life and order. Like the setting of the sun, He will retreat at times, leaving the moon as a reminder that the light is still there; it's just hidden for a moment. Each day repetitiously reminds us of this truth.

The purpose of this discussion is that if we want to understand Yahweh's timeline, we need to become familiar with His methods of timekeeping. We read that the celestial bodies (sun, moon, and stars) are for "signs and seasons," the term sign or "*oth*" in Hebrew (Strong's H226) is easily explained. Along the pathway of time, there will be "signposts" that point us to important seasons or events important to Yahweh, that is. These signs are discovered by understanding Yahweh's cycles, which are set in time. A very obvious sign is that a month starts at every new (dark) moon or that a full moon reveals that it is the middle or 15ᵗʰ day of the month. This knowledge would be important for determining biblical Feast Days, for example.

This leads us to the word for seasons or "*moed*" or plural "*moedim*" in Hebrew. Strong's number is H4150. מוֹעֵד moed or מֹעֵד moed or מוֹעָדָה moadah; (from H3259, *yaad* to appoint) and means – appointed time, place, or meeting.

What Yahweh is showing us is that He has appointed times

designated for us according to HIS calendar or timekeeping.

"The LORD spoke again to Moses, saying, "Speak to the sons of Israel and say to them, 'The LORD'S appointed times which you shall proclaim as holy convocations—My appointed times are these…"

Leviticus 23:1-2

Leviticus chapter 23 goes on to explain some of these appointed times: the seventh day Sabbath (which started at creation,) the seven annual feasts (all of which point to Yeshua,) the Shmitah or seven-year cycles (cancelling of debts and allowing the land to rest every seven years,) the seven sevens (49 years,) and the year of Jubilee, the 50th year (the redemption of the land, liberty to the captives, and the return of people to their inheritance,) these are all repeating cycles on the timeline. It is not my intention to describe in detail each of the appointed times, except to say that these are the timepieces used by Yahweh in His interaction with mankind.

An example of this is found by examining the biblical feast of Passover. The Passover lamb was sacrificed on the 14th day of the month of Nissan. Yeshua was the fulfillment of the Passover; he was the true Passover Lamb, and He is seen in the book of Revelation (5:6) as the slain lamb, standing before the Throne. Yeshua was crucified on the 14th day of Nissan, the exact appointed time on Yahweh's calendar as the killing of the Passover Lamb, connecting the two events.

As a matter of fact, every one of the seven biblical feasts is connected to Yeshua's first and second coming. The first four spring feasts outline four major achievements (His death, burial, resurrection, and giving of the Spirit) to the exact day and month accomplished in His first coming, and the three Fall feasts foreshadow the events of His second coming.

They revolve around the agricultural cycles of spring planting and fall harvesting. Yeshua came and planted the seeds of His message in the hearts of the believers and became the first fruits of resurrection during the spring feasts. Then, for two thousand years, the church has grown during this metaphoric *summertime*. He will return to harvest or gather His crop, the believers, during the time of the fall feasts. The Feasts are literal yearly cycles or rehearsals to keep us in remembrance of His plan. We may not know the day or hour of Yeshua's return, but we know it will be in the harvest season (Fall) and in the Hebrew month of Tishri (the month of all three Fall feasts.)

Many of Yeshua's parables reference these agricultural concepts; parables like the wheat and the tares, the farmer who sows his seed, the Mustard seed, the fig tree, and the vineyard owner, to name a few. All of these rely on an understanding of the agricultural calendar cycles …and a little botany, too.

It is interesting to note that major calamities seem to have occurred on the same day, years apart on the calendar. The 9th of Av (the fifth month on the Hebrew calendar), also known as Tish B'Av,[11] claims some of the most difficult events in Jewish history; it has become known as the Day of Mourning.

There are five major events occurring on that day.

1. The Twelve spies return and give the bad report, sentencing Israel to wander in the wilderness for forty more years.

2. The First Temple, Solomon's Temple, was destroyed by Nebuchadnezzar on that day in 586 BC.

3. The Second Temple was destroyed on the same day of the year as the first temple's destruction, the 9th of Av, in 70 CE.

4. The crushing of the Bar Kokhba's revolt in 135 CE happened on that day, killing over 500,000 Jewish civilians.

5. Following the Bar Kokhba revolt, Roman Commander Quintus Tineius Rufus plowed the site of the temple in Jerusalem and the surrounding area.

There is another period of time that is known to Yahweh as "the last days" or "the end times."

*"He said, "Behold, I am going to let you know what will occur at the final period of the indignation, for it pertains to **the appointed time** [moed] **of the end**."*

Daniel 8:19 (emphasis and brackets added)

This is also an "appointed time," as shown by the use of the Hebrew word *moed* here. The time of the end will reveal the rise of the final empire, the restoration of Yahweh's Holy Land, and the salvation of His people. These are all foretold by the ancient writings of the prophets of scripture, showing how He "declares the end from the beginning." (Isaiah 46:10). Even Yeshua brings the focus of His entire ministry to bear on the fact that he will return and establish His everlasting Kingdom on earth after executing judgement on the nations.

All these events will happen at their appointed times. We are living in appointed times! Are you ready to take your appointed place as a believer in Yeshua in these last days?

Many prophetic events are understood by counting days, months, or years. You can find many examples of this counting throughout the scriptures. The understanding of time has always been, and will continue to be, an exercise for the wise.

Now with more context, let's come back to the Four Horsemen and add some much needed detail.

Chapter 3 – Four Horsemen

We have already learned that the Four Horsemen are responsible for patrolling the earth and that timing is critical. Their entry is always centered around a mission; we need to identify the mission.

*"'We have patrolled the earth, and behold, all the earth is peaceful and quiet.' Then the angel of the LORD said, 'O LORD of hosts, how long will You have no compassion for Jerusalem and the cities of Judah, with which You have been indignant **these seventy years?'***

*The LORD answered the angel who was speaking with me with gracious words, comforting words. So the angel who was speaking with me said to me, 'Proclaim, saying, **Thus says the LORD of hosts**, **'I am exceedingly jealous for Jerusalem and Zion**. But I am very angry with the nations who are at ease, for while I was only a little angry, they furthered the disaster.'*

*Therefore, thus says the LORD, **'I will return to Jerusalem with compassion; My house will be built in it**,' declares the LORD of hosts, 'and a measuring line will be stretched over Jerusalem.' Again, proclaim, saying, 'Thus says the LORD of hosts, My cities will again overflow with prosperity, and the LORD will again comfort Zion and again choose Jerusalem.'"*

Zechariah 1:11-17 (emphasis added)

According to the prophet Jeremiah and the angelic message to Zechariah, time was running out. The seventy-year mark was coming up fast and the angel asks Yahweh; *"How long will you have no compassion for Jerusalem and the cities of Judah?"* in other words, the time is up, and something needs to be done to change this situation. Yahweh makes the mission clear, *"I will return to Jerusalem with compassion; My house will be built in it,"*

Once the King makes a decree, His advisors must begin working on it. The strategists engineer a plan, the horns are sent to begin moving the players around the board, and the Horsemen will ride with force to bring about the desired outcome. Almost like playing a massive living game of chess against a sinister opponent, but this is no game, and it's much more important!

The White Horse

*I looked, and behold, **a white horse**, and he who sat on it had a bow; and a crown was given to him, and he went out conquering and to conquer.*

Revelation 6:2 (emphasis added)

I believe we can see the mission of the riders by the color of their horses. The horses and their respective colors are revealed in the books of Zechariah (chapters 1 and 6) and Revelation (chapter 6). These passages give us more context to understand them.

The descriptive terms for the white horse and rider are:

1. The rider has a bow (a weapon),

2. ...a crown was given to him (a *Stephanos* in Greek, meaning a victor's crown, as opposed to a royal crown),

3. ...he went out conquering and to conquer.

The white horse is a war horse. The rider is carrying a bow, and a crown was given to him. The giving of a crown is telling. He is given authority by the Divine Council to conquer new territories or take power away from existing rulers.

The phrase "conquering and to conquer" is textually considered the "reduplication" of a word. It is the repeating of a word or subject for the purpose of emphasis. In this case, it means that the rider will be successful in his conquest and will definitely achieve his goals. It implies that political powers will change hands. Kingdoms or nations will rise or fall; be strengthened or weakened. The winds of geopolitical change will blow.

More importantly, the rider is sent on a mission from God, and the color of the horse reveals a specific part of the plan devised to reshape the current global situation.

It is tempting at this point to speculate on the passage of Revelation, what political changes will be made, and who these human agents will be. But I will cover that later in this book. We need much more context before any speculation will make sense.

The color white is used in other instances of prophecy. For example, there is a white throne judgment; the saints are clothed in white robes, and there is a white stone given to the overcomer. Each of these has one thing in common: it represents a final state or a completion of a process and purpose. White means finality.

Finality with the white horse can mean a final political outcome locally, regionally, or globally, for now, or all of time. In the case of our Revelation 6 rider, it means that this is the final conquering before the Messiah returns, and He puts an end to human governance. It is the rise of the last governmental system, a massive global power that seeks domination. They will try to take control of Yahweh's Land and His people, once and for all, but they will completely fail!

In Daniel's interpretation of the king of Babylon's dream, we see a picture of human government represented by a great statue. Daniel explains that the five different types of metal in the image represent five great empires that will rule the world, each in its succession until a heavenly stone is sent to topple the image. The final state of the image is its complete destruction.

*"In the days of those kings, **the God of heaven will set up a***

kingdom which will never be destroyed, *and that kingdom will not be left for another people; it will crush and put an end to all these kingdoms, but it will itself endure forever.* **Inasmuch as you saw that a stone was cut out of the mountain without hands and that it crushed the iron, the bronze, the clay, the silver, and the gold,** *the great God has made known to the king what will take place in the future."*

Daniel 2:44-45 (emphasis added)

Spoiler alert: Yeshua is The Stone (Psalms 118:22) that grows into a large mountain (Daniel 2:35) and strikes the image at its feet. He will come to the earth in those days riding on a…wait for it…A WHITE HORSE! In a final victory, He returns as the conquering King of Kings (Revelation 19:11).

The transfer of political power and how it is achieved becomes a key component in the study of geopolitics. The White Horse reveals "what" is going to happen, and the next horse will reveal the "how" factor.

The Red Horse

*"...**a red horse**, went out; and to him who sat on it, it was granted to take peace from the earth, and that men would slay one another; and a great sword was given to him."*

Revelation 6:4 (emphasis added)

So far, the red horse and the previous white horse are war horses. The attributes of a horse are what inspired their use in this imagery. In the days before mechanical vehicles were invented, animals accomplished transportation. Typically, donkeys, mules, and camels (in the ancient Near East) were used for common transportation. Oxen were used for plowing fields and other farming tasks. The horse was saved for carrying soldiers and pulling chariots. Horses are strong, swift, and easier to maneuver on the battlefield.

Early in human history, horses were the warriors' transportation of choice. The steppe Barbarians, for example, like the Scythians, the Huns, and the Mongols were known for their marauding bands and heavily relied on horsepower. It is believed that horses were first domesticated in the Eurasian Steppe around 3500 B.C.[12]

The imagery of the heavenly patrols is that of a powerful force ready to fight when necessary. There is a reason we see four horsemen and not four donkey riders in this imagery.

The descriptive terms for the red horse and rider are:

1. ...it was granted to him to take peace from the earth,

2. ...that men would slay one another,

3. ...a great sword was given to him.

After the end of WWI, the United States experienced a rise of political unrest into the 1920s and 30s due to the rise of communism. This led to a national concern, which was eventually called the Red Scare. During the Red Scare, many feared that recent immigrants and dissidents, particularly those who embraced communist, socialist, or anarchist ideology, were going to disrupt the freedoms of our democracy.

"In 1917, the Bolshevik Revolution brought a Communist government to power in Russia. With the USSR firmly in its control, the Communist Party began to spread out to other nations. The American Communist Party began in 1919. By 1929, it had 7,000 members, and it reached its peak during the World War II alliance with the USSR, at which time it had some 85,000 members."[13]

In the years following, the movement escalated, and many people lost their jobs as a result of various blacklists.

The soviet flag was red with the emblem of a hammer and sickle, set below a star, and is most likely the inspiration for the Red Scare color reference. The label Red Scare and the Red Horse may not be coincidental, at least prophetically speaking. Communism was and still is a threat to peace on the earth.

American historian Martin Malia states,

"Communism has been the great story of the twentieth century," and "it had come to rule a third of mankind and seemed poised to advance indefinitely. For seven decades, it haunted world politics, polarizing opinion between those who saw it as the socialist end of history and those who considered it history's most vital tyranny."[14]

Communism is part of a list of ideologies that have subjugated humanity. We can add to that list socialism, fascism, anarchism, totalitarianism, and more recently, (radical) feminism and environmentalism, to name only a few, as a means of controlling people. Forms of these ideologies have existed throughout history. These strongly held beliefs divide humanity at the deepest levels. The rise of communism has taken much peace from the earth and has been the cause of much bloodshed.

There is another force, equally as strong, deeply seated in the souls of men. It solicits our most devoted worship and, in some, the strongest hatred. The topic is religion. We are warned not to talk about politics and religion; they can invoke the strongest emotions, which is why we need to talk about them in relation to the Red Horse.

The Red Horse represents ideological and religious conflicts; this is the "how" factor mentioned earlier. Great wars have been fought to silence those with opposing convictions. The ancient world is rife with myths of pagan deities who became the inspiration for many human battles and conquests. The Greeks tried to Hellenize the world with their beliefs. They defiled the temples of any foreign gods to establish their own. The Romans completely renamed the pantheon of gods after conquering the Greeks and forced the world to comply with their ideals or die. The Romans even weaponized Christianity in their later history. Roman armies were sent to subjugate the entire world. Their motto was, convert or die!

Every one of these ideologies and others could be studied at length (and there are those who do). In the upcoming chapters, we'll breakdown a few of these historical moments where these belief systems clashed and reveal the heavenly horseman that ride the winds of change.

All three missions of the Red Horse are covered; These ideological and religious wars take peace from the earth, causing men to polarize against one another and ultimately slay one another. That describes the great sword that is wielded when he rides. The Red Horse is a key component in the study of geopolitics and understanding the purpose of the Four Horsemen.

The Black Horse

*"I looked, and behold, **a black horse**, and he who sat on it had a pair of scales in his hand. And I heard something like a voice in the center of the four living creatures saying, "A quart of wheat for a denarius, and three quarts of barley for a denarius; and do not damage the oil and the wine."*

Revelation 6:5-6 (emphasis added)

The black horse presents the idea of a change in economic conditions, which dramatically affects food sources and availability, a basic component of human life. This ties to regional or even global famine, either man-made or weather related. The "pair of scales" in the rider's hand suggests the rider's mission is to cause a rationing of food through economic depression.

The descriptive terms for the black horse and rider are:

1. The rider is given a pair of scales (used for measuring),

2. …wheat and barley WILL increase in cost,

3. …the oil and wine will not be damaged.

In this instance, the wheat and barley would be affected, but the oil and wine would not. There is a recent example of this occurring in 1930's America. It is referred to as the Dust Bowl.

"The phenomenon was caused by a combination of both natural factors (severe drought) and manmade factors (a failure to apply dryland farming methods to prevent wind erosion, most notably the destruction of the natural topsoil by settlers in the region). The drought came in three waves: 1934, 1936, and 1939–1940, but some regions of the High Plains experienced drought conditions for as many as eight years."[15]

This happened during The Great Depression between 1930-1940 and was a contributing factor to that crisis. The area affected was the U.S. Midwest, the breadbasket of the country. The dust storms started in the eastern states in 1930, affecting agriculture from Maine to Arkansas. By 1934, they had reached the Great Plains, stretching from North Dakota to Texas and from the Mississippi River Valley to the Rocky Mountains.

These severe dust storms greatly damaged the ecology and agriculture of the American and Canadian prairies. They created choking billows of dust named "black blizzards" or "black rollers" that traveled across the country.

"The Dust Bowl forced tens of thousands of poverty-stricken families, who were unable to pay mortgages or grow crops, to abandon their farms, and losses reached $25 million per day by 1936 (equivalent to $490 million in 2021)."[15]

One particularly severe dust storm occurred on April 14, 1935. It was one of the worst dust storms in American history, and it caused immense economic and agricultural damage. The day is known as Black Sunday.[16]

There were other factors globally that contributed to this food shortage. The exportation and importation of food commodities from around the world were already struggling. The convergence of these conditions caused the price of wheat and other crop commodities to increase greatly.

"The combined effects of the disruption of the Russian Revolution, which decreased the supply of wheat and other commodity crops, and World War I increased agricultural prices;"[17]

Although affected, the Oil industry was not damaged during this time.

"In 1930, the second largest producer [of petroleum] was Venezuela, while in 1931 Russia came second on the list, the United States taking as hitherto prior place. In 1932, the production of Venezuela still further decreased, Russia again taking second place to the United States, the total output of which was 781 million barrels, or about 60 per cent of the world's total."[18]

It appears that the Black Horse of Revelation 6 was the one actually riding on the winds of the dust storms. Again, is the label "black" a coincidence? Maybe, but I don't think so. We will discuss later the reasons for the possible riding of this Horseman in 1935. The world was on the cusp of a huge prophetic event that would occur a decade later.

This was not the first famine to occur in the history of the world, nor was it the most severe. There are other famines that have recorded much greater starvation and death. The point is that when they occur, the balance of power in a region changes. When economies are depressed and famines occur, the power of a people is weakened, making them susceptible to other influences.

Another phenomenon in history, known as the Black Plague, was more insidious. We will explore that with the rider of the next horse.

The Pale or Ashen Horse

"I looked, and behold an ashen horse, and he who sat on it had the name Death, and Hades was following with him. Authority was given to them over a fourth of the earth, to kill with sword and with famine and with pestilence and by the wild beasts of the earth."

Revelation 6:8

The descriptive terms for the Pale Horse and rider are:

1. The rider's name is Death, and Hades followed with him.

2. …authority was given to him over a fourth of the earth (in our current world population, that would be over 2 billion people)

3. …to kill with the sword (terror events)

4. …with famine (or starvation)

5. …with pestilence (this would include plagues, diseases, and pandemics)

6. …and by wild beasts of the earth (creatures that carry death)

The Pale Horse represents terror events that end in death. The sources of these events will vary according to the list. Pestilence, for instance, is a deadly force that was referenced in a previous section. The Black Death was a strong example of such an event.

The Black Death was an epidemic of bubonic plague that spread across Europe and Asia in the mid-1300's; it is estimated to have killed over 20 million people in Europe—almost one-third of the continent's population.

"The plague arrived in Europe in October 1347, when 12 ships from the Black Sea docked at the Sicilian port of Messina. Most sailors aboard the ships were dead, and those still alive were gravely ill and covered in black boils that oozed blood and pus."[19]

These would become known as the "death ships."

"They know that the bacillus travels from person to person through the air, as well as through the bite of infected fleas and rats. Both of these pests could be found almost everywhere in medieval Europe, but they were particularly at home aboard ships of all kinds—which is how the deadly plague made its way through one European port city after another."[20]

In any case, when the Black Death reached Europe, it attacked a population that was already weakened and malnourished by the brutal nature of the feudal system economy.

"I think a good argument can be made that [the Black Death] hit at a time when the health of the poor was compromised by the stress of famines, poverty, and the very nature of serfdom."[21]

In one report, they observed that the disease was spread by bites of infected fleas and rats. You could say that the "wild beasts of the earth" were responsible for those deaths. Events that wipe out large populations of the earth are what this hideous rider of death is revealed in.

Another such event happened in the U.S. in 1918, called the Spanish Flu.

"The 1918 influenza pandemic was the most severe pandemic in recent history. It was caused by an H1N1 virus with genes of avian origin. Although there is no universal consensus regarding where the virus originated, it spread worldwide during 1918-1919. In the United States, it was first identified in military personnel in the spring of 1918.

It is estimated that about 500 million people, or one-third of the world's population, became infected with this virus. The number of deaths was estimated to be at least 50 million worldwide, with about 675,000 occurring in the United States. Mortality was high in people younger than 5 years old, 20-40 years old, and 65 years and older. The high mortality in healthy people, including those in the 20-40 year age group, was a unique feature of this pandemic."[22]

One more example of a killer diseases should be mentioned here since it has played a major role in the resettling of the Americas.

Smallpox was endemic to Europe, Asia, and Arabia for centuries, a persistent menace that killed three out of ten people it infected and left the rest with pockmarked scars. However, the death rate in the Old World paled in comparison to the devastation wrought on native populations in the New World when the smallpox virus arrived in the 15th century with the first European explorers.

The indigenous peoples of modern-day Mexico and the United States had zero natural immunity to smallpox, and the virus cut them down by the tens of millions.

"There hasn't been a kill off in human history to match what happened in the Americas—90 to 95 percent of the indigenous population wiped out over a century," says Mockaitis. "Mexico goes from 11 million people pre-conquest to one million."[23]

We have seen historically how these terror events reshaped our societies. It's easier to believe that these were just a random convergence of conditions that led to major catastrophes. What if they weren't so random? What if they are guided by forces unseen? We need to look to the Bible for more answers.

*"Thus says the LORD, the God of the Hebrews, 'Let My people go, that they may serve Me. For **this time I will send all My plagues on you** and your servants and your people, so that you may know that there is no one like Me in all the earth. For if by **now I had put forth My hand and struck you and your people with pestilence, you would then have been cut off from the earth.'"***

Exodus 9:13-15 (emphasis added)

*"When they fast, I am not going to listen to their cry; and when they offer burnt offering and grain offering, I am not going to accept them. Rather, **I am going to make an end of them by the sword, famine, and pestilence."***

Jeremiah 14:12 (emphasis added)

It is hard to imagine why a benevolent God would suggest or allow such plague and death to come upon mankind. What is clear is that it is a form of judgement passed on to people who have been wicked and deserving of harsh punishment. We do not sit in the seat of the Judge of the world. Nor do we understand what is required to keep the entire world safe from self-destruction.

It's not hard to believe that humanity is capable of destroying itself or the world Yahweh created. Events like the Great Flood can be seen as acts of mercy by God to preserve humanity. I wouldn't want His job! Still, we've seen how these decisions are not made by God alone, but by an entire council of advisors, a panel of other created beings. There is much to learn about the unseen realm.

The entirety of the history of the world reveals that civilization begins with a city. A case could be made that all our troubles started with cities and those who rule them. In the next section we will travel back in time and study the first city builders.

Chapter 4 - The First City Builders

"The LORD God planted a garden toward the east, in Eden; and there He placed the man whom He had formed. Out of the ground the LORD God caused to grow every tree that is pleasing to the sight and good for food...

Then the LORD God took the man and put him into the garden of Eden to cultivate it and keep it."

Genesis 2:8-9,15

Before discussing the first city builders, we must discuss the first people. Much discussion, speculation, and theories exist about how the first human beings organized into cities outside of the biblical narrative. Where did different people groups come from? How long ago was that? We are not going to attempt here to resolve all these deep questions. But I believe we can shed some much needed light on the subject.

We will be working off the premises of a biblical worldview. I believe that the foundational facts are given to us by God in the writings of the bible, but the smaller details are out there for us to discover. The Bible states that God created man. The first two people were placed in a garden, and it was their job to cultivate and keep it.

Let's review a quick pre-civilization account based on the Genesis story. The short of a long story is that the Garden of Eden proved to be a temporary assignment for Adam and his wife, Eve. Their new assignment thrust them into a much harsher environment. They would learn to work with their hands in the dirt, and by the sweat of their brow, they would grow food. Cain, the first son, was a tiller of the ground, and Abel, the second son, was a shepherd of flocks.

A family would have been the first basic community. The first family would grow into a large community when we factor in reproductive multiplication and passage of time. Cain was eventually driven away from that community for killing his brother Abel, and human expansion began. In essence, Cain was scattered so he could multiply, and multiply he did.

Archeologists and scholars tell us that the first cities were found to exist in the fertile crescent of Mesopotamia (more on that later). This area is most likely where the Garden of Eden was located. The same geographical markers are given in the Bible and our current maps, like the Euphrates and Tigris Rivers and the lush, well-watered plain of lower Mesopotamia.

*"Cain had relations with his wife, and she conceived and gave birth to Enoch; **and he built a city, and called the name of the city Enoch**, after the name of his son."*

Genesis 4:17 (emphasis added)

According to the Bible, Cain was the first city builder. If we add the lifespans given in the biblical account and if Cain lived anywhere close to the age of his brother Seth, he would have had about 900 years or so to build cities.

To add perspective, in a very rough analysis, the United States was settled by a small group of Europeans in Jamestown, Virginia, in 1607, and about 425 years later, we now have a population of over 350 million people. Given the longer lifespans, it is not inconceivable for there to be enough people to populate several large cities or city-states in the pre-flood world.

The first true towns or villages are sometimes considered large settlements where the inhabitants were no longer simply farmers of their lands but began to take on specialized occupations and where trade, food storage, and power were centralized. In 1950, Gordon Childe attempted to define a historic city with ten general metrics.[24] In Childe's analysis, these metrics are:

1. The size and density of the population should be above normal.

2. Differentiation of the population. Not all residents grow their own food, leading to specialists.

3. Payment of taxes to a deity or king.

4. Monumental public buildings.

5. Those not producing their own food are supported by the king.

6. Systems of recording and practical science.

7. A system of writing.

8. Development of symbolic art.

9. Trade and import of raw materials.

10. Specialist craftsmen from outside the kin group.

This categorization is descriptive and used as a general pattern when considering ancient cities, although not all have each of its characteristics.

Archeological sites as well as the earliest written records indicate that Eridu was one of the earliest cities and is believed to have existed from 5400 BCE – 600 BCE[25]. It is located in southern modern-day Iraq, in the fertile crescent of Mesopotamia.

Ancient Mesopotamia, the area of the Tigris and Euphrates rivers within modern-day Iraq and Syria, was home to many cities by the third millennium BCE. These cities formed the basis of the Sumerian and Akkadian cultures. Cities such as Jericho, Uruk, Ur, Nineveh, and Babylon, made legendary by the Bible, have been located and excavated, while others such as Damascus and Jerusalem have been continuously populated."[26]

Although there is much more to say about the pre-flood era, it is not the subject of this book except to the extent that civilizations existed prior to the flood. These preflood cities were, in some instances, most likely repopulated after the flood waters receded and became the source of ancient mystery and lure.

Civilization was abruptly interrupted by a divine force of nature, The Great Flood. Was there a reason God interrupted the growth of civilization and reduced the world's population?

The Great Flood

"Now the earth was corrupt in the sight of God, and the earth was filled with violence. God looked on the earth, and behold, it was corrupt; for all flesh had corrupted their way upon the earth.

Then God said to Noah, "The end of all flesh has come before Me; for the earth is filled with violence because of them; and behold, I am about to destroy them with the earth."

Genesis 6:11-13

We can define the earliest civilizations by either pre-flood, also called anti-diluvian, or post-flood historically. Although scholars don't quite agree on the actual date of the flood, most still acknowledge that a great flood occurred.

Archeology suggests that early anti-diluvian empires like Akkad and Sumer were repopulated shortly after the flood. Writings from Mesopotamian cities, such as the Eridu Genesis, a Sumerian epic, or a Babylonian epic called The Epic of Gilgamesh, share similar stories.

"According to Eridu Genesis, an ancient Sumerian religious epic, deities fashioned humankind from clay to cultivate the ground, care for flocks, and perpetuate the worship of the gods. Cities were soon built, but, for some reason, the gods determined to destroy humankind with a flood. Enki (Akkadian: Ea), who did not agree with the decree, revealed it to Ziusudra, a man well known for his humility and obedience. Ziusudra did as Enki commanded him and built a huge boat, in which he successfully rode out the flood. Afterward, he prostrated himself before the gods An (Anu) and Enlil, and, as a reward for living a godly life, Ziusudra was given immortality.

In the related Babylonian Gilgamesh epic, Utnapishtim and his wife are the survivors of the mythological flood, having preserved human and animal life in the great boat he built. The couple were then deified by the god Enlil as a reward for heeding the divine instruction to build an ark."[27]

In these accounts we see Ziusudra and Utnapishtim loosely taking on the role of Noah. As with Noah, each saved the animals and repopulated the world. They also believed their patron god gave them their mandate.

The biblical account is clear that Noah, his wife, his three sons, and their wives survived the flood and reset the genetic stock from which all modern people came.

Again, we are working on the premise of a biblical worldview. We must then seek to trace post-flood civilizations back to Noah's sons and grandsons. The biblical record can be found in Genesis 10, commonly called the Table of Nations.

There is another matter of importance surrounding the flood narrative. It is the subject of a later section of this book called The Great Rebellion. We'll continue that discussion there. For now, we will see how God orchestrated or guided the repopulation of the world. The result of the flood was that one family survived the deluge, and one set of human genetics repopulated the earth. The animals (not including sea creatures) were also hand-picked by God to ensure good genetic stock. Does history support this enormous Biblical claim that one family repopulated the earth?

The Table of Nations - The Sixteen Grandsons of Noah

"Now the sons of Noah who came out of the ark were Shem and Ham and Japheth; and Ham was the father of Canaan. These three were the sons of Noah, and from these the whole earth was populated."

Genesis 9:18-19

The biblical account of Noah and his family, as well as the subsequent generations and nations that descended from them, is indeed a central narrative in the Old Testament. According to the Bible, Noah and his family were the sole survivors of a great flood that covered the Earth, and it fell upon his three sons, Shem, Ham, and Japheth, and their wives to repopulate the world through their descendants.

Genesis chapter 10 provides a list of 16 grandsons of Noah, representing the heads of family clans that went on to establish various populations in different regions of the ancient world. The Bible offers these names as historical figures, although further research into the original languages may be required for precise identification.

In the generations following the Flood, people were reported to have lived exceptionally long lives, often outlived their children, grandchildren, and great-grandchildren. These extended lifespans set them apart from later generations.

As the descendants of Noah's grandsons spread across the Earth, several practices emerged:

1. **Naming After Ancestors:** In various regions, people began to identify with their common ancestor's name, tracing their lineage back to one of Noah's grandsons.

2. **Naming of Lands and Features:** Similarly, they named their lands, major cities, and prominent rivers after their ancestral forefathers, a tradition that can be seen in the naming of places in ancient histories.

3. **Ancestor Worship:** In some cases, these nations or groups turned to ancestor worship, deifying their long-lived ancestor, or naming their gods after them.

This tradition of naming, ancestor worship, and preserving historical narratives has been passed down through generations, contributing to the rich tapestry of human history. The biblical account serves as a foundational text for many cultures and religions and continues to shape the understanding of humanity's ancient past.

The Seven Sons of Japheth

"Now these are the records of the generations of Shem, Ham, and Japheth, the sons of Noah; and sons were born to them after the flood. The sons of Japheth were Gomer and Magog and Madai and Javan and Tubal and Meshech and Tiras."

Genesis 10:1-2

The first of Noah's grandsons mentioned is **Gomer**. Ezekiel locates the early descendants of Gomer, along with Togarmah (a son of Gomer), in the north quarters (Ezekiel 38:6.)

In modern Turkey is an area which in New Testament times was called **Galatia**. The Jewish historian Flavius Josephus records that the people who were called Galatians or Gauls in his day (c. AD 93) were previously called Gomerites.

They migrated westward to what are now called **France** and **Spain**. For many centuries, France was called Gaul, after the descendants of Gomer. North-west Spain is called Galicia to this day.

Some of the Gomerites migrated further to what is now called **Wales**. The Welsh historian, Davis, records a traditional Welsh belief that the descendants of Gomer 'landed on the Isle of Britain from France, about three hundred years after the flood,' he also records that the Welsh language is called Gomeraeg (after their ancestor, Gomer.)

Other members of their clan settled along the way, including in **Armenia**. The sons of Gomer were 'Ashkenaz, and Riphath, and Togarmah' (Genesis 10:3). Encyclopedia Britannica says that the Armenians traditionally claim to be descended from Togarmah and Ashkenaz. Ancient Armenia reached into **Turkey**. The name Turkey probably comes from Togarmah. Others of them migrated to

Germany. Ashkenaz is the Hebrew word for **Germany**.

The next grandson mentioned is **Magog**. According to Ezekiel, Magog lived in the northern parts (Ezekiel 38:15, 39:2.) Josephus records that those whom he called Magogites, the Greeks called Scythians. According to Encyclopedia Britannica, the ancient name for the region, which now includes part of **Romania** and the **Ukraine,** was Scythia.

The next grandson is **Madai**. Along with Shem's son Elam, Madai is the ancestor of our modern-day Iranians. Josephus says that the descendants of Madai were called **Medes** by the Greeks. Every time the Medes are mentioned in the Old Testament, the Hebrew word *Madai* (maday) is used. After the time of Cyrus, the Medes are always (with one exception) mentioned along with the Persians. They became one kingdom with one law— 'the law of the Medes and Persians' (Daniel 6:8, 12, 15). Later, they were simply called **Persians**. Since 1935, they have called their country **Iran**. The Medes also 'settled **India**'.

The name of the next grandson, **Javan**, is the Hebrew word for **Greece**. Greece, Grecia, or Grecians appears five times in the Old Testament and is always the Hebrew word Javan. Daniel refers to 'the king of Grecia' (Daniel 8:21), literally 'the king of Javan.' Javan's sons were Elishah, Tarshish, Kittim, and Dodanim (Genesis 10:4), all of whom have connections with the Greek people. The Elysians (an ancient Greek people) obviously received their name from Elishah. Tarshish or Tarsus was located in the region of Cilicia (modern **Turkey**.)

Encyclopedia Britannica says that Kittim (also the name of Javan's third son) is the biblical name for **Cyprus**. The people who initially settled around the area of Troy worshipped Jupiter under the name of Jupiter Dodonaeus, possibly a reference to the fourth son of Javan (Dodanim), with Jupiter a derivative of Japheth. His oracle was at Dodena. The Greeks worshipped this god but called him Zeus.

Next is **<u>Tubal</u>**. Ezekiel mentions him along with Gog and Meshech (Ezekiel 39:1.) Tiglath-pileser I, king of Assyria in about 1100 BC, refers to the descendants of Tubal as the Tabali. Josephus recorded their name as the Thobelites, later known as Iberes.

'Their land, in Josephus' day, was called by the Romans Iberia, and covered what is now (the former Soviet State of) **Georgia,** whose capital to this day bears the name Tubal as Tbilisi. From here, having crossed the Caucasus mountains, these people migrated north-east, giving their tribal name to the river Tobol and, hence, to the famous city of Tobolsk.'

<u>Meshech</u>, the name of the next grandson, is the ancient name for **Moscow**. Moscow is both the capital of Russia and the region that surrounds the city. To this day, one section, the Meshchera Lowland, still carries the name of Meshech, virtually unchanged by the ages.

According to Josephus, the descendants of grandson **<u>Tiras</u>** were called Thirasians. The Greeks changed their name to Thracians. Thrace reached from **Macedonia** on the south to the Danube River on the north to the Black Sea on the east. It took in much of what became **Yugoslavia**. World Book Encyclopedia says, "The people of Thrace were savage Indo-Europeans, who liked warfare and looting," Tiras was worshipped by his descendants as Thuras, or Thor, the god of thunder.

The Four Sons of Ham

Next, we come to the sons of Ham: Cush, Mizraim, Phut, and Canaan (Genesis 10:6.)

The descendants of Ham live mainly in south-west Asia and Africa. The Bible often refers to **Africa** as the land of Ham (Psalms 105:23,27; 106:22.) The name of Noah's grandson, **Cush,** is the Hebrew word for old Ethiopia (from Aswan south to Khartoum). Without exception, the word **Ethiopia** in the English Bible is always a translation of the Hebrew word Cush. Josephus rendered the name as Chus and said that the Ethiopians 'are even to this day, both by themselves and by all men in Asia, called Chusites.'

Noah's next grandson mentioned was **Mizraim**. Mizraim (mitsrayîm, מצרים) is the Hebrew word for **Egypt**. The name Egypt appears hundreds of times in the Old Testament and (with one exception) is always a translation of the word Mizraim. For example, at the burial of Jacob, the Canaanites observed the mourning of the Egyptians and so-called the place Abel Mizraim (Genesis 50:11.)

Phut, the name of Noah's next grandson, is the Hebrew name for **Libya**. It is translated three times in the Old Testament. The ancient river Phut was in Libya. By Daniel's day, the name had been changed to Libya (Daniel 11:43.) Josephus says, "Phut also was the founder of Libia [sic] and called the inhabitants Phutites, from himself."

Canaan, the name of Noah's next grandson, is the Hebrew name for the general region later called by the Romans **Palestine**, i.e., modern Israel and Jordan. Here we should look briefly at a few of the descendants of Ham (Genesis 10:14–18.)

There is Philistim, obviously the ancestor of the Philistines (clearly giving rise to the name Palestine,) and Sidon, the founder of the ancient city that bears his name, and Heth, the patriarch of the ancient Hittite empire. Also, this descendant is listed in Genesis 10:15–18 as being the ancestor of the Jebusites (Jebus was the ancient name for Jerusalem—Judges 19:10,) the Amorites, the Girgasites, the Hivites, the Arkites, the Sinites, the Arvadites, the Zemarites, and the Hamathites, ancient peoples who lived in the land of Canaan.

The most prominent descendant of Ham was **Nimrod**, son of Cush, the founder of Babel (Babylon) as well as of Erech, Accad, and Calneh in Shinar (Babylonia.)

The Five Sons of Shem

Last, we come to the sons of Shem: Elam, Asshur, Arphaxad, Lud, and Aram (Genesis 10:22.)

<u>Elam</u> is the ancient name for **Persia**, which is itself the ancient name for **Iran**. Until the time of Cyrus, the people here were called Elamites, and they were still often called that even in New Testament times. In Acts 2:9, the Jews from Persia who were present at Pentecost were called Elamites. Thus, The Persians are descended from Elam, the son of Shem, and from Madai, the son of Japheth (see above). Since the 1930s, they have called their country Iran.

It is interesting to note that the word 'Aryan,' which so fascinated Adolf Hitler, is a form of the word 'Iran,' Hitler wanted to produce a pure Aryan 'race' of supermen. But the very term 'Aryan' signifies a mixed line of Semites and Japhethites!

<u>Asshur</u> is the Hebrew word for **Assyria**. Assyria was one of the great ancient empires. Every time the words Assyria or Assyrian appear in the Old Testament, they are translated from the word Asshur. He was worshipped by his descendants.

'Indeed, as long as Assyria lasted, that is until 612 BCE, accounts of battles, diplomatic affairs, and foreign bulletins were daily read out to his image, and every Assyrian king held that he wore the crown only with the express permission of Asshur's deified ghost.'

<u>Arphaxad</u> was the progenitor of the **Chaldeans**. This 'is confirmed by the Hurrian (Nuzi) tablets, which render the name as Arip-hurra—the founder of Chaldea.' His descendant, Eber (Heber), gave his name to the **Hebrew** people via the line of Eber-Peleg-Reu-

Serug-Nahor-Terah-Abram (Genesis 11:16–26). Eber's other son, Joktan, had 13 sons (Genesis 10:26–30), all of whom appear to have settled in **Arabia**.

Lud was the ancestor of the **Lydians**. Lydia was in what is now **Western Turkey**. Their capital was Sardis—one of the seven churches of Asia was at Sardis (Revelation 3:1).

Aram is the Hebrew word for **Syria**. Whenever the word Syria appears in the Old Testament, it is a translation of the word Aram. The Syrians call themselves Arameans, and their language is called Aramaic. Before the spread of the Greek Empire, Aramaic was the international language (2 Kings 18:26). On the Cross, when Jesus cried out, 'Eloi, Eloi, lama sabachthani' (Mark 15:34), he was speaking Aramaic, the language of the common people.

Conclusion

We have only taken the briefest glance at Noah's sixteen grandsons, but enough has been said to show that they lived, were who the Bible says they were, and that their descendants are identifiable on the pages of history. The Bible is not a collection of myths and legends, but it stands as an important key to the history of the world's earliest civilizations.[28]

Seventy Nations and The Seventy Sons of God

*"When the Most High gave the nations their inheritance, when He separated the sons of man, He set the boundaries of the peoples **according to the number of the sons of [God].** 'For the LORD'S portion is His people; Jacob is the allotment of His inheritance.'"*

Deuteronomy 32:8-9 (emphasis added)

The seventy "sons of God" is a topic that connects to a greater subject of the Divine Council in scripture. Historically, we are covering this topic out of order since the division of nations happens at the Tower of Babel. An event we'll cover in a subsequent section. It does, however, become relevant in discussing the division and repopulation of the world.

The passage above declares that when the nations and languages of the world were divided at Babel, seventy principalities were assigned, by Yahweh, one for each nation or territory, presumably. These principalities are referred to as the sons of [God] (In many translations the name, Israel, is inserted instead of God in the highlighted passage above. According to the Septuagint, it is rendered as "angels of God." Since Israel did not exist at the time when the boundaries of the nations were set after the Tower of Babel event. It is more accurately translated "sons of God". A good case for that translation is made by Michael Heiser in his book, "The Unseen Realm," in which He renders them as sons of El. These are lesser Elohim created by Yahweh, and now given authority over the nations.

We are not given much more detail about these territorial principalities except that they are hinted to in several ways throughout scripture. Deuteronomy 32:8-9 states that the Sons of God were appointed over the nations; this becomes an established fact. How they function is where we lack detail.

We know that they answer to an appointed council or divine council. We also know they are given authority to influence their respective territories, the cities, and people that reside in them, more specifically, the power structures in those regions. The apostle Paul understood this when he wrote,

*"For our struggle is not against flesh and blood, but against the rulers, against the powers, **against the world forces of this darkness**, against the spiritual forces of wickedness in the heavenly places."*

Ephesians 6:12 (emphasis added)

Paul makes another reference to these supernatural authorities,

*"...so that the manifold wisdom of God might now be made known through the church **to the rulers and the authorities in the heavenly places.**"*

Ephesians 3:10 (emphasis added)

In our previous example of the principality of Persia in Daniel chapter 10, we read,

"But the prince of the kingdom of Persia was withstanding me for twenty-one days; then behold, Michael, one of the chief princes, came to help me, for I had been left there with the kings of Persia."

Daniel 10:13

We would like to believe that these "sons of God" would always be compliant to Yahweh, but we see here that the "prince of Persia" was in opposition to Gabriel the angelic messenger sent to Daniel. It is in these rare glimpses that an unseen realm unfolds and reveals a whole other-dimensional reality at work in our world.

These seventy Elohim are reflected in the pattern repeated on Mount Sinai as we spoke about earlier, when the seventy Elders of Israel had a meal on the mountain in the presence of Yahweh. Where did these seventy elders of Israel come from? They were instructed to be chosen from the appointed elders and officers and then they were anointed by Yahweh Himself.

"The LORD therefore said to Moses, "Gather for Me seventy men from the elders of Israel, whom you know to be the elders of the people and their officers and bring them to the tent of meeting, and let them take their stand there with you. Then I will come down and speak with you there, and I will take of the Spirit who is upon you, and will put Him upon them; and they shall bear the burden of the people with you, so that you will not bear it all alone."

Numbers 11:16-17

They were both appointed by Moses and anointed by Yahweh as a part of Moses' council.

In similar fashion Yeshua forms an appointed and anointed group around Himself. The group consisted of twelve disciples or apostles and seventy appointed ambassadors who were to go out ahead of Him and proclaim, "the kingdom of God is at hand".

"Now after this the Lord appointed seventy others, and sent them in pairs ahead of Him to every city and place where He Himself was

going to come… and say to them, 'The kingdom of God has come near to you.'"

Luke 10:1-2, 9

Eventually the ambassadors of the New Testament were sent out to all the nations, represented by seventy, with their message of hope.

*"The seventy returned with joy, saying, 'Lord, even the demons are subject to us in Your name.' And He said to them, **'I was watching Satan fall from heaven like lightning. Behold, I have given you authority to tread on serpents and scorpions, and over all the power of the enemy, and nothing will injure you.** Nevertheless do not rejoice in this, that the spirits are subject to you, but rejoice that your names are recorded in heaven.'"*

Luke 10:17-20 (emphasis added)

There is a pattern here of seventy appointed members which connects us to the division of seventy nations after the Tower of Babel incident. We must remember that all these represent not only the nations of the world but more specifically, the principalities set over those nations. These will continue to have their role in the unfolding of human history and have their part in shaping the geopolitics of the world.

Yahweh's Portion

Yahweh separates a portion for Himself. This portion is the Land of Israel according to the boundaries described to Moses. This geography will be marked as His land and given as an inheritance to His people Israel. The promise of this inheritance started in Genesis 12.

> *"Now the LORD said to Abram, 'Go forth from your country, and from your relatives and from your father's house,*
> ***To the land which I will show you****; and I will make you a great nation, and I will bless you, and make your name great;'"*

Genesis 12:1-2 (emphasis added)

And in another place, He says,

> *"The LORD said to Abram, after Lot had separated from him,*
> ***'Now lift up your eyes and look from the place where you are, northward and southward and eastward and westward; for all the land which you see, I will give it to you and to your descendants forever.*** *I will make your descendants as the dust of the earth, so that if anyone can number the dust of the earth, then your descendants can also be numbered. Arise, walk about the land through its length and breadth; for I will give it to you.'"*

Genesis 13:14-17 (emphasis added)

This was Yahweh's portion to give to whomever He would choose. Yahweh chose Abraham and his descendants through his son Isaac and his son Jacob. It was prophesied that Abraham's descendants would live in Egypt for a period of time but return 430 years later, back to this land.

During this return or the Exodus from Egypt, Yahweh reiterates to His people through Moses this intention, and defines the boundaries of His territory.

"I will fix your boundary from the Red Sea to the sea of the Philistines, and from the wilderness to the River Euphrates;"

Exodus 23:31

Later, in Deuteronomy, Moses declares that Yahweh may enlarge their territory, bringing it back to His original plan.

"If the LORD your God enlarges your territory, just as He has sworn to your fathers, and gives you all the land which He promised to give your fathers..."

Deuteronomy 19:8

The Prophet Ezekiel gives a future establishment of boundaries,

"This shall be the boundary of the land: on the north side, from the Great Sea by the way of Hethlon, to the entrance of Zedad; Hamath, Berothah, Sibraim, which is between the border of Damascus and the border of Hamath; Hazer-hatticon, which is by the border of Hauran. The boundary shall extend from the sea to Hazar-enan at the border of Damascus, and on the north toward the north is the border of Hamath. This is the north side."

"The east side, from between Hauran, Damascus, Gilead and the land of Israel, shall be the Jordan; from the north border to the eastern sea you shall measure. This is the east side."

"The south side toward the south shall extend from Tamar as far

*as the waters of Meribath-kadesh, to the brook of Egypt and to the
Great Sea. This is the south side toward the south."*

*"The west side shall be the Great Sea, from the south border to a
point opposite Lebo-hamath. This is the west side."*

Ezekiel 47:15-20

These expanded boundaries of the Nation of Israel are not yet
realized currently. Ezekiel prophesied of a future date when Israel will
enjoy these newly defined boundaries.

In addition to the physical boundaries of the Land, there is a
spiritual aspect to consider. This quote is from Eliezer Schweid, an
Israeli scholar, writer, and professor of Jewish Philosophy at the
Hebrew University of Jerusalem.

"Eliezer Schweid sees Canaan as a geographical name and Israel
the spiritual name of the land. He writes: "The uniqueness of the Land
of Israel is thus **"geo-theological"** and not merely climatic. This is
the land that faces the entrance of the spiritual world, that sphere of
existence that lies beyond the physical world known to us through our
senses. This is the key to the land's unique status with regard to
prophecy and prayer, and also with regard to the commandments."[29]

This is Yahweh's Land! There is a city in Israel named Beth-El,
meaning "house of God"; the original name comes from Jacob. In
Genesis 28:10-22, Jacob falls asleep on a stone pillow and has a
dream of the heavens opening and a ladder descends upon the earth.
The angels of God were ascending and descending on it. Yahweh
stood above it and declared that Jacob and his descendants would be
brought back to this Land. Jacob awoke and realized that he was in a

92

place like no other.

> *"Then Jacob awoke from his sleep and said, "Surely the LORD is in this place, and I did not know it." He was afraid and said, "How awesome is this place! This is none other than the house of God,* ***and this is the gate of heaven****."*

Genesis 28:16-17 (emphasis added)

Yahweh reveals through the dream that there is a supernatural connection between heaven and this land. The ladder imagery of the dream represents a gateway to Heaven and from heaven to earth. Is it possible that this geographical area holds a hidden portal between the two realms?

Yahweh continues to choose this area over and over again. It would be several hundred years later that Yahweh's presence would come and rest in the Temple at Jerusalem (2 Chronicles 7:1.)

It is also prophesied in Zechariah (Zechariah 14:4) that in the future, Yahweh will set His feet on the Mount of Olives (just outside the city of Jerusalem.)

Modern-day Beth-El is only about 10 miles from the city of Jerusalem, but some rabbinical sources believe that the location of Jacob's dream was on Mount Moriah. The same Mount that Abraham offered Isaac on. This is also where the Temple was eventually built almost 800 years later. Whether Jacob's dream was on Mount Moriah or not, it still puts them in very close proximity to each other and on Yahweh's real estate.

Another interesting fact is that when Israel conquered the land of Canaan, the Ark of the Covenant (the Ark of Presence) first came to rest in the city of Bethel (Judges 20:26-27) before being moved to Shiloh. The Tabernacle was re-assembled and kept in Shiloh (Joshua 18:1) for 369 years until King David moved the Ark to a tent in Jerusalem (2 Chronicles 1:3-4), and an altar was built in Gibeon where they offered sacrifice on the high place (1 Chronicles 21:29), and eventually it was placed in the temple in Jerusalem by King Solomon.

The point of this discussion is that on occasion, these principalities, sent to govern the nations, rebel against the Most High. They overstep their bounds and try to take His portion of land for themselves. It is only when Israel is in rebellion themselves that Yahweh gives permission to the nations to inhabit His Land, only to serve His purposes. The entire end-of-days scenario is a battle for His Land, His Holy city, and the salvation of His people. We know who ultimately wins.

In the next section, we will discuss the rise of a warrior-king who strategically established several city-states in opposition to Yahweh. He was the son of one of the sixteen grandsons of Noah, the son of Cush; his name was Nimrod.

Chapter 5 – The Rebellion of Nimrod

"Now Cush became the father of Nimrod; he became a mighty one on the earth. He was a mighty hunter before the LORD; therefore it is said, "Like Nimrod a mighty hunter before the LORD." The beginning of his kingdom was Babel and Erech and Accad and Calneh, in the land of Shinar. From that land he went forth into Assyria, and built Nineveh and Rehoboth-Ir and Calah, and Resen between Nineveh and Calah; that is the great city."

Genesis 10:8-12

The name Nimrod comes from the Hebrew root word, *marad* (Strong's H4775,) meaning "revolt" or "rebellion."

Nimrod is the first Warrior-King revealed in the bible. He was celebrated as both a great warrior and a kingdom builder. He established cities in southern Mesopotamia and later in northern Mesopotamia; both areas are near the Euphrates and Tigris Rivers. He is possibly the historical king known as Sargon, the Great, of Akkad. Nimrod is credited with building the cities of Babel, Akkad, Erech, Calneh in the land of Shinar, and Nineveh, Calah, and Resen in Assyria.

The phrase, "a mighty hunter before the Lord," gives insight into his charisma as a recruiter and leader of the first military forces. This is not likely an epithet of his ability to hunt wild game but as a hunter of men. With these military forces, he could subjugate people to his cause. It is the only plausible way he could maintain control of these great cities.

Archeology has given us insight into these ancient cities. One unique feature of these cities is that the inhabitants built walls around themselves, with narrowed entry points or gates. Walls can be built to define territory, but more importantly, they are built for protection. They needed to protect their resources, way of life, and structures from those who would want to forcibly take them away.

The first military could have simply been formed for protection, but that same organized militia could also be used to acquire new territories. In the control of a tyrant, these same forces could be enlisted to subjugate other peoples. Nimrod was a mighty hunter, a subjugator of people.

There is another aspect to the nature of Nimrod's tour-de-force. As his name implies, he was a rebel, in rebellion against the God of his fathers. Nimrod chose the side of the antagonists to Yahweh and His sovereignty over mankind. This takes us back to the Garden of Eden, where the first rebellion occurred, and the first adversary was revealed.

The First Rebellion

"Then the LORD God said to the woman, "What is this you have done?" And the woman said, "The serpent deceived me, and I ate."

Genesis 3:13

Adam and Eve were given an idyllic lifestyle. Their home was a garden, food was plentiful, and most importantly, they were in a close relationship with their Creator and maker of this new world. An adversary was let into the garden, and their loyalty would ultimately be tested. They had explicit instructions not to partake of the fruit of one tree: the Tree of the Knowledge of Good and Evil.

The label given to this fruit tree defines its nature not only as a physical tree but also as a spiritual gateway to knowledge from a hidden realm. The voice of this adversary was full of half-truths and lies, and access to that secret knowledge would come at a price. Yeshua addresses the religious of His day and declares,

*"You are of your father the devil, and you want to do the desires of your father. He was a murderer from the beginning, and does not stand in the truth because there is no truth in him. Whenever he speaks a lie, he speaks from his own nature, **for he is a liar and the father of lies**."*

John 8:44 (emphasis added)

*"... You serpents, **you brood [offspring] of vipers**, how will you escape the sentence of hell?"*

Matthew 23:33 (emphasis added)

This type of soft-pedaled rebellion is always based on believing lies or being convinced that God has lied to you. The idea or concept of deception was introduced by Satan, the Father of Lies. The serpent deceived Eve.

Deceit, by definition, is the action or practice of misdirecting someone by concealing or misrepresenting the truth; to carry one away on a false premise.

The Adversary twisted what Yahweh said, and when the Serpent said, "You will not surely die," the contradiction gave birth to the LIE. That lie continues to be the poison in the apple; repeatedly, he changes the truth of God into a lie.

*"When the woman saw that the tree was good for food, and that it was a delight to the eyes, and that **the tree was desirable to make one wise**, she took from its fruit and ate; and she gave also to her husband with her, and he ate."*

Genesis 3:6 (emphasis added)

"A tree to make one wise" is how the adversary sets himself up as the possessor of secret knowledge, only revealed when you rebel against Yahweh and follow the serpent's "wisdom". The occult has always been synonymous with secret or hidden mysteries, secret societies, and secret rituals, and even promises to reveal the secrets to wealth and power. The description of the Serpent conveys this idea.

The word for serpent in Genesis is the Hebrew word *nachash*, it is connected to a prime root word meaning "divination or one who practices divination" (Strong's H5172). In short form, The Serpent was the first medium to reveal this secret wisdom and its occultic practices and give man an alternative to Yahweh's true path.

*"Behold, to obey is better than sacrifice, And to heed than the fat of rams. **For rebellion is as the sin of divination, And insubordination is as iniquity and idolatry. "***

1 Samuel 15:22-23 (emphasis added)

Rebellion against the instructions or commands of Yahweh opens a door for another spirit to enter a person's heart; this is divination. This truth will play out over and over again throughout human history. We will find the occult at the center of every rebellious city-state. It is the pattern!

Adam and Eve's rebellion was met with harsh consequences, and they were expelled from the sacred space of Eden. They were now compromised with a different spirit. Remember, they ate from the tree that offered a new knowledge or awareness of good, AND EVIL. They were now under the influence of the adversary.

Their rebellion did not stop there; after Cain and Abel were born, the adversary pursued Adam's firstborn son. Cain was confronted personally by Yahweh after his sacrifice was rejected.

Yahweh states, *"Sin is crouching at the door, and its desire is for you, but you must master it."*

Genesis 4:7

The term "crouching" reveals the personal nature of this evil, like a lion crouching in wait for its prey.

Cain was instructed to master this evil, to resist its temptation. He chose rather to act in rebellion towards his brother Abel's right to life and killed him. Like his father and mother's exile from Eden, and as a consequence of his sin, Cain was exiled from his family's territory. He was sentenced to be a wanderer on the earth.

An additional meaning to the *nachash* is its connection to "mixed" metals. This technology would eventually be introduced to Tubal-Cain (Genesis 4:22) by the "fallen ones," but more later. The word for mixed metals like bronze (modern bronze is typically 88% copper and 12% tin) is *nechosheth*, taken from the same root word as *nachash* (serpent). This does not render the meaning that bronze is evil; it means it's a mixture. The Serpent in Eden was a mixture of an earthly creature and a spiritual being. This type of mixture produced an evil outcome. Now combine that with the idea of *nachash,* meaning "one who practices divination," and you have an evil adversarial spirit mixing with man. This is forbidden, according to Deut. 18:10-14,

*"There shall not be found among you anyone who makes his son or his daughter pass through the fire, one who uses divination, one who practices witchcraft, or **one who interprets** [nachash] **omens**, or a sorcerer, or one who casts a spell, or a medium, or a spiritist, or one who calls up the dead.*

***For whoever does these things is detestable to the LORD**; and because of these detestable things the LORD your God will drive them out before you…"*

"For those nations, which you shall dispossess, listen to those who practice witchcraft and to diviners, but as for you, the LORD your God has not allowed you to do so."

Deuteronomy 18:10-14

The required condition is that to obtain these secrets or hidden wisdom, one must act in rebellion against the instructions/laws of Yahweh, the true God. Adam and Eve had to eat the fruit of the forbidden tree, then they would become "wise like God!" or would they? Through this deception, the adversary achieved power over mankind, specifically, the power of death itself.

Satan cleverly used God's own punishment of "death for disobedience" to ensnare his victims. He deceives Adam into relinquishing the dominion over the earth that was given to him and to mankind. Satan assumes sovereignty for himself and becomes the "god of this world" (2 Corinthians 4:4; Ephesians 2:1).

It was an ingeniously diabolical plan, teaching us that we should never underestimate the cunning of our adversary!

Many theologians attribute the identity of the serpent to Satan. Although not wrong, the Hebrew word *satan*, Strong's H7854 - śāṭān, simply means "adversary", it is not a proper name. The Adversary takes on different names and forms at various times, but his function remains the same. For example, Rev 12:9 calls him the great dragon, the serpent of old, the devil, and Satan (adversary).

In Isaiah 14:12, he is called the "shining one" or Lucifer. These names or titles are descriptive. Each one reveals more about this adversary, and (a teaser) there may be more than one.

Before we can get back to Nimrod, we need to explore one more important thing about the first rebellion. The clue is in Genesis 3:15. In this passage, Yahweh is speaking to the serpent or, more specifically, the entity behind the serpent.

*"And I will put enmity between you and the woman, **and between your seed and her seed**; He shall bruise you on the head, and you shall bruise him on the heel."*

Genesis 3:15 (emphasis added)

The race is now on for dominion over creation, as Yahweh pronounces punishment as a consequence of man's disobedience. Adam gave up dominion of the earth, and the adversary was given boundaries for this new sovereignty he stole from man. Now, one would think that Yahweh should have just taken it away from The Satan (the adversary), but He created the world with a divine order, and that order is regulated by divine law. Yahweh is a God of order, and to keep it, He must work "legally" - or He is no longer a God of order. Adam legally gave away sovereignty, and Yahweh must legally get it back.

Yahweh declares that He will restore order through "the seed of the woman," but there will be another seed spoken of in this prophecy, "the seed of the serpent," to challenge the regaining of that authority. Here is where the Nachash's mixing will take place: the mixing or hybridization of human seed.

Genetically altered humans will be on Satan's agenda as he desires to build an army of rebellion against the Creator. Sounds preposterous? This will become a cosmic battle that will continue until the restoration of all things at the end-of-days. We will explore this reality in the next section, The Great Rebellion.

You have just been introduced to the entirety of the Bible through the Genesis 3:15 prophecy. It is through the seed of the woman that

Yahweh will take a people to Himself through whom He will restore order, and they will become kings and priests on the earth He created and sons in His heavenly realm. Divine order will be restored!

We can now see Genesis 3:15 as a profound prophecy, hidden in plain sight: Yahweh will bring restoration back to the world through a future child of mankind, the seed of the woman. But Yahweh informed us that there was going to be an antagonist to this offspring, who would bruise His heel. Not only the heel of Messiah, but the heels of every son of righteousness leading up to His advent and anyone after who dares to follow after Messiah.

The "seed of the Serpent?" - we really need to think about this. Is Yahweh suggesting that snakes are going to be a nuisance to Yeshua, nipping at His heels as He walks around on His earthly mission? I don't think so. Is the serpent's seed only referring to all the "bad people" in the world?

It's more supernatural and more literal than that. Messiah is more than just a man; His origin is in the spirit realm. It stands to reason then that the seed of the serpent is also more than a mere man (or reptile). This seed of the serpent must be spiritual in origin and then manifest itself in the physical realm.

Is there any biblical reference to an event like this, a supernatural event that produces a physical seed for the Serpent? Yes…there is.

The Great Rebellion

The Satan is not without a plan of his own. Man must now contend with the seed of the serpent. The Adversary will not give up this newly acquired power and authority easily. This brings us to Genesis 6.

*"Now it came about, when men began to multiply on the face of the land, and daughters were born to them, that the **sons of God** saw that the **daughters of men** were beautiful; and they took wives for themselves, whomever they chose."*

*"...The Nephilim were on the earth in those days, and also afterward, when the sons of God came into the daughters of men, **and they bore children to them**. Those were the mighty men who were of old, men of renown."*

Genesis 6:1-2,4 (emphasis added)

This passage of scripture has been difficult to understand. It has been discussed by theologians for millennia. There are several theories as to the meaning of this passage, and many books have been written on the subject. The question starts with who "the sons of God" and "the daughters of men" are.

The second question is, what was the result of their unholy union? Some have explained this away as a taboo relationship with Adam's righteous descendants through his son Seth, referred to as "the sons of God," and the unrighteous line of women born to Cain, referred to as the "the daughters of men." The idea is that their offspring were simply important people in history (a rough summation). This is called the Sethite view. The following is a quote from Dr. Michael Heiser's well-documented book, The Unseen Realm.

"Exposing the deficiencies of the Sethite view isn't difficult. The position is deeply flawed. First, Genesis 4:26 ("men began to call on the name of the Lord") never says the *only* people who "called on the name of the Lord" were men from Seth's lineage. That idea is imposed on the text. Second, the view fails miserably in explaining the Nephilim. Third, the text never calls the women in the episode "daughters of Cain." Rather, they are "daughters of humankind." There is no actual link in the text to Cain. This means the Sethite view of the text is supported by something *not* present in the text, which is the very antithesis of exegesis. Fourth, there is no command in the text regarding marriages or any prohibition against marrying certain persons. There are no "Jews and Gentiles" at this time. Fifth, nothing in Genesis 6:1-4 or anywhere else in the Bible identifies people who come from Seth's lineage with the descriptive phrase "sons of God." That connection is purely an assumption through which the story is filtered by those who hold the Sethite view."[30]

The most plausible interpretation and the view held by most Jewish writers and historians of Old Testament literature is that the "sons of God" refer to rebellious angelic beings that left their "first estate" (2 Peter 2:1-10) and took for themselves human women and mated with them, and through this unholy union, created a hybrid race of giants or genetically altered humans on the earth. These would be considered the "seed of the serpent", both a physical seed and a supernatural, evil seed, creating a human-angel hybrid.

Because of their earth-bound and genetically wild nature, scripture refers to them at times as beasts. These altered humans' lust for power and control drive them to dominate men. They find their way into royalty, governments, and military organizations and have become the driving rebellious forces of the nations, i.e., Daniel's four beasts or the Revelation chapter 13 beasts.

This would explain why Yahweh would choose to destroy "all flesh" on the earth. The flood became a supernatural cleansing of the genetics of creation.

*"Now the earth was corrupt in the sight of God, and the earth was filled with violence. God looked on the earth, and behold, it was corrupt, **for all flesh had corrupted their way upon the earth**. Then God said to Noah, "**The end of all flesh has come before Me; for the earth is filled with violence because of them; and behold, I am about to destroy them with the earth.**"*

Genesis 6:11-13 (emphasis added)

The extra biblical book of 1 Enoch chapter 6 tells the Genesis 6 story more descriptively.

"And it came to pass when the children of men had multiplied, and in those days, they were born unto them beautiful and comely daughters. And **the angels**, the children of the heaven, saw and lusted after them, and said to one another: "**Come, let us choose us wives from among the children of men and beget us children**." And Semjâzâ, who was their leader, said unto them: "I fear ye will not indeed agree to do this deed, and I alone shall have to pay the penalty of a great sin." And they all answered him and said: "Let us all swear an oath, and all bind ourselves by mutual imprecations not to abandon this plan but to do this thing." Then sware (sic), they all came together and bound themselves by mutual imprecations upon it. **And they**

were in all two hundred; who descended in the days of Jared on the summit of Mount Hermon, and they called it Mount Hermon, because they had sworn and bound themselves by mutual imprecations upon it."

A section from 1 Enoch ch 7,

"And all the others together with them took unto themselves wives, and each chose for himself one, and they began to go in unto them and to defile themselves with them, **and they taught them charms and enchantments, and the cutting of roots, and made them acquainted with plants.** And they **became pregnant, and they bare great giants**, whose height was three thousand ells: Who consumed all the acquisitions of men. And when men could no longer sustain them, **the giants turned against them and devoured mankind**. And they began to sin against birds, and beasts, and reptiles, and fish, and to devour one another's flesh, and drink the blood. Then the earth laid accusation against the lawless ones."

To summarize, 200 watcher class angels made a covenant with each other to leave their domain in the heavenlies and rebel against Yahweh and his creation. They came down to earth on Mount Hermon and took on human form. They had forbidden unions with human women, and as a result, their hybrid offspring, the Nephilim, became the giants of old men of renown. These "men" became violent and bent on destroying the human race. It goes on later to explain that these hybrids died, and they became the "wandering spirits" that we now call demons.

The cult of the dead venerates these fallen angels and their offspring and draws ancient knowledge and power from them through the occult, even still today. Most, if not all, of the ancient civilizations that have been discovered have some form of ancestral worship (communicating with their dead relatives) and deep ties to the cult of the dead.

The reason seems apparent: the gods they worshiped were now dead and sent to the lowest parts of the underworld. The fallen angels are now held in chains of darkness awaiting judgment, and their hybrid offspring wander on earth as spirits of the cursed. These part human, part spirit-beings, want to continue their reign of terror by inhabiting human hosts, the ancient warrior-kings. These become *"the mighty men who were of old, men of renown."* Genesis 6:4

If you haven't studied these concepts before, I'm sure this sounds like a crazy conspiracy theory and like nothing more than an ancient myth. But consider what the New Testament writers have to say about this.

The Apostle Peter understood this interpretation of Genesis 6. In 2 Peter, he states,

> *"...God did not spare **angels when they sinned**, but cast them into hell and committed them to pits of darkness, reserved for judgment; and did not spare the ancient world, but preserved Noah."*

> *2 Peter 2:4-5 (emphasis added)*

The context of Peter's message was regarding sexual sin, and he compared the angels' imprisonment to the judgment of the cities of Sodom and Gomorrah. The only event referencing angels sinning in the bible is this interpretation of Genesis 6, and he ties it to sexual sins.

Jude has a similar warning,

*"And **angels who did not keep their own domain**, but abandoned their proper abode, He has kept in eternal bonds under darkness for the judgment of the great day, just as Sodom and Gomorrah and the cities around them, since they in the same way as these **indulged in gross immorality and went after strange flesh**, are exhibited as an example in undergoing the punishment of eternal fire."*

Jude 1:6-7 (emphasis added)

Peter and Jude would have drawn from their understanding of Jewish literature, specifically second temple writings such as the book of Enoch. This idea is also found in the Dead Sea scroll works from the first century BCE. The book of Enoch was accepted reading among the Qumran community. But we can go back farther than that. Early Mesopotamian writings, much older than the written Old Testament, have the story of creation, fallen angels and their half-human offspring, a great flood, and the tower of Babel incident. Research done by Dr. Michael Heiser reveals the following,

"Mesopotamia had several versions of the story of a catastrophic flood, complete with a large boat that saves animals and humans. They include mention of a group of sages (the apkallus), possessors of great knowledge, in the period before the flood. These apkallus were divine beings. Many apkallus were considered evil; those apkallus are integral to Mesopotamian demonology. After the flood, offspring of the apkallus were said to be human in descent (i.e., having a human parent) and "two-thirds apkallu."

In other words, the apkallus mated with human women and produced quasi-divine offspring.

The parallels to Genesis 6:1–4 are impossible to miss. The "two-thirds divine" description is especially noteworthy since it precisely matches the description of the Mesopotamian hero Gilgamesh. Recent critical work on the cuneiform tablets of the Epic of Gilgamesh has revealed that Gilgamesh was considered a giant who retained knowledge from before the flood."[31]

History continues to reveal the "fallen angels and their offspring" theme in Babylonian, Greek, and Roman cultures. In the tales of the Greeks, their deities and demigods were twisted versions of the true story. For example, the Titans, like Cronus or Oceanus, are the fallen "sons of God" who came into the "daughters of men." The heroes of the Golden Age were their offspring, like Heracles, Achilles, Hector, and Perseus. These were "the mighty men of old, the men of renown," also known as the Nephilim or giants.

The Romans had a similar mythos, only the names changed. Their deities were planetary, like Jupiter and Saturn. They had their list of demi-gods as well. Each of these myths is built around this same familiar theme. Even though these civilizations span approximately three thousand years, The "origin" stories remain close versions of each other. Again, containing a kernel of truth.

A note from the author:

Each chapter of this book builds on the other. The passages in Genesis 3:15 and 6:1-4 are key to establishing one's biblical worldview. It lays the contextual foundation for the cosmic chess match that began in Genesis and continues through Revelation.

I say this to those unfamiliar with this topic. I find myself hard-pressed to want to give many more details and examples to help you, as the reader, understand the enormous amount of information that exists to aid in your understanding. If you research some of the works I cite in this book, it will get you started. Let me rest by saying if you search for it, you will find it.

Babel – National Rebellion

"Now the whole earth used the same language and the same words. It came about as they journeyed east that they found a plain in the land of Shinar and settled there."

Genesis 11:1-2

The tone in the opening passage of Genesis 11 is "the whole earth used the same language and the same words." There existed a cohesiveness in the human family up to this point. Historically, the descendants of Noah were multiplying on the earth and spreading south and eastward from the place where the ark had rested in Northern Anatolia, the mountains of Ararat. Geographically, it would have been natural to follow the waterways of the Euphrates and Tigris rivers south into the southern Mesopotamia region. Some of them settled there and built the city of Babel.

It was a single purpose of mind that allowed the people to unite and build this ancient city. The central edifice of their new city was a tall tower. It would have taken great effort to build this ancient ziggurat, but what was the reason for this massive undertaking? What motivation did they find that caused them to invest in such hard work and with great expense?

Their leader Nimrod was a rebel; as we learned earlier, he disagreed with the beliefs of his ancestors. He rejected the God of his fathers and embraced the Fallen Ones as gods. It was this impetus that inspired the building of the massive central tower and rallied the people together. They desired "to reach into heaven and make a name for themselves." This was not just a simple act of pride but an altar of invitation, calling out to the fallen (supernatural) beings who would wish to rule the world, but still, it was more than that.

Babel represents a hostile takeover of mankind and the world. Of course, just because it was attempted doesn't mean it would happen, or does it?

*"The LORD said, 'Behold, they are one people, and they all have the same language. And this is what they began to do, **and now nothing which they purpose to do will be impossible for them.**'"*

Genesis 11:6 (emphasis added)

The rebellion in the Garden led to the rebellion of Cain, the first city builder. The great rebellion of the Fallen Ones inspired the rebellion of Nimrod, and they became his new gods, and coincidently, he was also a city builder.

What took place on the ziggurat of Babel? A look into ancient ziggurats reveals a dark secret. The Fallen Ones were venerated and worshiped at these places, and they required human sacrifices from their followers. The reality is that animal or human sacrifices open a gateway between the underworld and the physical world, and life-blood is the key. This is actually a twisting of scriptural truth.

"For the life of the flesh is in the blood, and I have given it to you on the altar to make atonement for your souls; for it is the blood by reason of the life that makes atonement."

Leviticus 17:11

From the blood of the lamb of Abel's sacrifice to the Levitical sacrifices, atonement or a covering came from blood. Ultimately, the righteous blood of Yeshua allows mankind access to God's heavenly realm.

When considered in reverse, the sacrificial method of idolatrous shedding of blood opens a gateway for beings from another realm to enter ours. Perhaps this is why almost every ancient culture became obsessed with human sacrifice, as revealed by the practices of such deities as Chemosh and Molech in Canaanite cultures and the practices demanded by the deities of the Mayan and Aztec cultures, just to name a few.

Babel became the first "high place" of idolatrous worship, opening a gateway to "the gods" that promised dominion to all that bow to them. This model of city building would be the model on which empires were eventually patterned, each having at its core this occultic gateway to the underworld.

The occult is obsessed with all-things death, taking us right back to the first rebellion, the day Adam ate of the cursed tree, he would "surely die". The occult's source is the underworld or abode of the dead. As we mentioned earlier, it is the place where the Fallen Ones are imprisoned until the day of judgment. Like a mob boss who is sent to prison for his crimes but still manages to run his businesses from behind bars, these Fallen Ones still live vicariously through their living counterparts, trying still to dominate the world. The occult is their access to our world through people who allow the mixing or possession of their souls.

To put a finer point on this subject, Nimrod has been known throughout history as an occultic figure. Stories and legends have kept the spirit of Nimrod's rebellion alive. Like most legends, it is a mix of facts and fiction. Stories are spun to create the most unimaginable tales. The reality is not in the story so much as in what people perceive and believe about the legend. This type of legend tends to shape reality to inspire others to emulate these inflated characters; over time, these beliefs can evolve from veneration to deification, creating new objects of worship. So is the case with Nimrod.

Nimrod was a man, possibly a Nephilim, as some stories suggest, or at least a gibborim (a mighty man). He has become a symbol of rebellion to all those who seek to rebel against the true creator God, Yahweh.

The story shaped around his legend is a dark trinity, a family with a twisted identity. Nimrod became the great warrior-king in this legend, and his wife was Semiramis, whom some stories portray as his mother or mother-wife. As the story goes, Nimrod eventually dies, and Semiramis promotes the belief that Nimrod is a god. She then assumes his place of power and authority as Queen, or Queen Mother.

A few years later, Semiramis bore a son, Tammuz, also known later as Gilgamesh. She declared that she had been visited by the spirit of Nimrod, who left her pregnant with the boy. Tammuz, she maintained, was Nimrod, reincarnated. With a father, mother, and son deified, a deceptive, perverted trinity was formed.

Through her scheming and designing, Semiramis became the Babylonian "Queen of Heaven," and Nimrod, under various names, became the "divine son of heaven," Semiramis and Tammuz were worshipped as "Madonna and child," As the generations passed, they were worshipped under other names in different civilizations and languages. Many of these are recognizable: Isis and Horus in Egypt, Fortuna and Jupiter in Rome, Aphrodite and Adonis in Greece, and Ashtoreth/Astarte and Molech/Baal in Canaan.[32]

This is how legends are born (and reborn). This mythos eventually makes its way into the Catholic Church and is replaced by Mary and Jesus as Madonna and Child, a perversion of the true nature of Mary and the birth of Messiah.

My commentary on this is that the adversary is always seeking to create a plausible and believable backstory. He often mimics or imitates the narrative of Yahweh's true story, only with a dark or perverted twist. This art of deception is necessary if you want to convince people of a lie, and Satan is the master of deception.

It doesn't matter at some point whether the story is true or not; the legend is born! This legend shaped the ancient world. It shows up as a core religious belief in most, if not all, ancient civilizations in one form or another.

We could spend more time exploring how the fallen ones of the occultic underworld benefited from keeping this story alive. We would learn that the impetus behind this legend was more supernatural than natural. It has served to keep these deified Nephilim and their progenitors in power for millennia, and this lie is still at work today!

Chapter 6 - Post-flood Cities and Kingdoms

*"They must not arise and take possession of the earth
And fill the face of the world with cities."*

Isaiah 14:21

Why are we looking at cities, you ask? Understanding geopolitics in relationship to the spiritual realm starts with the fundamental idea that people have already been centralized in cities, and those cities have come together under a federalized system. It is also important to understand that these city-states developed a relationship with the underworld through their temples and priests. The pagan pantheon of principalities, these "sons of God," wanted to dominate humanity. Cities then become the power centers from which they control the world.

In our example, Nimrod built several cities. We will assume that the people of these cities cooperated and traded with each other, shared a system of commerce, and loosely held to the same religious ideology. These cities were built in general proximity to each other in two separate regional groups: Upper and lower Mesopotamian groups. The waterways (the Euphrates and Tigris rivers) would have allowed for transportation between the two. Most of this information has been discovered through archaeology and ancient texts. The Biblical text doesn't reveal much detail about that time period, but it would stand to reason that these factors existed.

This could possibly have been the start of what would become known as the Akkadian Empire. A few Mesopotamian Empires existed starting around 3500 B.C.; according to most scholars, they are Sumer and Akkad. One of the cities that Nimrod built was Akkad (Accad, Genesis 10:10) in the land of Sumer (Shinar).

"…the most likely historical person, as suggested by archaeologist Murray AdaMounthwaite in an article in CMI's Journal of Creation, and in the New Bible dictionary, is Sargon the Great, or Sargon of Akkad, the founder of the dynasty of Akkad. (Sargon (Šarru-kin: "the king is legitimate") is a dynastic name taken centuries later by King Sargon I of the Old Assyrian Empire (fl. 1850 BC) and a thousand years after that by King Sargon II (reigned 721–705 BC) of the Neo-Assyrian Empire.)."[33]

There are benefits to living in a city. One of those benefits is convenience. In a city, you have access to food stores, water sources, and other people who have skills and trades you may need from time to time. There are social benefits to a community; people like having neighbors nearby and other children with whom their child can play. Their friends and extended families remain closer to them.

That all sounds good until you factor in human bad behavior. It's a lot harder to get away from an undesirable neighbor or to be privy to fights and arguments best not seen. Increased opportunity leads to increased crime, resulting in the loss of property and life.

There are health concerns as well. Historically, cities have been the breeding grounds of disease and epidemics. Waste and sewage removal are some of the biggest challenges for cities, which contribute to sickness and disease. Remember, the black plague of the 1300's was spread into homes by city sewer rats.

Beyond the pros and cons of city dwelling, there are more important concerns. These concerns are rarely seen by the average person. They are kept behind the walls of government buildings and the controlling arms of its agencies.

Cities are the key component to the collection and centralization of power and a magnet for those seeking control. When these powers fail to manage their differences, it leads to conflict. This conflict is fueled by other bad human behavior like greed, hatred, and the lust for more control. A city can bring out the best in us or reveal the worst in us.

If you want to control a nation, you must first divide that authority into regions or states, then counties or providences, and finally cities, large and small. So, in reverse, you can see that organizing a city is the first step in controlling the world.

This is the part where I give a brief message about the fundamental tools given to mankind, The Ten Commandments. God gave us laws to govern ourselves, with His help, of course. He knew we had the potential to destroy ourselves. Many of the laws that govern our cities have their roots in the basic Ten Commandments. I believe there is evidence that God's commandments did not begin with Moses; they were just codified at that time.

From the beginning, God has taught man the values of these commandments. For example, the ancient ruler Hammurabi established a codex of laws that are similar to God's Commandments. The United States of America was founded on many biblical laws, as represented by a relief of Moses, the great lawgiver, who's image resides over the US Capitol Building to this day.

Babel – The Prototype City

The first biblical mention of a major city would be Babel in Genesis 11. There are key elements about this city that give insight into the development of civilization. I have identified a list of six key elements or building blocks; they are language, location, religion or ideology, commerce, a formidable leader, and a military.

1. **Language** – (culture, ethnicity) The earth was all one language when Babel was built by Nimrod. Language would be divided by the end of the Babel event. This caused the rise of many cities where language was the common factor. People of like languages pooled together.

Language can be spoken and written. It is a unifying force in bringing people together to accomplish a purpose. When a community starts to produce written records and stories, it marks a transition into becoming more civilized. The discovery of written records is one way we have been able to learn about the rise of ancient civilizations.

2. **Location** – (geographical boundaries, climate, land usability factors) Finding a suitable place to locate a city is important to its survival. Babel was located in the Land of Shinar (Sumer) in what is known as the fertile crescent. It gave them access to farmable land for growing food. It was in close proximity to rivers and waterways, and having access to water was also important for transportation and trade. There was an abundance of natural resources for building. The first cities were made from mud bricks (fire-hardened), which would eventually be replaced by stone, centuries later. Then, the

proximity to quarries became important. For example, in the Egyptian civilization, large stones were hewn from quarries. These enormous building projects (i.e., the pyramids) needed to be located near a source of stone. Egyptian cities were built along the Nile River, which gave them access to water and transportation. But I digress.

3. **Religion** – (philosophies, Ideologies) is the hidden force behind the efforts. Because of its deep inner connection with people, religion is a strong motivator. What motivates people to want to build a city? There are several natural forces, such as food, safety, and even a sense of accomplishment, but Babel reveals that there were supernatural forces behind the effort.

The pagan religions played a vital role in the development of cites. The city of Babel was centered around a tower or ziggurat; it was used for religious purposes. Babel represents rebellion against God and His authority. The Ziggurat was a gateway to connect to "other gods." Ancient cities had a patron god and a pantheon of other or lesser gods and demi-gods. I suggest these deities were not just fictitious myths, but powerful beings given authority over the nations. Even so, the stories surrounding these ancient deities were often fabrications of human imagination.

The seed bed of the rebellious pagan religions is discovered in the narrative of Genesis 6, which was incited by the fallen ones! The entirety of human civilization outside of Yahweh's people will ultimately be driven by the forces of the fallen ones, which we call the "small g" gods. As we have already discussed, these Elohim are defined as spirit beings more powerful than men but not equal to Yahweh, God. They are the sons of God, as spoken about in Gen. 6 and elsewhere, created beings from another realm, a spiritual realm.

Over time, less superstitious or spiritually minded people would replace these deities with philosophy. Philosophy was viewed as "higher thinking" in a progressive world. The Pseudo-religions or ideology of "isms", i.e. Buddhism, Taoism, Hinduism, atheism, communism, and socialism, were introduced as alternatives.

4. **Commerce** – (economics) Every large community needs a system of commerce to buy and sell. They create the ability to gather money, gold, silver, or any other type of monetary system. Commerce creates wealth and, consequently, more powerful individuals. Someone once called this "The Golden Rule;" he who has the gold, rules.

With more money comes more influence. Leaders would gravitate to those who could make money or own great possessions. Cities are built around those who can produce goods and services. A city government, out of necessity of its growing infrastructure, found ways to tax the people. Wealthy people paid more taxes and were more desirable than the poor.

Most cities had a spoken or unspoken class system. Your worth to the king was based on your wealth or your ability to produce it. With wealth comes privileges to be measured out by the king.

5. **Leaders** – (Politics, governing bodies) Every great city has a person who is the embodiment of power, like a king, emperor, president, or governor; the title warrior-king is given to the

ones capable of conquering other cities or kingdoms. In the case of Babel, it was Nimrod who was a great warrior king.

This means if you want to study a city, you must study its leader. The leader controls (or tries to control) the language, location, commerce, religion, and military. This system exists until anarchy rises and another becomes ruler.

Historically, these Kings have had a deep connection to the underworld. Nimrod was driven to build a ziggurat or tower. It served as a point of connection to these gods. The phrase, "If you build it, they will come," comes to mind. "They" referring to the power-hungry lords of the underworld. The King's complete devotion or worship to these deities was required, and in return, they would empower him and give him secret knowledge. You will recall, according to Enoch, that the fallen angels brought with them the secrets of alchemy, charms and enchantments, the use of plants and roots, and the forging of metals and weapons.

The people were promised wealth and fame, and even immortality, which they never physically achieved, only through their legacies. This opened the door for ancestral worship and veneration of the dead. The cult of the dead would become the main essence behind paganism. It is important to note the goal of the fallen ones was to forcibly take over Yahweh's creation. Therefore, things like armies, wars, seizing control, were all part of their sinister agenda. Killing humanity by mass events would be a high objective for the underworld. This is just yet another proof of who or what was behind the provocation to dominate the world…and still is.

6. **A Military** – (including Technologies) might start as a city police force or be used for protecting its borders. It can ultimately grow into a tool of advancement. The leader seeks to recruit the strong and brave to fight others who would try to subjugate them. The military can also be used to force others into subjection to its own authority. Much can be said about building powerful armies. History is full of military conquests and heroic battles. Military forces are a key factor in the study of geopolitics. Let's remember Nimrod was a (rebellious) mighty hunter before Yahweh.

Equipped with this information, we can begin to identify key components that will need to be considered if one desires to change the geo-political landscape. It is interesting to note that six is understood to be the number of, or associated with, mankind. Man was created on the sixth day of creation. Six days in a week are allotted to man for work; the seventh day is God's Day (of rest).

A man can sow in his fields for six years, and the seventh year is a rest for the land, called the Shemitah. There were six cities of refuge in ancient Israel for a man to run to for safety. Multiple sixes are important also; for example, 66 persons went with Jacob to Egypt (Gen 46:26), and Revelation 13:30 says the number of mankind is 666.

666 is the number of the beast system; the beasts of the earth (land animals) were created on the sixth day. Metaphorically, when a man is devoid of a moral compass and higher reasoning, he is likened to an animal or a beast. Just like an animal that functions on basic instincts and passions, these beastly systems of men are driven by

their own animal instincts. They lust for power, greed, and deviant desires fueled by a dark underworld.

Cities are central to the rise of the beast systems, and we have now identified the six key elements of their existence.

We learned earlier that Yahweh's headquarters for the Divine Council is also referred to as the "Mount of Assembly" (Isaiah 14:13) and is associated with a mountain. The Garden of Eden was considered to have been the gateway to the Mount of Assembly. Perhaps the reason the guardian Cherub was placed at Eden's entrance after the fall of mankind was to prevent Adam's re-entry and access to the heavenly Mount in his fallen state. Access to the Divine Council was, at that point, forbidden.

In Ezekiel's polemic of the ruler of Tyre, most scholars agree that it is directed at the Nachash, the serpentine supernatural being who rebelled against the authority of Yahweh in Eden.

*"**You were in Eden, the garden of God**; Every precious stone was your covering…You were the anointed cherub who covers, And I placed you there. **You were on the holy mountain of God;** You walked in the midst of the stones of fire. **Therefore, I have cast you as profane. From the mountain of God**. And I have destroyed you, O covering cherub, From the midst of the stones of fire."*

Ezekiel 28:13-16 (emphasis added)

The connecting point in our discussion of Babel is a mountain. The Tower of Babel, or ziggurat, was an artificial or man-made mountain. Babel was humanity's attempt to force its way back into the Divine Council and replace it with new leadership. The name Babel is derived from the original Akkadian words *bab ilu,* which means "gate of god" or "gate of the gods," it is replaced in the Bible with the Hebrew word Babel, derived from *balal,* meaning "to confuse." Hebrew writers often liked to substitute words for poetic impact, and it is most likely a jab at pagan deities, reducing the "gate of the gods" to nonsense or confusion. [34]

It is easy to confuse the tower of Babel with the ancient city of Babylon. There is a problem linking Babylon to the Tower of Babel. Babylon didn't even become a city until a thousand years after the tower incident.

Although Babel may not be a physical match to the time and location of Babylon, there is a connection; it is the earliest prototype of how ancient cities would develop. At the heart of these cities was an occultic "seat of the gods." They summoned the spirits of the underworld upon their ziggurats and in their temples. They have the potential to open a portal from the netherworld realm into our physical world.

Babylon's Origins

Archeological discoveries have found that the oldest and largest ziggurat in Mesopotamia was at Eridu. The connection of Babel to Eridu is significant. The city of Eridu dates back to the pre-flood era in Ancient Sumer. The author Derek Gilbert, in his book The Great Inception, does an excellent job of analysis connecting the city of Babel to Eridu and Eridu to the first city, most likely built by Cain. Derek writes,

"Remember, the oldest and largest ziggurat in Mesopotamia was at Eridu, the first city built in Mesopotamia.

In recent years, scholars have learned that the name "Babylon" was interchangeable with other city names, including Eridu. So, "Babylon" didn't always mean "Babylon in ancient texts." Even though Eridu never dominated the political situation in Sumer after its first two kings, Alulim and Alalgar, the city of [the patron god] Enki was so important to Mesopotamian culture that more than three thousand years later, Hammurabi, the greatest king of the old Babylonian empire, was crowned not in Babylon, but in Eridu—even though Eridu had ceased to be a city about three hundred years earlier. Even as late as the time of Nebuchadnezzar, 1,100 years after Hammurabi, the kings of Babylon still sometimes called themselves LUGAL.NUNki—King of Eridu.

Why? What was the deal with Eridu? Yes, it was the first city, the place where "kingship descended from heaven," a city possibly built by Cain or his son and maybe named for Cain's grandson, Irad. Think about that for a moment. Eridu—its name interchangeable with Babylon—may have been established by the first murderer on earth.

It may have been Cain, not Nimrod, who founded the original Babylon!

Archaeologists have uncovered eighteen levels of the temple to Enki at Eridu. The oldest levels of the E-abzu, a small structure less than ten feet square, date to the founding of the city around 5400 B.C. Fish bones were scattered around the building. Enki seems to have been a fan of the Euphrates River carp.

Now, stop and take that in. The first small shrine to Enki may have been built by Cain or one of his immediate descendants. The spot remained sacred to Enki long after the city was deserted around 2000 B.C. The temple remained in use until the fifth century B.C., nearly five thousand years after the first crude altar was built to accept offerings of fish to the god of the subterranean aquifer, the abzu.

Now, at this point, we should tell you that abzu (ab = water + zu = deep) is very likely where we get the English word "abyss." Ah, the fog lifts! Another clue: The name Enki is a compound word. En is Sumerian for "lord," and ki is the word for "earth." Thus, Enki, god of the Abzu, was "lord of the earth."

Do you remember Jesus calling someone "the ruler of this world"? Or is Paul referring to "the god of this world"? Who were they talking about? Yeah. Satan."[35]

The *spirit* of Babylon originates with Babel/Eridu and continues to manifest itself through the Babylonian Empires. The essence of Babylon is not limited to the empire of Babylon but often is still called by its name. It is referred to as *"Mystery, Babylon the Great, Mother of all harlots and abominations of the earth"* in Revelation 18:3. It is synonymous with the spirit of Jezebel and is known as the great city (Revelation 17:18). This Babylonian spirit manifests through the

Roman Empire, and later the Roman-Catholic Church, the city of Rome with its seven hills in comparison to the seven mountains that the beast in Revelation 17:9 sits on. This spirit is constantly at war with true believers in Yahweh. Its final manifestation in the Book of Revelation describes it as the last rebellious city, and it is ultimately destroyed forever!

When the word of Yahweh came to the prophet Jeremiah regarding the looming judgment that was coming upon Jerusalem, He referred to Babylon as the "enduring nation' and an "ancient city."

*"'Behold, I am bringing a nation against you from afar, O house of Israel,' declares the LORD. **It is an enduring nation, It is an ancient nation**, A nation whose language you do not know, Nor can you understand what they say."*

Jeremiah 5:15 (emphasis added)

Even though the physical city of Babylon only historically existed for roughly 1400 years between the Old and Neo-Babylonian empires, the spirit of Babylon continues to resurface and remains very much alive today. We will see the progression of this spirit through multiple civilizations. It will come to be known as the Great Harlot of Mystery Babylon.

Babylon and its origins are an important part of our study. There is an interminable relationship between Babylon and Jerusalem and these two cities are locked in a supernatural struggle for dominance. There are observable forces at work fighting for each to be victorious. We know the outcome, but the journey is an epic series of battles. It teaches us how heaven must work in synchronous movement with men to achieve humanity's God-given destiny.

Early Jerusalem, The Foundation Stone

The city of Jerusalem originated around the same time as Babel. It was not called by its full name but a shorter version, Salem or Shalem. The Hebrew word *Shalem* is a root word meaning "peace". Its later iteration, Jerusalem, is a compound from West Semitic yrw or *Jeru*, meaning 'to found, to lay a cornerstone', and the Hebrew *shalom* or "peace" to form the meaning, "The Cornerstone of Peace" or "The City of Peace."

*"Therefore, thus says the Lord GOD, "Behold, I am laying in Zion a stone, a tested stone, **A costly cornerstone for the foundation**, firmly placed. He who believes in it will not be disturbed."*

Isaiah 28:16 (emphasis added)

The language of this verse carries a secondary meaning. It is a literary play on words, between the name of the city, Jerusalem, and the nature of Messiah, Yeshua. Both are referred to as foundational cornerstones of Yahweh's city (Psalm 118:22).

The Biblical Hebrew form of the city's name is Yerushalayim (ירושלם). The ending -ayim indicates a dual form in Hebrew, thus leading to the suggestion that the name refers to the two hills on which the city sits. It can also refer to two Jerusalems: the city above, which is heavenly and sometimes referred to as the New Jerusalem (Rev 21:2,10), and the one below, earthly, situated on two-hilled Mount Moriah.

The "Aramaic Apocryphon of Genesis" of the Dead Sea Scrolls (1QapGen 22:13) equates Jerusalem with the earlier "Salem" (שלם),

said to be the city of Melchizedek in Genesis 14.

*"And **Melchizedek, king of Salem,** brought out bread and wine; now he was a priest of God Most High. He blessed him and said, "Blessed be Abram of God Most High, Possessor of heaven and earth; And blessed be God Most High, Who has delivered your enemies into your hand. He gave him a tenth of all."*

Genesis 14:18-20 (emphasis added)

Now, let's look at the city's king. The name Melchizedek is a compound of *Melek*, "king," and *Zedek*, "righteous" or "king of righteousness." His second title is "king of Shalem," a word with a dual meaning. Peace as an attribute, as in the "King who brings peace," and it is also the name of "the city of peace." Scholars are divided on the issue of Shalem being the original city of Jerusalem. The Psalms record this statement,

*"God is known in Judah; His name is great in Israel. **His tabernacle is in Salem; His dwelling place also is in Zion**."*

Psalms 76:1-2 (emphasis added)

My reading of this passage is that Shalem (Salem) and Zion (Mount Zion in Jerusalem) are synonymous. Some historians disagree with this assertion, but what seals the idea in my mind is its first king, Melchizedek.

There are a couple of views on who Melchizedek is. Genesis 14 establishes the fact that he was King of Shalem and priest of God Most High. The historian Josephus, the Genesis Apocryphon, and Rabbinical sources support the theory that this King-Priest was Shem, Noah's eldest son.

Shem lived five hundred years after the Flood and at the time of His encounter with Abram, he would have been over five hundred and fifty years old (roughly), making him the oldest person alive at the time. As the firstborn son of Noah, Shem would have inherited the priestly role from his father. He would also have been the first to establish that city after the Flood.

As the oldest person alive, it would have qualified him to be the High Priest of Yahweh for all people alive at that time. This qualification is based on an ancient king-priest order called the "Order of Melchizedek" handed down to the qualified firstborn from the time of Adam.[36]

The Order of Melchizedek refers to a priestly order in which the roles of king and priest are combined, in contrast to the Levitical (or Aaronic) priesthood, which is only a priestly order. According to the extra-biblical Book of Jasher, the title Melchizedek was an ancient King-Priest Order that began with Adam and was passed-on through firstborn succession all the way up to the time of the flood. Noah would have passed on this role to his eldest son, Shem.

The Psalms identify Melchizedek as a foreshadow of Yeshua, Messiah,

*"The LORD has sworn and will not change His mind, **'You are a priest forever, according to the order of Melchizedek.'** The Lord is at Your right hand; He will shatter kings in the day of His wrath. He will judge among the nations."*

Psalms 110:4-6 (emphasis added)

It is Yeshua Messiah, heaven's King-Priest, who will shatter the kings of the nations and rule from Jerusalem. He is also the great High Priest of the Heavenly Temple (Hebrews 8:1-2).

Was Shem guarding the cornerstone or foundation stone of peace, (Jeru)Shalem, the city of Yahweh? I think so. When Shem met Abram, he passed on the priestly torch to its successor. Abraham became the Father of Faith and exalted Father of the family of Yahweh and took on a priestly role as mediator between God and men. I am reminded of the quote in Hebrews 11:10, *"[Abraham] was looking for the city which has foundations, whose architect and builder is God."* He was looking for the greater Jerusalem, the city that comes down out of heaven in Rev 21.

During the Second Temple period, after Zerubbabel returned from exile and rebuilt the Temple in Jerusalem, they did not have the Ark of the Covenant to place in it. According to the Mishnah (Middot 3:6), the Foundation Stone stood where the Ark used to be, and the High Priest offered up the incense and sprinkled the blood of the sacrifices on it during the Yom Kippur service.[37]

The Foundation, or the Noble Rock, is the rock at the center of the modern Dome of the Rock in Jerusalem. It is also known as the Pierced Stone because it has a small opening or hole on the southeastern corner that enters into a cavern beneath the rock, known as the Well of Souls.[38]

In 1974, while on a trip to Israel, I visited the Dome of the Rock and entered this cavern, the Well of Souls. I was only eleven years old and had no idea of the significance of this site or that it would be closed off from the world several years later. I literally planted my feet on the foundation stone that day. It reminds me of the words of king David, "And He set my feet upon a rock making my footsteps firm." Psalms 40:2

There are times in history when people are so close to the truth yet still do not realize it. I am speaking about the foundation stone on the Temple Mount; the symbolism here is rich with enlightenment.

What is the meaning of this foundation stone, you ask?

There is a great mystery to uncover here. The second Jewish temple was built over this Noble Rock, which still exists on the temple mount today, which is currently covered by the golden topped, Dome of "The Rock". This ancient bed rock was under the place where the ark rested in the Holy of Holies at one time. The Ark of the Covenant was then assumed lost upon the return of the exiled Jews from Babylon; all that was left was this great stone. This stone symbolism is the same symbology used to describe Yeshua, the cornerstone or foundation stone of Psalms 118,

The stone which the builders rejected. Has become the chief corner stone.
This is the LORD'S doing; It is marvelous in our eyes.

Psalms 118:22-23

Yeshua is the Noble Rock, or Kingly (Noble) Stone, that sits in The Temple, and he also was pierced and was able to release the souls held captive underground in the proverbial well of souls or Sheol (the grave). He is the embodiment of the Ark of the Covenant and the essence of the atoning Yom Kippur sacrifice. This foundation stone has pointed to Yeshua since the beginning, and His identity is not yet understood by many of the Jewish people to this day.

The Roman-Era midrash Tanchuma, Kedoshim 10:1, sums up the centrality and holiness of this site in Judaism:

"As the navel is set in the centre of the human body, so is the land of Israel the navel of the world... situated in the centre of the world, and Jerusalem in the centre of the land of Israel, and the sanctuary in the centre of Jerusalem, and the holy place in the centre of the sanctuary, and the ark in the centre of the holy place, and the Foundation Stone before the holy place, because from it, the world was founded."[39]

There is still another deeper layer of revelation to this Foundation Stone, which is discovered by looking into the "stone that the builders rejected." Our journey starts with the Hebrew word for stone used in Psalm 118:22; it is *eben* (commonly pronounced *even*). Like many Hebrew words, we can find multiple smaller words used to form a concept in a larger word. In the word *eben,* we find two words, the words *ab* and *ben,* that share the *"b"* or *beit.* Each word has a distinct meaning, but combined, it reveals a hidden truth.

Ab means "father," and it is found in words like **Ab**raham (father of many nations) and Jo**ab** (Yah is Father). Yah is a shorten version of God's official name, Yahweh.

Additionally, *Ben* means "son," as in **Ben**jamin or **Ben**yamin (son of my righthand) or Rue**ben** (son of vision).

Then there is the letter *b* by itself, pronounced *Beit* in Hebrew, and It simply means "house" as in *Beit Lechem* or Bethlehem, meaning "house of bread."

When you put all this together, you have a message, "the father and son sharing the house," a(b)en, encapsulated in the word for stone. This is "the stone" that the builders rejected, the idea that the Father and the Son share the house, and this rock of revelation is the foundation stone lying in the holiest place under the (former) temple in Jerusalem. It has been there from the beginning.

*"He [Yeshua] said to them, "**But who do you say that I am?**" Simon Peter answered, "**You are the Christ, the Son of the living God.**" And Jesus said to him, "Blessed are you, Simon Barjona, because flesh and blood did not reveal this to you, but My Father who is in heaven. I also say to you that you are Peter, and **upon this rock, I will build My church**, and the gates of Hades will not overpower it.*

Matthew 16:15-18 (emphasis added)

"Upon this rock, I will build my church," Peter is not the rock; it is the rock of the revelation of who Yeshua is; this is the foundational principle of truth at the center of all things. The Jews could not accept that Yeshua claimed to be Yahweh. As a matter of fact, they tried to "stone" him three times (ironically) for statements like this. This is why he is known as "the stone which the builders rejected." They didn't reject Yeshua, the man; they rejected Yeshua as the Son of Yahweh.

Yeshua reveals this truth in the parable of the landowner.

"Listen to another parable. There was a landowner who PLANTED A VINEYARD, AND PUT A WALL AROUND IT, AND DUG A WINE PRESS IN IT, AND BUILT A TOWER, and rented it

out to vine-growers and went on a journey. When harvest time approached, he sent his slaves to the vine-growers to receive his produce. The vine-growers took his slaves and beat one, killed another, and stoned a third. Again, he sent another group of slaves larger than the first, and they did the same thing to them. ***But afterward, he sent his son to them, saying, 'They will respect my son.'*** *But when the vine-growers saw the son, they said among themselves,* ***'This is the heir; come, let us kill him and seize his inheritance.' They took him and threw him out of the vineyard and killed him.*** *Therefore, when the owner of the vineyard comes, what will he do to those vine-growers?"*

Matthew 21:33-40 (emphasis added)

In this passage, Yeshua continues to reveal that this son of the vineyard owner is the stone that the builders rejected.

Jesus said to them, "Did you never read in the Scriptures, 'THE STONE WHICH THE BUILDERS REJECTED, THIS BECAME THE CHIEF CORNER stone; THIS CAME ABOUT FROM THE LORD, AND IT IS MARVELOUS IN OUR EYES'? Therefore, I say to you, the kingdom of God will be taken away from you and given to a people, producing the fruit of it. ***And he who falls on this stone will be broken to pieces; but on whomever it falls, it will scatter him like dust."***

Matthew 21:42-44 (emphasis added)

The overarching message is that we must all humble ourselves, fall on this foundational message, and be broken. Falling onto this Stone must break our self-will, pride, arrogance, and rebellion, and we must receive Him as our Savior, the Son of the Living God. The revelation to be realized is that The Father and The Son share the house, and they are One. It is upon this revelation that Yeshua said He would build His Church.

If we don't willingly fall on this Stone, we will eventually be crushed by it and be scattered like dust. An even greater significance is that this will be the same stone (Eben) that is "cut out of the mountain without hands" in King Nebuchadnezzar's Dream. This stone crushes the great image, toppling all the governments of the world represented in that image, and then becomes a great mountain that fills the whole earth.

In the movie "Raiders of the Lost Ark," Indiana Jones outran the huge stone that was trying to crush him. If we reject Yeshua, we will not be so lucky on that day.

And finally, the Apostle Peter has this to say about it,

*"And coming to Him as to a living stone which has been rejected by men, but is choice and precious in the sight of God, **you also, as living stones, are being built up as a spiritual house for a holy priesthood**, to offer up spiritual sacrifices acceptable to God through Jesus Christ. For this is contained in Scripture: BEHOLD, I LAY IN ZION A CHOICE STONE, A PRECIOUS CORNER stone, AND HE WHO BELIEVES IN HIM WILL NOT BE DISAPPOINTED."*

1 Peter 2:4-6 (emphasis added)

Peter declares that we are to be living stones ourselves, built up as a spiritual house for a holy priesthood. We carry with us the revealed Messiah, the true Foundation Stone.

Peter, upon receiving this revelation, was given a new name.

*"I also say to you that **you are Peter**, and upon this rock, I will build My church; and the gates of Hades will not overpower it."*

Matthew 16:18 (emphasis added)

Prior to this life-changing moment, Peter was known as Simon BarJona (son of Jonah). His new name is transliterated from the Greek word *petros,* which means "a stone," identifying him with this revelation he received from heaven, that is, that Yeshua is the *eben.* This is the "rock of revelation" that would inspire Peter to write about this very thing in his first epistle, 1 Peter 2:4-9. To continue the passage previously quoted above,

"This precious value, then, is for you who believe, but for those who disbelieve, THE STONE WHICH THE BUILDERS REJECTED, THIS BECAME THE VERY CORNER stone, and,
A STONE OF STUMBLING AND A ROCK OF OFFENSE;
for they stumble because they are disobedient to the word, and to this doom, they were also appointed."

1 Peter 2:7-8

This truth is now synonymous with his name, Peter. He would eventually be seen as the object of this rejection of the Jewish Messiah.

"On the next day, their rulers and elders and scribes were gathered together in Jerusalem; and Annas, the high priest, was there, and Caiaphas and John and Alexander, and all who were of high-priestly descent.

*When they had placed them in the center, they began to inquire,
'By what power, or in what name, have you done this?'*

Then Peter, filled with the Holy Spirit, said to them,

*'Rulers and elders of the people, if we are on trial today for a
benefit done to a sick man, as to how this man has been made well,
let it be known to all of you and to all the people of Israel, that by
the name of Jesus Christ the Nazarene, whom you crucified, whom
God raised from the dead—by this name this man stands here before
you in good health.*

*He is the STONE WHICH WAS REJECTED by you, THE
BUILDERS, but WHICH BECAME THE CHIEF CORNER stone.*
***And there is salvation in no one else; for there is no other name
under heaven that has been given among men by which we must
be saved.'"***

Acts 4:5-12 (emphasis added)

Peter was chosen to be the first to receive this revelation and he
would be the first to defend it. He declares this to be the cornerstone
truth on which the entire New Testament teaching is built, yet the
concept pre-existed Yeshua's advent in the foundation stone in
Jerusalem, under the Temple, from the beginning.

*"There is no other name [Yeshua Messiah, the eben] under heaven
that has been given among men by which we must be saved."*

More importantly, the heavenly Temple is being built upon this
truth, of which Peter writes that we are all "living stones' in this great
divine construct.

Joshua, Son of Nun

As we move to the next biblical mention of Jerusalem, we come to the book of Joshua. Joshua was the successor of Moses, and he led the children of Israel into the promised land. He was anointed for the task, and his commission was confirmed by heaven itself (Numbers 27:18-23).

The name Joshua is derived from the same linguistic cognate as Yeshua; he is a foreshadowing of Yeshua. In the concept of biblical study, the person of Joshua is seen as a type or shadow, and from it we can see the ministry and purpose of Yeshua revealed through Joshua's life. In a broad stroke, just as Joshua led Israel into the conquest of Canaan, Yeshua led us into the heavenly Promised Land. Yeshua demonstrated this leading when He said, *"I go to prepare a place for you, that where I am, there you may also be"* (John 14:1-3). There are a few other parallels we'll mention here.

The bible states that Joshua was the "son of Nun" according to Exodus 33:11. Nun was not only his father's name, but it is the name of the fourteenth letter of the Hebrew alphabet. We must consider again the fact that every detail given in scripture is given to us for a reason, whether it is numbers, names, or dates; each detail points us to a deeper understanding.

These details are not in the text by accident but by design. Nor are they interjected into the text by the minds of men, for the minds of the Jewish writers knew nothing of Yeshua, the Messiah. To this day, there is disdain in the minds of many religious Jews over the name Yeshua, or Jesus, when speaking of the Messiah. This must be the hand of God that guided these details, and it is the Spirit of God that reveals them.

A father's name is not only given in scripture as a simple moniker, but the name appears to be added when it reveals something relative (no pun intended) to that person's identity. The name *Nun* contains a hidden meaning and points us to a prophetic discovery about Joshua.

In a simple definition, the word or letter *Nun* means "fish," but there is another word for fish in Hebrew, *dagah* (Strong's #1710), so what is the difference? Nun is a prime root word that carries the meaning "to propagate," and it is connected to fertility, continuity, and the ability to increase and multiply. We see this concept in the Genesis creation story. On the fifth day of creation, Yahweh filled the waters with "teeming swarms of living creatures".

*"Then God said, "**Let the waters teem with swarms of living creatures**, and let birds fly above the earth in the open expanse of the heavens." God created the great sea monsters and every living creature that moves, with which the waters swarmed after their kind, and every winged bird after its kind, and God saw that it was good."*

Genesis 1:20-21 (emphasis added)

These were the first of the "living" parts of creation; they represented the introduction of life to the world. They were created to swarm or teem in the waters, meaning they quickly multiplied to fill the seas and skies. This propagation and multiplication were considered signs of life. *Nun,* by implication, then points us to the source of life through the "fish." This has led some to consider the meaning of *Nun* to be a representation of the introduction to life itself, or in short, the *Nun* can also mean "life." This is also supported by the fact that in ancient Hebrew, the letter Nun was represented by the picture of a sprout or seed, which is the beginning of life.[40]

The hidden message in Joshua's father's name is that Joshua, figuratively, is the "son of life," which is the reason for its inclusion in the text of scripture. When you consider the entire story of Joshua's role in the Exodus and his succession of Moses, his identity takes on a new layer of meaning. As discussed earlier, Joshua is a type and shadow of Yeshua (Jesus), and to complete this imagery, we are informed that just as Joshua is the "son of life", so Yeshua also is the "Son of Life," suggesting to us that there is a deeper connection between the life of Joshua and Yeshua. Let's look further.

*"So the LORD said to **Moses**, "Take **Joshua the son of Nun**, a man in whom is the Spirit, and lay your hand on him; and have him stand before **Eleazar, the priest** and before all the congregation, and commission him in their sight. **You shall put some of your authority on him** in order that all the congregation of the sons of Israel may obey him."*

Numbers 27:18-20 (emphasis added)

This is the record of Yahweh's instruction to Moses to appoint Joshua as his successor. This parallels another commission orchestrated by Yahweh in the New Testament.

*"Then Jesus arrived from Galilee at the Jordan coming to John, to be baptized by him. But John tried to prevent Him, saying, 'I have need to be baptized by You, and do You come to me?' But Jesus answering said to him, 'Permit it at this time; for **in this way it is***

***fitting for us to fulfill all righteousness.** ' Then he permitted Him. After being baptized, **Jesus** came up immediately from the water; and behold, the heavens were opened, and he saw the **Spirit of God** descending as a dove and lighting on Him, and behold, **a voice** out of the heavens said, **'This is My beloved Son, in whom I am well-pleased.'**"*

Matthew 3:13-17 (emphasis added)

This was actually a ceremony or "rite of passage" that transitioned Yeshua from being the (alleged) son of a carpenter (Joseph) to beginning His earthly ministry as the "Son of God." After His baptism, He was immediately driven into the wilderness to be tested, and after 40 days, He emerged as the Messiah (the anointed one). This immersion event is when Yeshua was commissioned.

There are interesting aspects to this scene. First, the one officiating the ceremony is John (the Baptist), who was actually the son of an Aaronic priest, Zechariah, technically allowing the mantle of the priesthood to fall on him as well, making him an excellent choice to officiate this event.

Next, we see a dove descend in this ceremony as a representation of The Spirit of God as a witness. And finally, we hear "a voice" from heaven declaring Yeshua as the beloved Son of God. So, there are two witnesses here, The Father (a voice) and the Spirit (a dove), officiated by a Priest (John), all attesting to Yeshua's identity and commission.

Now, jump back to Joshua's commission. We also see two witnesses there that are parallel in nature. Moses, the lawgiver, figuratively represents God, the true Law Giver, and Eleazar, the priest, represents the Spirit of God as a second witness. The name Eleazar (Strong's #499 'El`azar) has a hidden meaning relevant to these stories. Eleazar means "God is helper" or sometimes coined "the helper." Yeshua informs us that "the helper" is another name for the Holy Spirit[41],

> *"But **the Helper, the Holy Spirit**, whom the Father will send in My name, He will teach you all things and bring to your remembrance all that I said to you."*
>
> *John 14:26* (emphasis added)

The result is that the name Eleazar points us to the Helper, the Holy Spirit, as it also does in the story of Abraham, his son Isaac, and his servant Eleazar, who is given the task of finding a wife for Abraham's son. We know from Mount Moriah, the binding of Isaac on an altar, that Isaac is a type of Yeshua. Eleazar becomes Abraham's helper to find his son a wife.

Who helps Yeshua find His bride? The figurative Eleazar, the Holy Spirit. End of rabbit trail, now back to Joshua.

In each story, the commission of Joshua and Yeshua is witnessed by two observers, one story foreshadowing the other. The amazing details of the Torah will always point us to Yeshua, who is the Living Word hidden in the written word.

The Jerusalem of Joshua

The book of Joshua records a famous battle with the king of Jerusalem, Adoni-Zedek. This is the first time the Bible uses the name Jerusalem (Yerushalayim, in the Hebrew text) in reference to this foundational city.

Adoni-Zedek is most likely a title rather than a name, which means "lord of righteousness," and he was an Amorite king. The Amorites had occupied several cities in Canaan at the time of Joshua. The city of Shalem was taken from the Shemites at some point in history during the 465 years between Abraham and Joshua.

When Israel had destroyed Jericho, captured the city of Ai, and brought the great city of Gibeon into subjection, the king of Jerusalem feared greatly. He made an alliance with four other Amorite kings to attack Gibeon because they had made peace with Israel.

The city of Gibeon was then surrounded by the armies of the five Amorite kings, and Gibeon sent word to Joshua for help.

*"Then the men of Gibeon sent word to Joshua to the camp at Gilgal, saying, "Do not abandon your servants; come up to us quickly and save us and help us, for all the kings of the Amorites that live in the hill country have assembled against us." So Joshua went up from Gilgal, and he and all the people of war with him and all the valiant warriors. **The LORD said to Joshua, 'Do not fear them, for I have given them into your hands; not one of them shall stand before you.'"***

Joshua 10:6-8 (emphasis added)

What we see next is Yahweh directly intervening in the affairs of men.

> *"So Joshua came upon them suddenly by marching all night from Gilgal. And the LORD confounded them before Israel, and He slew them with a great slaughter at Gibeon, and pursued them by the way of the ascent of Beth-horon and struck them as far as Azekah and Makkedah. [11] As they fled from before Israel, while they were at the descent of Beth-horon, **the LORD threw large stones from heaven on them as far as Azekah, and they died; there were more who died from the hailstones than those whom the sons of Israel killed with the sword.**"*

> *Joshua 10:9-11* (emphasis added)

The veil between the physical realm and the spiritual realm becomes very thin here as we see Yahweh engaging in this battle. It stands to reason that Yahweh Sabaoth worked through his heavenly armies to accomplish this outcome. I admit the next is speculative, but perhaps we are seeing the horsemen, the horns, and the craftsmen at work here. The story doesn't stop here, though. There is another even more spectacular part of this battle.

> *"Then Joshua spoke to the LORD in the day when the LORD delivered up the Amorites before the sons of Israel, and he said in the sight of Israel,*
> *"O sun, stand still at Gibeon,*
> *And O moon in the valley of Aijalon."*
> ***So the sun stood still, and the moon stopped,***
> ***Until the nation avenged themselves of their enemies.***

> *Joshua 10:12-13* (emphasis added)

This is the only time in history when God listened to the request of a man and stopped the sun from setting and the moon from rising. A review of online articles brings up a lot of controversy regarding proof of the bible event. There is a story of a man named Harold Hill who supposedly went to NASA and found a missing day. That story has been debunked, but the following information does provide some historical evidence that should be considered.

"It is reported by historians that records of the Chinese during the reign of Emperor Yeo, who lived at the same time as Joshua, report 'a long day.' Also, Heroditus, a Greek historian, wrote that an account of 'a long day' appears in records of Egyptian priests. Others cite records of Mexicans of the sun standing still for an entire day in a year, denoted as 'Seven Rabbits,' which is the same year in which Joshua defeated the Philistines and conquered Palestine.

In Velikovsky's "Worlds in Collision." If Joshua's long day (not "missing" day) occurred—and of course, I believe that it did—then we would expect its effects to show up in the historical records of other nations, and that is exactly what we find."[42]

…and something worth noting: this story did make it into the bible.

The Jerusalem of King David

Joshua started the Canaanite conquest, and it was completed by King David. There is no doubt that King David was the most influential leader in securing Jerusalem as Yahweh's city. Almost four hundred years had passed between Joshua and King David. In King David's day, the city was known as Jebus, and it was inhabited by the Jebusites. There isn't much historical evidence linking Jebus or the Jebusites to Shalem. Except that, Theophilus G. Pinches noted a reference to "Yabusu", which he interpreted as an old form of Jebus, on a contract tablet that dates from 2200 BC.[43]

The Jewish Encyclopedia says this,

"The 2200 BC date of the tablet is dated to the time Melchizedek would have inhabited the city of Shalem. Some scholars believe a possible explanation is that Jebus is a pseudo-ethnic name given to the city. However, an increasingly popular view, first put forward by Edward Lipinski, professor of Oriental and Slavonic studies at the Catholic University of Leuven, is that the Jebusites were most likely an Amorite tribe. This would be consistent with the Story of Joshua and the Amorite King, Adoni-Zedek, as we mentioned earlier. In David's day, it was referred to as Jerusalem of the Jebusites (2 Samuel 5:6), including both the city name and the ethnicity of its inhabitants."[44]

There is an interesting story from classical Rabbinic literature that argues,

"…as part of the price of Abraham's purchase of the Cave of the Patriarchs (Cave of Machpelah), which lay in the territory of the

Jebusites, the Jebusites made Abraham grant them a covenant that his descendants would not take control of Jebus against the will of the Jebusites, and then the Jebusites engraved the covenant into bronze;[1] the sources state that the presence of the bronze statues are why the Israelites were not able to conquer the city during Joshua's campaign."[45]

"The rabbis of the classical era go on to state that King David was prevented from entering the city of Jebus for the same reason, and so he promised the reward of captaincy to anyone who destroyed the bronzes – Joab performing the task, and so gaining the prize. The covenant is dismissed by the rabbis as having been invalidated due to the war the Jebusites fought against Joshua, but nevertheless, David (according to the rabbis) paid the Jebusites the full value of the city, collecting the money from among all the Israelite tribes, so that the city became their common property.

In reference to 2 Samuel 5:6, which refers to a saying about the blind and the lame,

> *"Now the king and his men went to Jerusalem against the Jebusites, the inhabitants of the land, and they said to David, 'You shall not come in here, **but the blind and lame will turn you away'**; thinking, 'David cannot enter here.'"*

> *2 Samuel 5:6* (emphasis added)

Rashi quotes a midrash which argues that the Jebusites had two statues in their city, with their mouths containing the words of the covenant between Abraham and the Jebusites; one figure, depicting a blind person, represented Isaac, and the other, depicting a lame person, representing Jacob."[46]

The story is interesting, but none the less, David conquers the Jebusite city and declares it to be the King's city, eventually making it the capital of Israel. There is one more event that seals the spiritual significance of this city, making Jerusalem - the Holy City. There is a supernatural story about how the Temple mount came to be.

The Adversary Stood Up

"Then Satan stood up against Israel and moved David to number Israel. So David said to Joab and to the princes of the people, "Go, number Israel from Beersheba even to Dan, and bring me word that I may know their number."

1 Chronicles 21:1-2

The city of Jerusalem would not be established without a supernatural clash of forces. In another behind-the-scenes view, we see Satan stand up in opposition to King David and, in a cunning attempt to subvert him, incites David to number Israel.

Now, taking a census of God's people was restricted in the Torah or Law of God. The writing of Moses gives instructions about how to do this.

"The LORD also spoke to Moses, saying, 'When you take a census of the sons of Israel to number them, then each one of them shall give a ransom for himself to the LORD when you number them **so that there will be no plague among them when you number them.**

This is what everyone who is numbered shall give: half a shekel according to the shekel of the sanctuary.'"

Exodus 30:11-12 (emphasis added)

David sent out Joab to count all of Israel without giving the proper temple half-shekel ransom. The consequence of the plague, forewarned about, was about to fall upon the people.

The prophet Gad was sent by Yahweh, to deliver three options to the King. They were either three years of famine, three months to be swept away before Israel's enemies, or three days of "the sword of the LORD, [which equated to] a pestilence in the land, and the angel of the LORD destroying throughout all the territory of Israel." (1 Chronicles 21:12).

Under great distress, David chose to "fall into the hands of Yahweh", which was option number three (the original consequence according to Torah).

*"**So the LORD sent a pestilence on Israel; 70,000 men of Israel fell**. And God sent an angel to Jerusalem to destroy it; but as he was about to destroy it, the LORD saw and was sorry over the calamity, and said to the destroying angel, "It is enough; now relax your hand." **And the angel of the LORD was standing by the threshing floor of [Araunah] the Jebusite**. Then David lifted up his eyes and saw the angel of the LORD standing between earth and heaven, with his drawn sword in his hand stretched out over Jerusalem."*

1 Chronicles 21:14-16 (emphasis and brackets added)

The Angel of Yahweh steps in as David and the Elders of Israel watch in horror during the three days of death.

*"Then the angel of the LORD commanded Gad to say to David, **that David should go up and build an altar to the LORD on the threshing floor of [Araunah] the Jebusite**."*

1 Chronicles 21:18 (Emphasis added)

Araunah, the Jebusite, offered to freely give David the threshing floor to stop the plague, but David said he would not make an offering to Yahweh on something that cost him nothing, so he purchased the land from Araunah. After paying 600 shekels, he built an altar there for Yahweh and offered up the oxen he had purchased.

Did you see what happened here? The Adversary tried to use Yahweh's own Law to destroy Jerusalem. The Angel of Yahweh holds back the plague and does a reversal on the Adversary, and in this supernatural upset, the Temple Mount is now purchased, and Jerusalem's cornerstone is established! The city of Jerusalem and the Temple mount are now safely in the hands of David. This will not be the last time that the city of Jerusalem is wrestled out of the enemy's grasp.

This mountain or mount holds a deep history, and the Adversary knows it. This was the city of the first king-priest Melchizedek, the place where Abraham offered Isaac, and (possibly) the "city of God, Beth-El, or Gate of Heaven," discovered by Jacob, the city conquered by Joshua (with Divine help). This threshing floor would later become the Temple Mount, the site of Solomon's Temple, the site of Zerubbabel's rebuilt Temple, the site of Herod's second Temple, and I would suggest, one of the most hotly debated pieces of real estate on the earth today.

Solomon Builds the Temple in Jerusalem

The Temple project started in the heart of David, but it was inspired by heaven. It was David who secured this site and truly wanted to build a "House for Yahweh." He was told by the prophet Nathan that he was not allowed to build the temple because there was too much blood on his hands. David's son Solomon was chosen to build this magnificent structure. David spent the rest of his life gathering materials and making plans.

"Then he called for his son Solomon and charged him to build a house for the LORD God of Israel. David said to Solomon, "My son, I had intended to build a house to the name of the LORD my God. But the word of the LORD came to me, saying, 'You have shed much blood and have waged great wars; you shall not build a house to My name because you have shed so much blood on the earth before Me. **Behold, a son will be born to you, who shall be a man of rest;** *and I will give him rest from all his enemies on every side; for* **his name shall be Solomon, and I will give peace and quiet** *to Israel in his days.* **He shall build a house for My name, and he shall be My son and I will be his father;** *and I will establish the throne of his kingdom over Israel forever."*

1 Chronicles 22:6-10 (emphasis added)

He shall be a "man of rest", "My son," "and I will establish the throne and his kingdom over Israel forever." It becomes obvious that this was more than a message about David's son, Solomon; it is a prophecy about the coming Son, Yeshua. This truth was also revealed in David's son's name.

The name Solomon in Hebrew is Shlomo; it is derived from the root word *shalom*. As we have learned, *shalom* means "peace" or "rest"; it has a deeper meaning of completeness or complete peace and rest. King David's son, Solomon, would have been a prince before becoming king. Combining these ideas, the Temple builder would be known as the "Prince of Peace"; does that sound familiar?

"For a child will be born to us, a son will be given to us;
And the government will rest on His shoulders;
And His name will be called *Wonderful Counselor, Mighty God,*
Eternal Father, ***Prince of Peace.***

There will be no end to the increase of His government or of peace,
On the throne of David and over his kingdom,
To establish it and to uphold it with justice and righteousness
From then on and forevermore.
The zeal of the LORD of hosts will accomplish this."

Isaiah 9:6-7 (emphasis added)

The prophesied descendant of David and true temple builder is Yeshua. Solomon is a type and shadow of Messiah, teaching us about the Father's future plans and revealing Messiah's connection to the City of Peace. It points to a future when peace will dominate the world, and Messiah will sit on His throne, the throne of David.

David was attributed to finishing the conquest of the Land that Joshua had started 400 years earlier. Yahweh had now established His inherited portion of land, separated from the allotment given to nations, and He also secured its capital city. The building of

Yahweh's great house, the first Temple, was now finished by Solomon, and Yahweh was ready to place His Name there and descend upon His earthly footstool.

"But will God indeed dwell with mankind on the earth? **Behold, heaven and the highest heaven cannot contain You; how much less this house which I have built***."*

"Yet have regard to the prayer of Your servant and to his supplication, O LORD my God, to listen to the cry and to the prayer which Your servant prays before You; **that Your eye may be open toward this house day and night, toward the place of which You have said that You would put Your name there***, to listen to the prayer which Your servant shall pray toward this place."*

2 Chronicles 6:19-20 (emphasis added)

The dedication of Yahweh's Temple was a spectacular sight to behold! There was a full array of Levitical priest's dressed in holy garments, singers assigned by the King to worship the Holy God of Israel, with instruments of praise, and with the ascent of a great sound. All of Israel was gathered in Jerusalem in anticipation that they would see The Lord of all the earth descend upon them, to dwell in their midst. They were not disappointed!

"Now when Solomon had finished praying, **fire came down from heaven and consumed the burnt offering and the sacrifices, and the glory of the LORD filled the house. The priests could not enter into the house of the LORD because the glory of the LORD filled the LORD'S house.** *All the sons of Israel, seeing the fire come down and the glory of the LORD upon the house, bowed down on the*

pavement with their faces to the ground, and they worshiped and gave praise to the LORD, saying, "Truly He is good, truly His lovingkindness is everlasting."

2 Chronicles 7:1-3 (emphasis added)

Yahweh appears to Solomon three times in his life; this time was to respond to his prayer. Here is what He said,

*"Then the LORD appeared to Solomon at night and said to him, <u>'I have heard your prayer and have chosen this place for Myself as a house of sacrifice. If I shut up the heavens so that there is no rain, or if I command the locust to devour the land, or if I send pestilence among My people,</u> **and My people who are called by My name humble themselves and pray and seek My face and turn from their wicked ways, then I will hear from heaven, will forgive their sin and will heal their land.** Now My eyes will be open and My ears attentive to the prayer offered in this place. For now I have chosen and consecrated this house **that My name may be there forever**, and My eyes and My heart will be there perpetually.'"*

2 Chronicles 7:12-16 (emphasis and underline added)

Yahweh takes full responsibility for preventing rain on the earth, sending locusts to devour the land, and sending pestilence upon the people. We need to stop and consider the weight of that. Does Yahweh directly intervene in men's affairs? Yes, He does! But He also gives them a way to change the course of that judgment and hold back the armies of heaven or the forces of an evil adversary. It is PRAYER, prayer toward this house! The gateway between heaven and earth, where the angels ascend and descend on Jacob's ladder. The city where He placed His Name, over the wings of the Cherubim, where atonement is made for His people. The city of peace!

158

Yeshua's blood was spilled on this same mountain, it is also called Mount Calvary, in Jerusalem! His message is not just to the nation of Israel but to ALL NATIONS, every person. In Solomon's prayer (2 Chronicles 6:29), He asks Yahweh to hear the prayer of "the foreigner who is not from Your people Israel," and for His great name's sake, answer their prayers.

In quoting the prophet Isaiah (Isaiah 56:7), Yeshua declares that the Temple is "a House of Prayer for all nations,"

"[Yeshua said,] Is it not written, 'MY HOUSE SHALL BE CALLED A HOUSE OF PRAYER FOR ALL THE NATIONS'?

Mark 11:17

Jerusalem is not just the capital of Israel; it is an international city. Sadly, the nations of the world would rather take it away from Yahweh and conquer it as their own. This will be the ongoing struggle between these two cities, Babylon and Jerusalem. History will show that Jerusalem will be a cup of trembling for all nations,

"Thus declares the LORD who stretches out the heavens, lays the foundation of the earth, and forms the spirit of man within him,
"Behold, I am going to make Jerusalem a cup that causes reeling to all the peoples around*; and when the siege is against Jerusalem, it will also be against Judah. **It will come about in that day that I will make Jerusalem a heavy stone for all the peoples; all who lift it will be severely injured. And all the nations of the earth will be gathered against it.***"*

Zechariah 12:1-3 (emphasis added)

But in the end, Jerusalem will endure, and the nations will flock to it to worship the King of Kings. It is no wonder that the Psalmist records these beautiful words,

> *"Great is the LORD, and greatly to be praised,*
> *In the city of our God, His holy mountain.*
> *Beautiful in elevation, the joy of the whole earth,*
> *Is Mount Zion in the far north,*
> *The city of the great King."*
>
> *Psalms 48:1-2*

Later on, we will discuss just how long Israel would be able to hold on to this sacred city.

Babylon Rising

As we discussed, the origins of Babylon were found in the ancient civilizations of Sumer and Akkad, and the first cities can be traced back to the rebel, Cain. The essence of Babylon was established by Nimrod through building his system of city-states. The Tower of Babel incident reminds us of their occultic connections to the spirits of the rebellious Watcher-class angels, now imprisoned in the underworld, and their offspring, the Nephilim. These spirits formed the Pantheon of gods and goddesses, which was a central part of Mesopotamian culture.

The spelling of the name, Babylon, is the Latin representation of Greek Babylṓn (Βαβυλών), derived from the native (Babylonian) Bābilim, meaning "gate of the god(s)" as we discussed earlier.

The point of this next cursor through history is to see how the rise of Babylon has affected the nation of Israel. First, we must give a brief historical overview.[47, 48]

During the Akkadian and Neo-Sumerian periods (c. 2334-2004 BC) before this period, Mesopotamia was fragmented into a number of city-states referred to as the Early dynastic period. The Akkadian Empire defines this new period culminating with the Third Dynasty of Ur. This date roughly coincides with the city of Ur that Abraham left in Genesis 12.

There are interesting stories from extra-biblical writings about the Patriarchs. In this quote from the Book of Jasher, Nimrod's wise men had a vision regarding Terah's newborn son, Abram. At the very least, this material places Nimrod and Abraham in the same historical time frame.

> *"And it was in the night that Abram was born, that all the servants of Terah, and all the wise men of Nimrod, and his conjurors came and ate and drank in the house of Terah, and they rejoiced with him on that night. And when all the wise men and conjurors went out from the house of Terah, they lifted up their eyes toward heaven that night to look at the stars, and they saw, and behold one very large star came from the east and ran in the heavens, and he swallowed up the four stars from the four sides of the heavens. And all the wise men of the king and his conjurors were astonished at the sight, and the sages understood this matter, and they knew its import. And they said to each other, This only betokens the child that has been born to Terah this night, who will grow up and be fruitful and multiply, and possess all the earth, he and his children forever, and he and his seed will slay great kings and inherit their lands."*[49]

Isin–Larsa and rise of Babylon (c. 2025–1750 BC). Isin and Larsa were two major city-states that ruled the Mesopotamian region. Southern Mesopotamia (the region where Babylon was located) was conquered by an Amorite king named Sumu-abum (1894-1881 BC). Sumu-abum became the first king of a list of kings that formed the **Amorite First Dynasty** in the later part of this period. This is when the city of Babylon became known and rose to prominence. One of the most well-known Kings of the Amorite dynasty was Hammurabi.

The Amorite king, Hammurabi, founded the short-lived Old Babylonian Empire (1792-1750 BC). He built Babylon into a major city and declared himself its king. Southern Mesopotamia became known as Babylonia. During his reign, he conquered Elam and the city-states of Larsa, Eshnunna, and Mari. Hammurabi ousted Ishme-Dagan I, the king of Assyria, and forced his son Mut-Ashkur to pay tribute, bringing almost all of Mesopotamia under Babylonian rule.[50]

"Hammurabi is best known for having issued the Code of Hammurabi, which he claimed to have received from Shamash, the Babylonian god of justice. Unlike earlier Sumerian law codes, such as the Code of Ur-Nammu, which had focused on compensating the victim of the crime, the Law of Hammurabi was one of the first law codes to place greater emphasis on the physical punishment of the perpetrator. It prescribed specific penalties for each crime and is among the first codes to establish the presumption of innocence. They were intended to limit what a wronged person was permitted to do in retribution. The Code of Hammurabi and the Law of Moses in the Torah contain numerous similarities."[51]

Under Hammurabi, Babylon achieved military supremacy and power. It stretched from the Persian Gulf to the upper reaches of the Tigris River. It became the leading literary and cultural center, the intellectual capital of Mesopotamia.

Babylonian civilization was highly advanced. Mathematical and astronomical texts reveal that Babylonians developed the 60-minute hour and the 360-degree circle. He introduced the cuneiform writing system, used to establish the Code of Hammurabi and is considered one of the most famous Mesopotamian advancements.[52]

Hammurabi extended Babylonian rule not only through conquest but also through trade. Babylon sat at the crossroads of world commerce and communication. Caravans brought rare and exotic products from far and wide. Clothes from Indonesia were among the many luxuries imported.

"Texts from Old Babylon often include references to Shamash, the sun-god of Sippar, treated as a supreme deity, and Marduk, considered as his son. Marduk was later elevated to a higher status, and Shamash lowered, perhaps reflecting Babylon's rising political power."[53]

The empire waned under Hammurabi's son Samsu-iluna, and Babylon spent long periods under **Assyrian, Kassite, and Elamite** domination (1749-1475 BC). Elam eventually invades Babylon and carries away two stele artifacts, including the statue of Marduk, the patron god of Babylon, marking the fall of the Kassite Dynasty. The Elamites of the Shutrukid dynasty ruled over Elam and Babylon starting around 1155 BC.

During this period, two Babylonian writings, the **Epic of Gilgamesh** and **Ludllel bel nemeqi** (Babylonian "Book of Job"), were composed. These writings have been re-discovered in modern times and are a source for understanding the cultural beliefs and way of life in Babylonia. Another discovery was made from that period, the Babylonian version of **Enuma Elish,** and in 750 BC, the Assyrians made their own version of Enuma Elish, naming their gods in the epic.

The Enuma Elish is a Babylonian creation myth, also known as the Seven Tablets of Creation. There are many parallels to the biblical account of Genesis. The Babylonian myths predate written copies of

Genesis, leading some scholars to speculate that Genesis was derived from Babylonian myths.

My analysis, taking into consideration a biblical worldview, is simply that all mankind came from one family, Noah, and consequently shared one story from the pre-flood era. It was passed on through oral tradition until it was eventually written down by various civilizations. The pagan nations embellished that story, each inserting their own beliefs about deities, the rebellious watchers, and their fallen offspring, the Nephilim. The important question here is whose version of creation and the Great Flood is correct? Is it possible that the truth of this story, as recorded in the Bible, could have survived the passage of time?

If you consider the ages of the pre-flood patriarchs, according to biblical genealogical records, **Adam** lived 930 years, overlapping the life of Methuselah. **Methuselah** lived 969 years and died in the year of the flood, passing the story to **Noah**. The true story of creation would have been passed from Adam, through one person, to Noah. Let that sink in for a minute. A strong case for the accuracy of the oral story can be made here.

In the following succession, the story was passed from Noah to **Shem**, to Abraham, to Isaac, to **Jacob** (Shem was still alive during Jacob's lifetime), to Levi, to **Kohath**, to Amram, to **Moses** (Kohath was alive during Moses' lifetime), considering ages and the overlap of generations, there are only four more people to consider from Shem to Moses. In case you haven't been counting, **that's five people between Adam and Moses** and, of course, many years. I know how that sounds, but in researching the timelines and using multiple sources, this is an accurate accounting if you accept the extended ages of the pre-flood generations. I was also amazed to discover the simplicity of this timeline and potential accuracy for the passing of critical information!

I believe these men (families) were commissioned by God to preserve the truth and pass it down from generation to generation. The writing of the creation story, as well as the first five books of the Old Testament, are accredited to Moses, who met personally with Yahweh on Mount Sinai. It was at that time that any details of the true story of creation and ancient history could have been questioned and confirmed before Moses codified them.

Some scholars are of the opinion that Moses didn't write Genesis and that it may have been penned at a later date. Regardless of that, the mountaintop experience with Yahweh would have reinforced the accuracy of the oral story as Moses heard it. And also, considering the fact that he could have and probably would have just asked Yahweh to clarify, I know I would have!

Babylonia and Assyria (c. 1475–539 BC). This period was marked by the expansion of dynastic rule over both Babylonia and Assyria. We will mention four, starting with the **Second Dynasty of Isin** (1153-1022 BC). The fourth King was Nebuchadnezzar I (1119-1098 BC, *not to be confused with the Babylonian King in the book of Daniel, Nebuchadnezzar II*); Marduk was temporarily dethroned as the patron deity during this time. The patron god of the Kassites, Enlil (considered the father of Marduk in the pantheon, by the Kassites), replaced Marduk until King Nabopolassar (629-605 BC) brought back the statue of Marduk from Elam.

The Assyrian king from the **Adaside dynasty**, Shalmaneser V (727-722 BC) (Shalmaneser was a title, not a name, given to several Kings during this time). He was the second king from this dynasty to rule over the combined empire of Assyria and Babylonia.

Shalmaneser raided the northern kingdom of Israel in 725 BC and besieged the capital city of Samaria. After three long years, Samaria was sacked, and the people were exiled to Assyria in 722 BC. This is where the term "the lost sheep of the house of Israel" (Matt 10:6; 15:24) was derived from.

*"**Israel is a scattered flock**; the lions have driven them away. **The first one who devoured him was the king of Assyria**, and this last one who has broken his bones is Nebuchadnezzar, king of Babylon."*

Jeremiah 50:17 (emphasis added)

This Assyrian king was used by Yahweh to bring judgment on the northern kingdom of Israel for their chronic sins of idolatry. Meanwhile, the King of Judah, in the south, was faithful to Yahweh and was protected from the advances of the Assyria.

In 722 BC, there was a dynastic change in Assyria, and the **Sargonid dynasty** (722-626 BC) came into power. The most notable Assyrian to rule was King Sennacherib (705-681 BC). He is mentioned in 2 Kings 18:23 as an adversary of Israel during the reign of Hezekiah, King of Judah. Sennacherib marched his army into Judah and threatened to do to Jerusalem what Shalmaneser did to Samaria.

"Now in the fourteenth year of King Hezekiah, Sennacherib, king

*of Assyria, came up against all the fortified cities of Judah and seized them. **Hear the word of the great king, the king of Assyria.** Thus says the king, 'Do not let Hezekiah deceive you, for he will not be able to deliver you from my hand; nor let Hezekiah make you trust in the LORD, saying, 'The LORD will surely deliver us, and this city will not be given into the hand of the king of Assyria.' **Do not listen to Hezekiah**, for thus says the king of Assyria, 'Make your peace with me and come out to me.'"*

2 Kings 18:13,28-31 (emphasis added)

Hezekiah, after hearing the words Sennacherib, tore his clothes and entered Yahweh's house.

*"and **he went up to the house of the LORD and spread it out before the LORD**. Hezekiah prayed before the LORD and said, "O LORD, the God of Israel, who are enthroned above the cherubim, You are the God, You alone, of all the kingdoms of the earth. You have made heaven and earth. **Incline Your ear, O LORD, and hear; open Your eyes, O LORD, and see; and listen to the words of Sennacherib, which he has sent to reproach the living God.***

*Truly, O LORD, the kings of Assyria have devastated the nations and their lands and have cast their gods into the fire, for they were not gods but the work of men's hands, wood, and stone. So they have destroyed them. **Now, O LORD our God, I pray, deliver us from his hand that all the kingdoms of the earth may know that You alone, O LORD, are God.**"*

2 Kings 19:14-19 (emphasis added)

Yahweh's response, given by the prophet Isaiah, is historically epic!

> *"'Because of your raging against Me, and because your arrogance has come up to My ears,*
> **Therefore, I will put My hook in your nose and My bridle in your lips,**
> **And I will turn you back by the way which you came,"** *...declares the LORD. "'For I will defend this city to save it for My own sake and for My servant David's sake.'"*

> *"Then it happened that night that **the angel of the LORD went out and struck 185,000 in the camp of the Assyrians; and when men rose early in the morning, behold, all of them were dead**. So Sennacherib, king of Assyria, departed and returned home and lived at Nineveh. [37] It came about as he was worshiping in the house of Nisroch, his god, that Adrammelech and Sharezer killed him with the sword, and they escaped into the land of Ararat. And Esarhaddon, his son, became king in his place.*

> *2 Kings 19:32-37* (emphasis added)

Hezekiah was successful (with divine help), and the southern kingdom of Judah had now bought themselves some time to turn their hearts back to Yahweh, but would they do it?

In 609 BC, after about a century of the kings of the Neo-Assyrian Empire ruling both Assyria and Babylonia, the Neo-Babylonian Empire destroyed Assyria and became the sole power in Mesopotamia. This paved the way for the famous "head of gold" ruler of the Chaldean dynasty to take the throne and conquer the entire then-known world.

The reign of the **Chaldean dynasty** began with the Chaldean King, Nabopolassar (629-605 BC). With the allied forces of Medes, Persians, and Scythians, he utterly destroyed the city of Nineveh and brought down the long reign of the Assyrian empire. Under Chaldean rule, The Babylonian Empire had reached its greatest influence in culture, wealth, and military power. This allied army was led by a young General, the son of King Nabopolassar, Nebuchadnezzar II.

There was one stronghold left to be conquered, the city of Carchemish (or Karchemiš), in the northern region of Syria. Remnants of the Assyrian army joined Carchemish, a city under Egyptian rule on the Euphrates. Egypt, a former vassal of Assyria, was allied with Assyrian King Ashur-uballit II and marched in 609 BC to his aid against the Babylonians.[54]

The Egyptian army of Pharaoh Necho II was delayed at Megiddo by the forces of King Josiah of Judah. Josiah was killed, and his army was defeated at the Battle of Megiddo.

We need to take a brief detour here to mention a story about this important king of Judah, Josiah.

Israel had reached its lowest point morally under Judah's most wicked King, Manasseh. He built high places for the Baals, made Asherim, and worshiped all the hosts of heaven. Manasseh defiled the Temple courtyard with altars for the host of heaven, and he made his sons pass through the fire. (2 Chronicles 33:3-9). Yahweh brought the army of the king of Assyria against Manasseh. They captured him with hooks, bound him with bronze chains, and took him to Babylon. His wicked son Amon reigned in his place for two short years and was assassinated.

From this dark time in Judah's history, one bright star emerged: an eight-year-old son of Amon named Josiah. Josiah takes the throne as a young boy and reigns in Judah for thirty-one years. The Bible says, *"he did right in the sight of Yahweh and walked in the ways of his father David."*

*"...**He began to purge Judah and Jerusalem of the high places**, the Asherim, the carved images, and the molten images. They tore down the altars of the Baals in his presence, and the incense altars that were high above them he chopped down; also the Asherim, the carved images, and the molten images he broke in pieces and ground to powder and scattered it on the graves of those who had sacrificed to them."*

2 Chronicles 34:3-4 (emphasis added)

Josiah repaired the house of Yahweh, and the priests found a copy of the Book of the Law that had been hidden away for years. Josiah's heart was moved as he read the words of Yahweh written by Moses. He read about the wrath that would come upon the nation if they turned from serving Yahweh to worshiping Idols. In haste, he gathered the people, the priests, and the Elders of Israel together and made a covenant before Yahweh.

"The king went up to the house of the LORD and all the men of Judah, the inhabitants of Jerusalem, the priests, the Levites, and all the people, from the greatest to the least; and he read in their hearing all the words of the book of the covenant which was found in the house of the LORD"

2 Chronicles 34:30

They made a covenant that day with all who were present in Israel to serve Yahweh, their Elohim. Throughout Josiah's lifetime, they did not turn away from following the LORD God of their fathers. (2 Chronicles 34:33)

This proved to be nothing more than a band-aid, a temporary stay of judgment for Israel. At the end of King Josiah's life, the king of Egypt would defeat him on the battlefield, and Israel would mourn the loss of a great king. From this time on, Jerusalem would be under the thumb of Babylon until it was finally captured just 18 years later, in 587 BC.

The site of this final battle was in the valley of Jezreel in Megiddo. It won't be the last time we see an important battle take place there. This is the site of the final battle known as Armageddon in the book of Revelation between Israel (Jerusalem) and the pseudo city, Babylon.

Pharoah Necho II and the Egyptian army continued on to Carchemish, where they encountered the forces of the powerful Babylonian army and its allies, led by Nebuchadnezzar II. This famous **Battle of Carchemish** (605 BC) is recorded on a tablet discovered in Babylon of Iraq in recent years. The Nebuchadnezzar Chronicle, also known as the Jerusalem Chronicle, is one of the Babylonian Chronicles and contains a description of the first eleven years of the reign of Nebuchadnezzar II.[55]

The tablet claims that Nebuchadnezzar,

"...crossed the river to go against the Egyptian army which lay in Karchemiš. They fought with each other, and the Egyptian army withdrew before him. He accomplished their defeat and beat them to non-existence. As for the rest of the Egyptian army, which had escaped from the defeat so quickly that no weapon had reached them in the district of Hamath, the Babylonian troops overtook and defeated them so that not a single man escaped to his own country. At that time, Nebuchadnezzar conquered the whole area of Hamath."[56]

The Battle of Carchemish is also recorded in the book of Jeremiah, chapter 46,

> *"That which came as the word of the LORD to Jeremiah the prophet concerning the nations.*
>
> *To Egypt, concerning the army of Pharaoh Neco king of Egypt, which was by the Euphrates River at Carchemish, which Nebuchadnezzar king of Babylon defeated in the fourth year of Jehoiakim, the son of Josiah, king of Judah."*
>
> *Jeremiah 46:1-2*

The prophet Jeremiah goes on to say,

> *"The LORD of hosts, the God of Israel, says, "Behold, I am going to punish Amon of Thebes, and Pharaoh, and Egypt along with her gods and her kings, even Pharaoh and those who trust in him. **I shall give them over to the power of those who are seeking their lives, even into the hand of Nebuchadnezzar, king of Babylon, and into the hand of his officers.** Afterward, however, it will be inhabited as in the days of old," declares the LORD.*
>
> *Jeremiah 46:25-26 (emphasis added)*

Why was this detour important?

As we compare history with the Bible, we find that Yahweh, through the prophet Jeremiah, revealed that this political upheaval was not just a random series of events. Yahweh was using Babylon and its armies like a hammer to crush the nations. Yahweh refers to Nebuchadnezzar as "His Servant." It is Yahweh who empowered him to conquer the nations.

> ***Now I have given all these lands into the hand of Nebuchadnezzar king of Babylon, My servant****, and I have given him also the wild animals of the field to serve him. All the nations shall serve him and his son and his grandson until the time of his own land comes; then many nations and great kings will make him their servant.*

> *"It will be that the nation or the kingdom which will not serve him, Nebuchadnezzar king of Babylon, and which will not put its neck under the yoke of the king of Babylon,* ***I will punish that nation with the sword, with famine, and with pestilence," declares the LORD, "until I have destroyed it by his hand.***

Jeremiah 27:6-8 (emphasis added)

It is clear here that Yahweh is effecting a monumental change in the politics of the then-known world. Earlier, He orchestrated the fall of Assyria, the subjugation of Egypt, and even brought judgment upon His own people, Israel and Judah, all by the hand of the king of Babylon.

> *"The LORD of hosts has sworn to say, "****Surely, just as I have intended so it has happened, and just as I have planned so it will stand, to break Assyria in My land****, and I will trample him on My*

174

mountains. Then his yoke will be removed from them and his burden removed from their shoulder. **This is the plan devised against the whole earth, and this is the hand that is stretched out against all the nations. For the LORD of hosts has planned, and who can frustrate it?**

Isaiah 14:24-27 (emphasis added)

Who devised this plan to break Assyria? This is considered a huge geopolitical change in the world. The Hebrew word for devise is *yaats* (Strong's H3289 - yāʿaṣ), which means "to advise or counsel." Hidden in this word is a possible reference to the Craftsmen or Strategists. They would be the ones responsible for giving Yahweh counsel on this type of plan of action. We should also consider that the Four Horsemen would have most likely rode alongside the armies of Babylon during their conquests.

Jerusalem Falls

Nebuchadnezzar is used by Yahweh to bring judgment on His people, Israel. He is the horn used by God to scatter His people and deliver the almost deadly blow to a nation once proud of its heritage. After the death of Josiah, king of Judah, Jerusalem was placed in the hands of vassal kings under the rule of Babylon. Four kings would govern Jerusalem for a total of 22 ½ years before Jerusalem would reach its prophesied fate.

Jerusalem fell in two stages, the first under the governance of Jehoiakim, king of Judah. The Bible says, "he did evil in the sight of the LORD his God," and revolted against the king of Babylon. Nebuchadnezzar came and besieged the city of Jerusalem and carried Jehoiakim away in chains back to Babylon (597 BC). He took with him some of the furnishings of the Temple in Jerusalem and placed them in his own temple.

By this time, the Ark of the Covenant had been removed from the Temple and had been hidden away. Nebuchadnezzar hauled off some of the leaders and elders, as well as many of the people, and brought them captive to Babylon.

The second fall was ten years later. Zedekiah was the final vassal king of Judah to reign in Jerusalem. According to history, on Tisha B'Av, either the 25th of August 587 BCE or the 18th of July 586 BCE, the Babylonians took Jerusalem, destroyed the First Temple, and burned down the city.

The small settlements surrounding the city and those close to the western border of the kingdom were destroyed as well. The Kingdom of Judah was abolished and annexed as a Babylonian province with its center in Mizpah. The Judean elite, including the Davidic dynasty, were exiled to Babylon.

Not All is Lost!

Secretly, Yahweh placed a prophet named Daniel, a young man from among the exiles of Judah, in the court of Nebuchadnezzar. This man-of-God would prove to be, for the king, an invaluable connection to the true and living God of heaven and helped guide the king in his divine assignment. This is not to say that Nebuchadnezzar was a godly man by any means – no, he was a tyrant! Nonetheless, Yahweh used the king of Babylon for his own purposes.

Yahweh sent a dream to Nebuchadnezzar, which he would not understand until Daniel the prophet gave the king its interpretation. The contents of this dream would reveal the plan that Yahweh has for the nations, not just for then but even now, as we are watching this prophecy unfold.

The story goes that Nebuchadnezzar had a dream, and when he awoke from that dream, he was alarmed and greatly troubled. There was one problem, though: he couldn't remember the dream. So, he called all the wise men of his realm who were skilled in astronomy and mathematics; they were the top thinkers of his day. Among their skills was an occultic awareness of the spirits and the ancient knowledge of the gods. The king thought that if anyone could help conjure the dream, it would be these Chaldeans, the wise men of Babylon.

The elusive dream proved to be impossible to decipher; no man would be able to unlock the secret dream Yahweh had given the king. In a desperate move, Daniel was allowed to come before the king and inform him there was a "God in heaven" who revealed secrets and dreams. The interpretation of this dream would unlock the mystery of the entire future of human government on earth, beginning with this Babylonian ruler until the end of days.

"Then the mystery was revealed to Daniel in a night vision. Then Daniel blessed the God of heaven; Daniel said, "Let the name of God be blessed forever and ever,
For wisdom and power belong to Him.
"It is He who changes the times and the epochs;
He removes kings and establishes kings;
He gives wisdom to wise men
And knowledge to men of understanding.
"It is He who reveals the profound and hidden things;
He knows what is in the darkness,
And the light dwells with Him."

Daniel 2:19-22 (emphasis added)

Daniel gives credit where credit is due; this is Yahweh's dream and His interpretation. Daniel states, "The mystery was revealed to him in a night vision." It seems like more than just the interpretation of Nebuchadnezzar's dream was revealed to Daniel. Daniels says, *"It is He who changes the times and the epochs; He removes kings and establishes kings,"* no man, no king, is in charge of kingdoms of men.

Daniel will become one the most influential, pivotal, and geopolitical prophets in human history. He will not only live through the transition of several great kings but will survive the fall and rise of two major empires. His understanding of the divine plan, as revealed to him by angels, will even guide us into our current day, over 2600 years later, and his writings continue to speak to a future we have yet to experience.

We will continue to see that there are off-world actors involved, territorial principalities, and adversarial opponents, but Yahweh will have the last say. The realm of men is under the jurisdiction of the highest court in the universe.

There is One Judge, and His counsel will stand; He will rule with all the forces of heaven. The Divine Council sits in session; the Four Horsemen will continue to patrol the earth and carry out their missions. The Craftsmen will be commissioned to devise plans that will effectively bring the kingdoms of men to an end and reveal a supreme divine Kingdom!

The Four Horns will push the nations to the north, south, east, and west until the nation of Israel recognizes who their True God is, and they turn their hearts back to him; then Yahweh will sit in His Temple, the nations will know Him, and the rebellion that began in Genesis will be crushed forever!

The ultimate road map for the nations is revealed in the interpretation of the king's dream. This dream goes on to become a tool of study for believers all over the world, but only for those who accept it as truth. History itself bears witness to the facts of its truth, its accuracy, and its profound prophetic value.

Chapter 7 – Daniel's Image of the Beast – 605 BCE

*"You, O king, were looking, and behold, **there was a single great statue;** that statue, which was large and of extraordinary splendor, was standing in front of you, and its appearance was awesome. <u>The head of that statue was made of fine gold, its breast and its arms of silver, its belly and its thighs of bronze, its legs of iron, its feet partly of iron and partly of clay.</u> **You continued looking until a stone was cut out without hands, and it struck the statue on its feet of iron and clay and crushed them.** Then the iron, the clay, the bronze, the silver, and the gold were crushed all at the same time and became like chaff from the summer threshing floors, and the wind carried them away so that not a trace of them was found. **But the stone that struck the statue became a great mountain and filled the whole earth."***

Daniel 2:31-35 (Emphasis and underline added)

The interpretation of the dream chronicles history as we now know it and it reveals a future yet to be fully comprehended. Nebuchadnezzar would discover that the world was laid at his feet, and up to this point in history, he was the greatest ruler to ever live.

"You, O king, are the king of kings, to whom the God of heaven has given the kingdom, the power, the strength, and the glory; and wherever the sons of men dwell, or the beasts of the field, or the

*birds of the sky, He has given them into your hand and has caused you to rule over them all. **You are the head of gold**.*"

Daniel 2:37-38

Nebuchadnezzar would need to learn that the true God gave him this kingdom and power. He would be matchless in strength and earthly glory, but the key to his success is found in three small words, "He has given." This phrase, "He [Yahweh] has given them into your hand

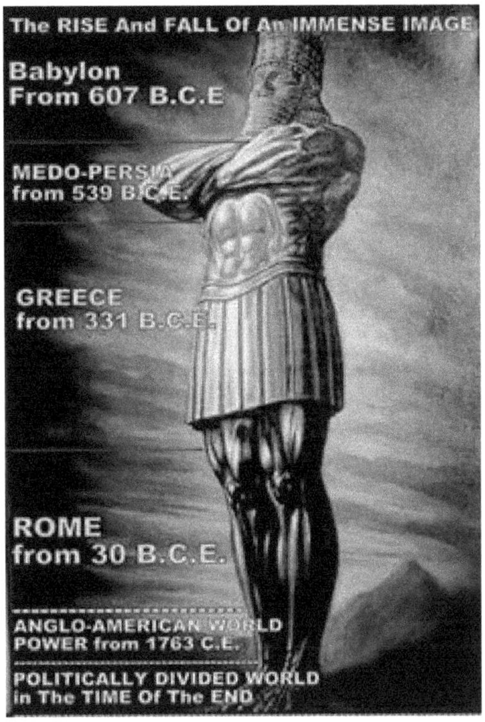

and has caused you to rule over them all," reveals the impartation of authority. Yahweh gave authority to Nebuchadnezzar to dominate all other human rulers and seats of power.

Authority can only be given by one who is greater than the receiving authority itself and Yahweh is and has always been the Supreme Authority. Man convinces himself that he is in control, but that is just an illusion. Yahweh forced this preeminent ruler – the Head of Gold, to see this reality as a lesson for all future rulers.

In a moment when Nebuchadnezzar was lifted up in pride and admiring his great kingdom, Yahweh gave him another dream.

" 'O Belteshazzar [Daniel], chief of the magicians, since I know that a spirit of the holy gods is in you and no mystery baffles you,

tell me the visions of my dream which I have seen, along with its
interpretation.'

'Now these were the visions in my mind as I lay on my bed: I was
looking, and behold, there was a tree in the midst of the earth

and its height was great.
The tree grew large and became strong
And its height reached to the sky,
And it was visible to the end of the whole earth.
It's foliage was beautiful, and its fruit abundant,
And in it was food for all.
The beasts of the field found shade under it,
And the birds of the sky dwelt in its branches,
And all living creatures fed themselves from it.
I was looking in the visions in my mind as I lay on my bed, and
*behold, **an angelic watcher, a holy one**, **descended from heaven**.'*
He shouted out and spoke as follows:
***'Chop down the tree and cut off its branches**,*
Strip off its foliage and scatter its fruit;
Let the beasts flee from under it
And the birds from its branches.
***Yet leave the stump with its roots in the ground**,*
But with a band of iron and bronze around it
In the new grass of the field,
And let him be drenched with the dew of heaven,
And let him share with the beasts in the grass of the earth.
Let his mind be changed from that of a man
And let a beast's mind be given to him,

And let seven periods of time pass over him.
This sentence is by the decree of the angelic watchers
And the decision is a command of the holy ones,
<u>In order that the living may know</u>
<u>That the Most High is ruler over the realm of mankind,</u>
<u>And bestows it on whom He wishes</u>
<u>And sets over it the lowliest of men.</u> '"

Daniel 4:9-17 (emphasis added)

This is the working definition of "Divine intervention." The passage states that the decision and decree were made by the holy ones.

First of all, the messenger was a Watcher class angel, according to the text. These special angels have a high rank in the heavens, and this watcher is called "a holy one." This is the same term given in Psalms 89 for the "assembly of the holy ones." The word "holy" in Hebrew is from the root *qadosh,* (Strong's H6918), which means set-apart, so these are "set-apart" ones. To put a finer point on it, this decision came down from the Divine Assembly (Council) of set-apart ones.

Secondly, how was this judgment carried out? Was this plan engineered by the Craftsmen? It truly was a unique method of dealing with a man's pride. Nebuchadnezzar would basically lose his mind for seven years. He ate grass like an ox and lived outdoors like an animal. He went from the throne room to crawling around in the back forty until such a time as he "recognized that the Most High is ruler over the realm of mankind and bestows it on whomever He wishes". At the end of the decreed time, he regained his sanity and had this to say,

"But at the end of that period, I, Nebuchadnezzar, raised my eyes
toward heaven, and my reason returned to me, and I blessed the
Most High and praised and honored Him who lives forever;
For His dominion is an everlasting dominion,
And His kingdom endures from generation to generation.
"All the inhabitants of the earth are accounted as nothing,
But He does according to His will in the host of heaven
And among the inhabitants of earth;
And no one can ward off His hand
Or say to Him, 'What have You done?'

Daniel 4:34-35

There is one more story regarding Nebuchadnezzar; it involves another image, a statue of gold. It's not the first time a king or ruler became so self-absorbed that he did something foolish. After learning that he was the head of gold in the dream, He made a ninety-foot-tall golden statue, most likely fashioned in the likeness of himself, and demanded that the rulers of all his provinces come and bow down to the image. The punishment for refusal would be a trip to a fiery oven. Daniel's friends, Shadrach, Meshach, and Abednego, would be put to the test.

I'm sure, if you have attended Sunday school, you know the rest of the story. Once again, Yahweh intervenes and makes his presence known - there is a fourth one in the fire. In a turn of events a Christophany called "one like the son of man," a reference to pre-incarnate Yeshua, stood with the three Hebrew men who were thrown alive into the fiery furnace. To the amazement of the king, their lives were spared by divine intervention.

The point of retelling this story is that in the future, another Babylon will make another image, and the image will seemingly come to life.

"And it was given to him to give breath to the image of the beast so that the image of the beast would even speak and cause as many as do not worship the image of the beast to be killed."

Revelation 13:15

Not only will it come to life, but it will cause many people to be killed. Doesn't this sound similar, if you don't worship the image, you will die. As I said earlier, history is not linear; it is cyclical. What has happened will happen again.

The war between Babylon and Jerusalem will repeat itself over and over until the end, but Babylon will not always be geographical Babylon. This is key to understanding how God operates and how he imparts authority. The principal authority of Babylon will be given to the next part of the image of Daniel, the chest and arms of silver, known as the kingdom of the Medes and Persians. The name Babylon will remain as an identifier until the end of time pointing us back to the influence, religion, culture, and rebellion that began in ancient Babylon.

After the reign of Nebuchadnezzar, the kingdom of Babylon would struggle to maintain its height of glory. In its later years, the city of Babylon was under the governance of Belshazzar, son of King Nabonidus. Daniel was still among the king's wise men when Belshazzar threw a banquet to honor his pagan gods. He commanded his servants to bring the vessels of gold and silver that were taken from Yahweh's Temple in Jerusalem. This did not turn out well for Belshazzar.

That same night, a mysterious hand appeared in the room and wrote on the wall. Belshazzar trembled at the sight, and they eventually called for Daniel. Daniel would interpret the words and deliver Babylon its final message directly and quite literally from the Hand of Yahweh Himself.

"Now this is the inscription that was written out: 'MENE, MENE, TEKEL, UPHARSIN.' This is the interpretation of the message: 'MENE'—God has numbered your kingdom and put an end to it. 'TEKEL'—you have been weighed on the scales and found deficient. 'PERES'—your kingdom has been divided and given over to the Medes and Persians."

Daniel 5:25-28

That very night, Babylon was invaded by Cyrus, King of Persia, in 539 BCE. The city was conquered and that began the reign of the Medes and Persians. We know from this type of geopolitical change that supernatural forces were at work. The White Horseman was leading the charge as the Persian armies entered Babylon that night. This was a planned takeover, a change of world powers. It was prophesied that Media and Persia would be the victors, and the clock was ticking.

The Horns were responsible for scattering the armies of Babylon, although as history shows, there wasn't much resistance to the takeover. A new era emerges, and Yahweh's people would soon find relief from their oppressors.

The Medes and Persians – 539 BCE

"Daniel said, "I was looking in my vision by night, and behold, ***the four winds of heaven were stirring up the great sea. And four*** ***great beasts were coming up from the sea****, different from one another… [The]second one, resembling a bear. And it was raised up on one side, and three ribs were in its mouth between its teeth; and thus they said to it, 'Arise, devour much meat!'"*

Daniel 7:2-5 (emphasis added)

In a separate vision, Daniel was shown the succession of empires again, but this time, a little more information was revealed. The vision begins with the Four Winds, aka the Four Horsemen, stirring up the great sea. We need to interpret the term "the great sea." It is the same term used in Revelation 13:1, *"Then I saw a beast coming up out of the sea."* The sea represents the masses of people, all the nations. Just as the ocean has currents and tides, people also move and shift in endless patterns and are referred to as "the sea."

The Four Horsemen were stirring the people of the nations, causing the beast empires to rise to power. Four beasts came up out of the nations, representing the same four empires as seen in Nebuchadnezzar's image. Babylon, Medo-Persia, Greece, and Rome. The implication is that the Horsemen were on the battlefield with the human generals and their armies, shaping the outcome with decisive victories or defeats: stirring the great sea.

In this case, the White Horseman controlled who would become the victor and aided by empowering them to dominate the opposing force. The other colored horses have different strategies. The black horse, for example, was not on the battlefield at all. Prior to any physical conflict, the black horse was behind the scenes, creating economic crises, food and supply chain issues, or controlling the flow of critical funds.

The pale horse rides silently on the winds of a more sinister type. For example, at a different time in history, one famous 14th-century account claimed,

"...that plague was introduced to Kaffa deliberately, through a Mongol biological warfare attack that involved hurling plague-infected corpses over the city's walls."

"This was the jumping point for the primary wave of the medieval Black Death from Asia to Europe in 1346-47 CE."[57]

The red horse would influence the outcome through ideological warfare, as in the idea of "fighting for a cause." There would be an ideological shift in philosophy between the Babylonians, and the Medes and Persians. While the Babylonians worshiped the ancient pantheon of Sumerians gods, the Persians were monotheistic and yet tolerant of many religions (including the religion of the Jews). This created much tension between people of opposing views, causing societal unrest, and invoking a reason to fight. There is evidence that the Persians believed in what is now called Zoroastrianism.

"Zoroastrianism[a] is an Iranian religion and one of the world's oldest organized faiths, based on the teachings of the Iranian-speaking prophet Zoroaster. It has a dualistic cosmology of good and evil within the framework of a monotheistic ontology and an eschatology, which predicts the ultimate conquest of evil by good. Zoroastrianism exalts an uncreated and benevolent deity of wisdom known as Ahura Mazda (lit. 'Lord of Wisdom') as its supreme being. Historically, the unique features of Zoroastrianism, such as its monotheism, messianism, belief in free will and judgment after death, the conception of heaven, hell, angels, and demons, among other concepts, may have influenced other religious and philosophical systems, including the Abrahamic religions and Gnosticism, Northern Buddhism, and Greek philosophy."[58]

I also suspect the beliefs of Cyrus and Darius were influenced by one of the wise men of their council, Daniel, a religiously devout man and prophet of Yahweh. Daniel was elevated to third in the kingdom of Nabonidus/Belshazzar (his son). This would have given the prophet access to the King's ear. These are also the same ancient Wisemen that discerned the timing of Messiah's birth almost 600 years later, and scripture says they "came from the East" to see this prophesied child. They could have very well deciphered this timeline from the teaching and writings of Daniel (the Seventy Weeks of Daniel chapter 9, for example).

Zoroastrianism is oddly similar to biblical beliefs in several ways, such as Monotheism, the dualistic concepts of good and evil, an uncreated benevolent deity, free will, and judgment after death, concepts of heaven and hell, angels and demons, for a partial list.

It is also notable that this list of core principles would be similar to, and possibly originally derived from, the beliefs of Noah and his family, as they were responsible for repopulating the earth after the flood. An early example of this would be the mysterious figure known in the Bible as Melchizedek.

As I discussed earlier, I believe this to be Shem, Noah's eldest son, who lived to be 600 years old (Gen 11:10). He would have lived 500 years after the flood and succeeded by his sons, Elam and Asshur, and Arpachshad, and Lud, and Aram. These names are connected to the names of ancient cities such as Elam and Assyria. (See the section on The Table of Nations)

Elam (/ˈiːləm/; עֵילָם ʿElam) in the Hebrew Bible (Genesis 10:22, Ezra 4:9) is said to be one of the sons of Shem, the son of Noah. The name is also used (as in Akkadian) for the ancient country of Elam, which existed in the west and southwest in what is now modern Khuzestān and Ilam, a providence of Iran.[59]

In ancient times, the Semites believed these people to be the offspring of Elam, son of Shem (Genesis 10:22). Their language was not one of the Semitic languages but was considered a linguistic isolate, suggesting they were influenced by a second culture. Elam would later become a key region in the Persian Empire.

Elam (the nation) is also mentioned in Genesis 14, describing an ancient war in the time of Abraham involving Chedorlaomer, the king of Elam at that time. This biblical reference places the Elamites there during the days of Shem (Melchizedek) of Shalem.

The prophecies of the Book of Isaiah (11:11, 21:2, 22:6) and the Book of Jeremiah (25:25) also mention Elam. The last part of Jeremiah 49 is an apocalyptic oracle against Elam, which states that Elam will be scattered to the four winds of the earth, but "It will be at the end of days, that I will return their captivity", a prophecy self-dated to the first year of Zedekiah, king of Judah (597 BC). Possibly a prophecy of the return of the modern nation of Iran.

The Book of Jubilees may be referring to an ancient tradition when it mentions a son (or daughter, in some versions) of Elam, named "Susan", whose daughter Rasuaya, married Arpachshad (Shem's son), progenitor of another branch of Shemites. A possible source for the name Shushan (or Susa), which was the ancient capital of the Elamite Empire. (Dan. 8:2)

A close look at the timeline puts almost 1300 years between Shem's death and Cyrus' conquest of Babylon. Any traces back to the beliefs of these patriarchs would have been difficult to maintain through successive generations, but not impossible. The Bible we have now in our modern day has survived over 3000 years (Moses to today).

So far, the analysis of this date suggests that Zoroastrianism could be a remnant of the beliefs (albeit distorted over time and culture) of the descendants of Noah, those apart from Abraham. The theory is that the Elamites eventually gave birth to the Persians, which gave us the kings, Cyrus and Darius. It is possible, then, that their religious systems could be roughly traced back to Noah.

The point of this discussion is that this is another element of the emerging Babylonian spirit. It is marked by an ecumenical collective of religious thought, a tolerance of multiple religious ideologies in one culture. We see how this continues to develop in the Greek culture.

Although the Greeks certainly had their Pantheon of gods and demi-gods, Greek philosophers like Socrates and Plato made the discussion of philosophy and other ideologies not only commonplace but acceptable in society. This is the purpose revealed in the riding of the Red Horseman, which is to affect these types of changes in the world.

It will be an element of the last iteration of (end time) Babylon to include an ecumenical one-world religion by combining the various beliefs and ideologies into one esoteric movement. To accomplish this, there will be a necessity to elevate someone or some group above all the religions of the world, including traditional Christianity. The likely candidate for this universal figure has already been identified in bible prophecy as The Antichrist, the two-horned beast from the earth in Revelation 13.

"Then I saw another beast coming up out of the earth; and he had two horns like a lamb and he spoke as a dragon. He exercises all the authority of the first beast in his presence. And he makes the earth and those who dwell in it to worship the first beast, whose fatal wound was healed. He performs great signs, so that he even makes fire come down out of heaven to the earth in the presence of men. And he deceives those who dwell on the earth because of the signs which it was given him to perform in the presence of the beast,"

Revelation 13:11-14

This is a supporting role to the final beast system, the last Babylon. It is an attempt to unify all humanity in rebellion against Yahweh. It is also a plan to subjugate all people and enslave them to the beast system, and in this case, The Beast (from the sea) is the embodiment of The Great Satan. Only the true believers in Yahweh and Yeshua (Jesus) will be able to see through this deception. We must resist the temptation to trust our world leaders to protect and provide for us during this time and turn our hearts to Yahweh.

Cyrus, The Great

Cyrus the Great (600–530 BC) was one of a short list of rulers that were prophesied to come in the bible. The Prophet Isaiah (approximately 740–701 B.C.) makes this declaration at least 100 years before Cyrus' birth,

*"**It is I who says of Cyrus, 'He is My shepherd!***
And he will perform all My desire.'
And he declares of Jerusalem, 'She will be built,'
And of the temple, 'Your foundation will be laid.'"

*'**Thus says the LORD to Cyrus His anointed**,*
Whom I have taken by the right hand,
To subdue nations before him
And to lose the loins of kings;

To open doors before him so that gates will not be shut.'

'I will go before you and make the rough places smooth;
I will shatter the doors of bronze and cut through their iron bars.
I will give you the treasures of darkness
And hidden wealth of secret places,
So that you may know that it is I,
The LORD, the God of Israel, who calls you by your name.'"

Isaiah 44:28, 45:1-3 (emphasis added)

Why did Yahweh foretell the life of this king, you ask? Because it would be important, even critical, to the future of Israel. Not only was Cyrus not born yet, but he would not even come from the current ruling nation. In order for Cyrus to have any impact on the geopolitics affecting Israel, Assyria and future Babylon would have to be overthrown, and a new political power would need to be put in its place. This seemed unlikely given the current ruler at the time Isaiah spoke was Sennacherib, the Assyrian king.

Sennacherib would go on to conquer Babylon, and the Chaldean dynasty would rise to power AND fall, before Cyrus could possibly become important. Secondly, the nation of Israel had not yet been conquered. This would happen 120 years after Isaiah's prophecy. So, you see, it would take a miracle for Cyrus to become a world ruler.

It was also included in this prophecy that Yahweh would open the gates of Babylon for Cyrus and his army and supernaturally give him access to the heavily fortified city of Babylon on the night of their conquest.

"I will go before you [Cyrus] and make the rough places smooth;
I will shatter the doors of bronze and cut through their iron
bars."

Isaiah 45:2

The rider of the White Horse, with bow-in-hand, would have been the one to cut through the iron bars, open the two-leaved gates of brass of the fortified city of Babylon, and lead Cyrus and his men to victory.

"The LORD has aroused the spirit of the kings of the Medes,
Because His purpose is against Babylon to destroy it;
For it is the vengeance of the LORD, vengeance for His temple."

Jeremiah 51:11

Cyrus (The Great), King of Medo-Persia, would ultimately give the decree in 536 BC that would allow the Jews to return from Babylonian exile and rebuild Jerusalem and its Temple.

As we mentioned earlier, the Persian Empire was more tolerant of other religious beliefs. This paved the way for Yahweh's people to be shown leniency and favor (a function of the Red Horse). Yahweh raised up a nation that would help his people find their way back home, but it wouldn't be easy. Yahweh inspired one man to start praying. It was Daniel who would receive a message from the angel Gabriel, declaring a timeline.

"So you are to know and discern that from the issuing of a decree to restore and rebuild Jerusalem until Messiah the Prince, there will be seven weeks and sixty-two weeks; it will be built again, with plaza and moat, even in times of distress."

Daniel 9:25

The rebuilding of Jerusalem's temple was done in stages (c. 536–516 B.C.) by the hands of Zerubbabel, Governor of Judah. First, the altar was built so that sacrifices could again be made (Ezra 3:2–3). The second phase was the laying of the foundation of the temple.

This work elicited mixed reactions from the people. Some rejoiced that the foundation was laid, while others, especially the elder priests, were sad, presumably because the quality of construction was inferior to that of the previous temple. Due to the opposition of the local population and the lack of motivation among the Jews, it took 20 years to complete the construction of the temple building.

After the building project came to a halt, the Prophet Haggai recorded this message to the people,

*"You look for much, but behold, it comes to little; when you bring it home, I blow it away. Why?" declares the LORD of hosts, **"Because of My house which lies desolate, while each of you runs to his own house.** Therefore, because of you, the sky has withheld its dew, and the earth has withheld its produce. I called for a drought on the land, on the mountains, on the grain, on the new wine, on the oil, on what the ground produces, on men, on cattle, and on all the labor of your hands."*

Then Zerubbabel the son of Shealtiel, and Joshua the son of Jehozadak, the high priest, with all the remnant of the people, obeyed the voice of the LORD their God and the words of Haggai the prophet, *as the LORD their God had sent him. And the people showed reverence for the LORD.*

Haggai 1:9-12

At this point in the timeline, King Darius (the Great) takes the throne in Babylon in 522 BCE. Daniel is still actively involved as wise counsel to the kings of Persia.

Through the prophet Zechariah, Yahweh revealed the heavenly instruments that were sent to assist his people. It's time to revisit the Four Winds of Heaven, aka The Four Horsemen. This is the verse we discussed earlier.

*"And the man who was standing among the myrtle trees answered and said, **"These are those whom the LORD has sent to patrol the earth."** So they answered the angel of the LORD who was standing among the myrtle trees and said, **"We have patrolled the earth, and behold, all the earth is peaceful and quiet."***

196

*Then the angel of the LORD said, "**O LORD of hosts, how long will
You have no compassion for Jerusalem and the cities of Judah,
with which You have been indignant these seventy years?**"*

Zechariah 1:10-1

*"Therefore thus says the LORD, "**I will return to Jerusalem with
compassion; My house will be built in it**," declares the LORD of
hosts, "and a measuring line will be stretched over Jerusalem."
Again, proclaim, saying, 'Thus says the LORD of hosts, "**My cities
will again overflow with prosperity, and the LORD will again
comfort Zion and again choose Jerusalem**."*

Zechariah 1:16-17 (emphasis added)

The King, Yahweh, makes the decree, the council is informed, and
now it is time. As in the story of the prophet Micaiah before Ahab,
the questions were asked: who will go, and how will you do it?

Yahweh would need to raise up leaders among the returning Jews
like Zerubbabel and Nehemiah that would champion His cause. He
called priests like Jeshua and Ezra who would restore the Temple
worship and teach the people about the Torah. Yahweh raised up
prophets that could relay the messages to the people like Haggai and
Zechariah. He needed builders who could rebuild the Temple and
walls of Jerusalem. Builders like Zerubbabel would need the help of
the people to accomplish this great task.

Zerubbabel Rebuilds - 536 BCE

*"This is the word of the LORD to Zerubbabel saying, **'Not by might nor by power, but by My Spirit,' says the LORD of hosts.** 'What are you, O great mountain? Before Zerubbabel you will become a plain; and he will bring forth the top stone with shouts of 'Grace, grace to it!'"*

*Also, the word of the LORD came to me, saying, **"The hands of Zerubbabel have laid the foundation of this house, and his hands will finish it."***

Zechariah 4:6-8

There are two key figures in the restoration of Jerusalem and the Temple: Zerubbabel, the Governor of Judah, and Jeshua, the high priest. These would later be joined by Nehemiah, a new governor, and Ezra, the priest. It is clear by Zechariah's prophetic message that it was not by Zerubbabel's own strength that this feat would be accomplished. The Spirit of Yahweh would be Zerubbabel's source of strength and inspiration.

*"So the LORD stirred up the spirit of **Zerubbabel the son of Shealtiel, governor of Judah**, and the spirit of **Joshua the son of Jehozadak, the high priest**, and the spirit of all the remnant of the people; and they came and worked on the house of the LORD of hosts, their God"*

Haggai 1:14

We will come back to Zerubbabel and Jeshua, but first we need to explore the topic of prophetic cycles.

Prophetic Cycles

We will take a short rabbit trail to examine a prophetic cycle that will reoccur in the future building of a Third Temple, an event which could possibly happen in our lifetime.

First, I would like to explain prophetic layers with an illustration. I attended high school during the early 1980's. This was an era before classrooms had computers and flat-screen monitors; teachers needed a way to share their ideas with the class. The method of choice was to use a pull-down screen with an overhead projector.

The overhead projector uses a strong bulb to project light through a clear glass lens in the tabletop of the device, up through a refractive mirror, and reflects an image on a screen or the classroom wall.

On the tabletop of the projector, the teacher would place transparencies; a sheet of clear plastic with words or images written or drawn on them. These images were then transferred from the tabletop to the screen where the class could view them.

What was interesting was how multiple layers of transparencies could create a uniquely combined image, each new sheet utilizing the one beneath it. The first transparency was sometimes called the master, on which the others were built. The final picture was made up of several individual pictures, somehow relating back to the master page.

I believe this is how prophecy works. One prophetic picture almost always points to multiple events layered on top of a master idea. These events occur in different time periods, yet each event plays out with precise synchronicity to the master pattern.

I refer to this concept as "prophetic cycles," a repeating pattern of separate but oddly similar events. They form a template that can be observed when overlayed on future events. Just as the teacher used the overhead projector in the classroom, I believe this is how Yahweh teaches us to understand prophetic events.

To my point, in Zechariah chapters 3 and 4, we find a series of events that seem to have layered references, meaning that not all of the message is explained by a single event. For example, after Jeshua (or Joshua) is introduced as "a brand plucked from the fire" and supernaturally cleansed and given a change in garments (Zech. 3), he is told that he and his friends are "symbols." Symbols of what, we ask? Then, this mysterious figure called "the Branch," along with "a stone with seven eyes," is introduced in the story. What does all this have to do with Jeshua, the high priest, and what is he a symbol of?

To make it even more confusing, in Zechariah chapter 6, the prophet is told to make a crown of gold and silver and put it on Jeshua's head. But wait, Jeshua is not a king; he's a priest, so what is the crown for?

"Take silver and gold, make an ornate crown, and set it on the head of Joshua, the son of Jehozadak, the high priest.

*Then say to him, 'Thus says the LORD of hosts, "Behold, **a man whose name is Branch**, for He will branch out from where He is; **and He will build the temple of the LORD**. Yes, it is He who will build the temple of the LORD, and **He who will bear the honor and sit and rule on His throne**. Thus, **He will be a priest on His throne**, and the counsel of peace will be between the two offices."*

Now, the crown will become a reminder in the temple of the LORD to Helem, Tobijah, Jedaiah, and Hen, the son of Zephaniah.

Those who are far off will come and build the temple of the LORD." Then you will know that the LORD of hosts has sent me to you. And it will take place if you completely obey the LORD your God."

Zechariah 6:11-15

Each new transparency adds a different symbolic element, e.g., the branch, the stone, and the crown. The added information was not intended to teach us about the first event but a future one.

This all becomes clear when we understand that this is a prophetic picture of both the current restoration and a future restoration of Jerusalem, including the building of a future Temple. This is an overlay of a future restoration imposed on this current one. The high priest, Jeshua, is a picture of another high priest, Yeshua HaMashiach (Jesus, the Messiah), who will come and rebuild the final Temple at the end of the days.

Understanding the Hebrew name Jeshua is important here. The English letter "J," in writing, is only about four hundred years old.[60] Prior to that the letter "Y" was originally used, making words like Judah, Yehudah, or Jerusalem, Yerushalem. So, the actual pronunciation of Jeshua was "Yeshua" (or, in English – Jesus); they are the same name.

Yeshua (Messiah) is "The Branch" (Isaiah 11:1) and also referred to as "My Servant" (Isaiah 42:1). He is "the stone" (Ps 118:22). He is the King-Priest who will come to His temple wearing "the crown" (a priest after the order of Melchizedek, as we discussed earlier) and it is Yeshua who will bring the counsel of peace between the two offices, and He will build the Third Temple.

Jeshua, the priest, was instrumental in restoring temple worship when the exiles returned to Jerusalem. He ushered in a renewed presence of Yahweh into the nation. In like manner, Yeshua, as King-Priest, will return to fully restore Jerusalem in the last days, but not before the great decisive battle between figurative Babylon (the nations) and Jerusalem. Zechariah 12:3 says,

"It will come about in that day that I will make Jerusalem a heavy stone for all the peoples; all who lift it will be severely injured. And all the nations of the earth will be gathered against it."

Zechariah 12:3

We can now see how the added information to the telling of the first story teaches us what to look for in future events. It teaches us how to recognize and interpret prophecy.

Now that we have shown the importance of cycles or layers in prophecy, there is one more prophetic cycle contained in Zechariah 4 that we need to look at. That is, the discussion by the prophet regarding Zerubbabel and the picture of the golden lampstand and two olive trees on either side of it.

We need to discover the meaning of the Lampstand and its relevance to this prophecy.

*"He said to me, "What do you see?" And I said, "I see, and behold, **a lampstand all of gold** with its bowl on the top of it, and **its***

seven lamps on it with seven spouts belonging to each of the lamps which are on the top of it; also two olive trees by it, one on the right side of the bowl and the other on its left side."

Zechariah 4:2-3

I will not attempt to give a full explanation of the meaning of the lampstand here. It is a fascinating subject to explore, but for a brief explanation, we will look at the vision John had in Revelation 1 to find more meaning.

"As for the mystery of the seven stars which you saw in My right hand, and the seven golden lampstands: the seven stars are the angels of the seven churches, and the seven lampstands are the seven churches."

Revelation 1:20

At first glance, it seems that John is describing seven individual lampstands, but I believe he is describing the seven-branched Menorah of the Temple. We learned earlier that Yeshua is described as the branch; the Menorah is described as having seven branches and patterned after a tree. The Menorah is actually fashioned after an Almond tree; its bowls are the budding almond flowers bearing its fruit. Yeshua is synonymous with the Menorah which interestingly is also called the Tree of Life in rabbinic commentary.

The passage in Revelation declares that the seven lamps "are the seven churches." This suggests that Yeshua and his followers were symbolically and secretly hidden in plain sight in the Temple for over a millennium.

In Revelation chapter 1, Yeshua is described as the one who walks in the midst of the golden candlestick. He is also the fire that lights the candles. Each lamp was filled with oil, allowing the flame to continue to burn. The oil is symbolic of the Holy Spirit, as seen in the parable of the Ten Virgins, who carried oil in their lamps. Five of the virgins, called the foolish ones, did not take enough oil for their lamps and were not ready when the bridegroom came. The analogies of the lamps, flames (light), and oil are all applied to the believers in Yeshua.

The Menorah is the light of the Temple; in contrast, Yeshua is the light of the world (John 8:12). Taking it further, the believers in Yeshua are called the lights of the world (Matt. 5:14). In John 15, the parable of the vine and the branches, believers in Yeshua are also referred to as branches. The template overlay suggests that the seven lights of the Menorah represent the Seven Churches of Yeshua as revealed in Revelation chapters 2-3.

To bring this into focus with our study, the Jerusalem Temple was restored by the returning exiles of Judah. They eventually restored the Menorah, which brought the light of Yahweh back to temple worship in the nation of Israel, signifying the restoration of spiritual enlightenment that was lost during the exile. The true restoration that Yahweh desired was meant to go beyond the nation of Israel and bring that same light to all the nations.

Yeshua sent his disciples out, as lights, into all the world. To some degree or another, this spiritual presence has been a constant moral voice among the nations for 2000 years. In the end, the nations will be judged according to how they walked according to that spiritual enlightenment. Judgment is revealed in this passage and is commonly referred to as "the judgment of the nations."

*"But when the Son of Man comes in His glory, and all the angels with Him, then He will sit on His glorious throne. **All the nations will be gathered before Him**, and He will separate them from one another, as the shepherd separates the sheep from the goats;"*

Matthew 25:31-32

We can now look deeper into the Menorah. According to Zechariah's vision, the Menorah is supplied with divine oil that flows from the two olive trees standing on either side of it. The oil represents the anointing of the Holy Spirit or Ruach HaKodesh.

The anointing is the portion of Yahweh's presence, power, and enlightenment that He gives to men to achieve His greater purposes. By that divine anointing, miracles are performed, knowledge is revealed, enemies are scattered, and it ultimately transforms the person possessing it. The three general types of service or vocations that operate under an anointing are prophets, priests, and kings. That is until Yeshua made it available to all true believers under the new covenant (those who make up the Menorah). The prophet Joel records,

"...and it shall be in the last days,' God says, 'that I will pour forth of My Spirit on all mankind; and your sons and your daughters shall prophesy, and your young men shall see visions, and your old men shall dream dreams..."

Acts 2:17

The olive tree represents the service of one who allows the Spirit of Yahweh (the oil of the Lamp) to work through him in the greatest measure. It is given to those who step up and say, "Here I am, use me!" It requires an empty vessel of a man, where pride is removed, and he (or she) is void of personal agendas, completely devoted to Yahweh and walking in a covenant relationship. The oil is always produced by The Holy Spirit; man is the vessel or, in this case, the olive tree. It is important to add that anointing oil is made from crushed olives. (Exodus 30:24)

The image of a tree, or specifically the fruit of the tree, holds a message as well. Like the tree, we are created to bear "good" fruit - the fruit of the Spirit. Yeshua instructs us that if we do not bear much fruit, we are cast forth as a withered branch and thrown into the fire (John 15:1-6). For this reason, the bible often uses the analogy of trees to describe men.

Oil is produced when the fruit of an olive tree is crushed and preserved. When a man produces fruit (of the Spirit), he will then go through a crushing series of trials or tribulations in life that is meant to crush his fruit so it can be preserved and made useful.

*"Then I said to him, **"What are these two olive trees on the right of the lampstand and on its left?"** And I answered the second time and said to him, "What are the two olive branches which are beside the two golden pipes, which empty the golden oil from themselves?"*
So he answered me, saying, "Do you not know what these are?"
*And I said, "No, my lord." then he said, **"These are the two anointed ones who are standing by the Lord of the whole earth."***

Zechariah 4:11-14

Let us apply the prophetic template of the Menorah. In the first layer, we can picture Zerubbabel and Jeshua, the high priest, as "the two anointed ones" who will restore the temple and the light of Menorah for the nation of Israel. This restoration was necessary for the first appearance of Messiah, for there needed to be a restored city and Temple when He came.

In a second layer, we get another picture in which we see Yeshua as the Menorah, and if we look closely at this next passage, we can see two corresponding anointed ones. Let's read about a heavenly vision that took place in the New Testament.

*"Six days later, Jesus took with Him Peter and James and John, his brother and led them up on a high mountain by themselves. And He was transfigured before them, and His face shone like the sun, and His garments became as white as light. **And behold, Moses and Elijah appeared to them, talking with Him**."*

Matthew 17:1-3

In this vision on the Mount of Transfiguration, Yeshua appears shining like the light of the sun and he is accompanied by Moses and Elijah. There is no mistake in connecting Yeshua to the Menorah here, as he shines in the brightness of the sun, but what about Moses and Elijah? These two prophets operated under a heavy anointing during their earthly ministries, performing many signs and wonders. They each represent pivotal roles: Moses, the lawgiver/leader, and Elijah, the great mouthpiece/prophet. They are pictured here as the two olive trees standing next to the Living Menorah in this heavenly vision.

There is a third layer to consider that shows us the final restoration of Jerusalem. In the last days, the true believers in Yeshua will be lights in a very dark world. It is during this turbulent time that two witnesses will be sent by Yahweh to Jerusalem. These two witnesses will declare their urgent message with signs and wonders for three and a half years; then, they will be killed as the whole world watches and celebrates their demise.

*"And I will grant authority to my two witnesses, and they will prophesy for twelve hundred and sixty days, clothed in sackcloth. **These are the two olive trees** and the two lampstands that stand before the Lord of the earth."*

Revelation 11:3-4

In this picture, the two witnesses prophesy on the earth with the power of a heavenly anointing but are connected to the lampstand that stands before the Lord.

It is my opinion that the final two witnesses will be men in our day who either come in the spirit of Moses and Elijah, just as John the baptizer came in the spirit of Elijah (Matt 11:12) … or they will actually be Moses and Elijah resurrected for a final showdown.

My reasoning for the latter has to do with the idea that a man is required to die as a consequence of sin, going all the way back to God's statement in Genesis, "The day you eat of the tree, you will SURELY DIE!"

In the book of Jude, it says,

*"But Michael the archangel, when he disputed with the devil and **argued about the body of Moses**, did not dare pronounce against*

Jude 1:9 (emphasis added)

Satan demanded the death, or proof of death (specifically, the body) of Moses.

What is alluded to here is that Satan couldn't find Moses' body, and he knew he was entitled to it. This goes back to the idea that because Adam obeyed the Serpent and sinned, Satan now has legal control over the dead (Heb 2:14). Therefore, from this passage, it seems that Moses did not experience a physical death.

Now, in full disclosure, the scripture says that Moses died on Mount Nebo, but according to Jude, his body was never found. Is it possible that Yahweh took him like he did with Elijah? I admit this is speculative, but it explains the conversation between the angel Michael and The Devil.

Satan can make the same claim for the prophet Elijah; he was taken up in a fiery chariot and escaped death. It was these two who appeared with Yeshua on the Mount of Transfiguration (a fact declared in the Gospels), and it would appear that these two still have to die. It makes them likely candidates for the Two Witnesses of Revelation 11, who are killed and then resurrected in front of the whole world; fulfilling their required deaths.

Also, they perform the same miracles that Moses and Elijah performed including no rain on the earth for three and a half years, turning water into blood, and striking the earth with plagues at will. I believe this makes a strong case for Moses and Elijah actually being the Two Witnesses.

Their final message will urge people to come out of that wicked city, Babylon. Not to take her mark or partake in her sins but to turn their hearts to Yahweh and pray for the restoration of Jerusalem and His people.

This is the point of Zechariah's prophecy: to enlighten us about the final message of restoration when Jerusalem becomes the source of light and righteousness to the nations. There will be no need for Babylon to exist anymore.

The takeaway here is that Yahweh will declare the end of a thing from its beginning because He works in repeating cycles. When we study the Horsemen, the Horns and Craftsmen, and the cities of Babylon and Jerusalem, the end is always declared from the beginning. We will continue to see that the job of these heavenly actors will also be understood in a similarity of repeating cycles. Events will change, but the purpose of each colored horse will remain the same.

> *"Remember the former things long past,*
> *For I am God, and there is no other;*
> *I am God, and there is no one like Me,*
> ***Declaring the end from the beginning,***
> ***And from ancient times, things which have not been done,***
> *Saying, 'My purpose will be established,*
> *And I will accomplish all My good pleasure"*
>
> *Isaiah 46:9-10*

A Final Analysis of the Restoration of Jerusalem

The circumstances surrounding the return of the Jewish exiles from Babylon and the rebuilding of the Temple were supernatural to say the least. An important fact was the prophecy by Jeremiah that determined the time frame; Israel would be exiled for 70 years. It was also prophesied by Isaiah that a King by the name of Cyrus would make the decree to free the exiles.

Here is the problem. Babylon was the dominant world power, and there were no obvious signs of that changing in 70 years. Yahweh worship was not tolerated by Babylon, leaving no opportunity for a return for the Jews or any hope of rebuilding the Temple in Jerusalem – that Babylon had destroyed. Finally, Medo-Persia would have to do battle with and conquer Babylon and install a king named Cyrus in the few short years that were left of the 70-year prophecy.

Yahweh would choose to enlist the help of the Four Horsemen. According to Zechariah 1:8, three were chosen: the red horse, the dappled (grey with black spots) horse, and the white horse. Each color represents a specific mission, as we discussed earlier in chapter three. The dappled horse represented a combination of the two ideas.

The Red Horse is the horse of chaos. His mission was to take peace from the earth and that he would cause men to slay one another. This chaos is achieved through ideological warfare.

The ideology that needed to change was the fact that Babylon did not tolerate monotheistic Yahweh worship; its beliefs were polytheistic (many deities or gods). The Persians, on the other hand, believed in the teachings of Zoroastrianism, a monotheistic religion (we discussed this earlier). History proves they were much more tolerant of other Abrahamic religions. They would become the nation that would allow the Jews to return to their homeland and rebuild the Temple.

The tension between the Babylonian and Persian religions was the beginning of the quest for dominance in the region. War would eventually break out.

Babylon needed to be weakened. There was another function of the Red Horse at work here. We need to learn some things about Babylon's last king. According to the book of Daniel, Belshazzar was the last king of Babylon, but the truth is a bit more complicated. What we know from the Babylonian record of kings is that Nabonidus was the last King of the Babylonian empire, and his son Belshazzar was most likely the regent of the city of Babylon.

Belshazzar was reigning in the place of his father, who had withdrawn himself to Tayma, Arabia, on what appeared to be a religious sabbatical.

"Throughout his reign, inscriptions and later sources suggest that Nabonidus worked to increase the status of the moon god Sîn and decrease the status of Babylon's traditional national deity Marduk. While some have suggested that Nabonidus wished to go as far as to completely replace Marduk with Sîn as the head of the Mesopotamian pantheon, the extent to which Nabonidus's devotion to Sîn led to religious reforms is debated. Nabonidus was in self-imposed exile in Tayma, Arabia, from 552 to 543/542 BC. The reason for this is unknown, though it might have been due to disagreements with the

Babylonian clergy and oligarchy. Belshazzar acted as regent in Babylonia during this period, while Nabonidus continued to be recognised as the king."[61]

Nabonidus was drawn to religious beliefs in Sîn, the moon god, that were in conflict with the history of Babylon's Marduk worship. His convictions may be attributed to the fact that his mother, Adad-guppi, was a priestess of the moon god, Sin. This conflict of ideologies brought great instability to the region and unrest to the followers of Marduk.

This was also exacerbated by the fact that the Persians were closing in on Babylon and themselves were more religiously tolerant of other beliefs. An appeal to the masses would potentially allow for both practices to coexist, as well as other belief systems. This had a significant political effect in the region.

"Babylonia was in an unpromising geopolitical situation; the Persian empire bordered it to the north, east, and west. It had also been suffering severe economic problems exacerbated by plague and famine, and its king, Nabonidus, was said to be unpopular among many of his subjects for his unconventional religious policies. According to Mary Joan Winn Leith, "Cyrus's success is credited to military acumen, to judicious bribery, and to an energetic publicity campaign waged throughout Babylonia, which portrayed him as a lenient and religiously tolerant overlord." On the other hand, Max Mallowan notes: "Religious toleration was a remarkable feature of Persian rule, and there is no question that Cyrus himself was a liberal-minded promoter of this humane and intelligent policy," and such a publicity campaign was, in effect a means of permitting his reputation to precede his military campaign."[62]

This ideological upheaval is a sign of the Red Horse riding, leading to a major political change. Apparently at work were also the Black and Pale Horses. The article goes on to say that the region "had also been suffering severe economic problems exacerbated by plague and famine." These conditions allowed the Persian forces to easily conquer the beleaguered Babylon. This overthrow was the successful campaign of Cyrus - and The Horsemen.

Chapter 8 – The Horn of Greece, Alexander the Great - 334 BCE

*"While I was observing, behold, **a male goat was coming from the west over the surface of the whole earth without touching the ground; and the goat had a conspicuous horn between his eyes**. He came up to the ram that had the two horns, which I had seen standing in front of the canal, and rushed at him in his mighty wrath. I saw him come beside the ram, and he was enraged at him; and he struck the ram and shattered his two horns, and the ram had no strength to withstand him. So he hurled him to the ground and trampled on him, and there was none to rescue the ram from his power. Then, the male goat magnified himself exceedingly. But as soon as he was mighty, the large horn was broken, and in its place, there came up **four conspicuous horns** toward the four winds of heaven."*

Daniel 8:5-8

The male goat in this imagery is Alexander the Great of Greece, and the four conspicuous horns are his four generals who inherited his kingdom after Alexander's untimely death in 323 BC in Babylon.

"Alexander the Great was a king of the ancient Greek kingdom of Macedon. He succeeded his father, Philip II, to the throne in 336 BC at the age of 20 and spent most of his ruling years conducting a lengthy military campaign throughout Western Asia and Egypt. By the age of 30, he had created one of the largest empires in history, stretching from Greece to northwestern India. He was undefeated in battle and is widely considered to be one of history's greatest and most successful military commanders."[63]

In 329 BC, Alexander the Great killed the last Persian king to rule, King Artaxerxes V, successfully defeating the "two horns" of the Medes and Persians. In the image in Nebuchadnezzar's dream, Greece is the "belly and thighs of Bronze" or, in the vision in Daniel 7, it is the third beast, a Leopard, which had four wings and four heads.

"After this I kept looking, and behold, another one, like a leopard, which had on its back four wings of a bird; the beast also had four heads, and dominion was given to it."

Daniel 7:6

The conquests of Alexander the Great are a perfect example of the "horn" imagery. Alexander pushed fast and hard to establish the rule of the Greek empire.

"In 334 BC, he invaded the Achaemenid Persian Empire and began a series of campaigns that lasted for ten years. Following his conquest of Asia Minor, Alexander broke the power of Achaemenid Persia in a series of decisive battles, including those at Issus and Gaugamela; he subsequently overthrew Darius III and conquered the Achaemenid Empire in its entirety."[64]

Over a millennium of civilization and the dominance of several great empires contributed to the ease at which Alexander and his armies moved through the region. The Assyrians, Babylonians, and Persians created vast road systems between the major city-states in their days. These roadways supported the supply lines of trade and commerce as well as other types of travel.

Gradually, over time, the entire world became more and more connected, from as far east as present-day China to as far west as Europe, even north into Great Britain. Merchants from the East and West would travel a route eventually known as the Silk Road. It would not only allow for the trading of new goods but also serve as a corridor for an exchange of ideas, religion, and technologies. All of this aided in the ease with which the Greek conquest was able to be achieved.

Like many ancient warrior-kings, Alexander believed he was chosen and aided by "the gods" in his life and his military campaigns. A few stories emerge from history that show this type of religious theme in Alexander's life. It starts with stories surrounding his birth.

There are a number of versions of the unexplained events surrounding the young king's birth (supposedly) on July 20, 356 BCE. According to one legend, on the day of Alexander's birth, the Greek goddess of the hunt, Artemis, was away attending his birth when her temple at Ephesos - one of the seven wonders of the ancient world - burned to the ground.

However, the one story that bolstered Alexander's belief in his own divinity was revealed to him before he left Macedon for Asia. His mother pulled him aside and recounted a series of events occurring the night before her wedding. Supposedly, Olympias was asleep in her bedchamber when a clap of thunder awakened her. Suddenly, a bolt of lightning (evidently, this was the god Zeus) shot into her room and struck her in her womb - miraculously without harming her - a flash of light immediately followed.[65]

Alexander's father, Phillip, claimed to be a descendant of Zeus's son Heracles (Hercules in Roman mythology), and his mother, Olympias, claimed her ancestors were descended from the famous Achilles - who had slain King Priam of Troy at the Altar of Zeus Herkeios.[66]

"To Alexander, the gods of Olympus were present everywhere, and their wishes were revealed to man through oracles and omens - this can be seen in his respect for the oracles at Delphi and Siwa. Alexander respected the rich history of the Greeks, sleeping with a copy of the Iliad under his pillow. He believed in both the labors of his forefather, Heracles and the exploits of his mother's ancestor Achilles. He sacrificed daily and even organized festivals as he travelled through Asia. Because his victories were sanctioned by the gods, before and after each battle, he would pray and sacrifice to them."[67]

Although Alexander considered himself a demi-god, I am not suggesting he was a demi-god or even a kind or godly man. He was a ferocious lion of a military leader, responsible for the deaths of many people. I am suggesting rather that his supernatural successes may have been driven by the "horn" forces described in the Bible.

It is my understanding that the Horns work in conjunction with the Four Horsemen. The Horns take the lesser role of influencing individual leaders (who themselves are called horns), while the Horsemen operate in the larger arena of entire armies and regional situations. This is speculative, though, because information about the

Horns is limited, except for the fact that they definitely exist according to scripture. Just like the wind, we can't see them; we can only observe the effects they have on what can be seen.

These forces are not to be confused with Yahweh himself. They are spirit beings that operate with permission to accomplish Yahweh's Divine will. Just like the Babylonian king Nebuchadnezzar and the Persian king Cyrus, who were ungodly men used to achieve a specific purpose, they were driven by territorial spiritual principalities.

Similarly, these Horns have their origin in the spirit realm, and their allegiance to a moral code may be questionable at times. This leads us to the understanding that all spirit beings, including angels, will find themselves under judgment in these situations. They must follow the same moral code we humans are subject to. Some types of insubordination are more egregious than others, as revealed in this passage.

"For if God did not spare angels when they sinned, but cast them into hell and committed them to pits of darkness, reserved for judgment...having made them an example to those who would live ungodly lives thereafter."

2 Peter 2:4,6

Yahweh is the creator of all things living and other; therefore, all created things are subject to His will, and all sentient beings are held to the standard of His moral laws. Those who break His laws will be judged, period. The Scripture says that God is the same yesterday, today, and forever. He does not change. (Heb 13:8; Mal 3:6)

The Horn Wars

*"In the third year of the reign of Belshazzar the king, a vision appeared to me, Daniel, subsequent to the one which appeared to me previously. I looked in the vision, and while I was looking, I was in the citadel of Susa, which is in the province of Elam; and I looked in the vision, and I myself was beside the Ulai Canal. Then I lifted my eyes and looked, and behold, **a ram which had two horns** was standing in front of the canal. Now the two horns were long, but one was longer than the other, with the longer one coming up last. I saw the ram butting westward, northward, and southward, and no other beasts could stand before him nor was there anyone to rescue from his power, but he did as he pleased and magnified himself.*

*While I was observing, behold, **a male goat was coming from the west over the surface of the whole earth without touching the ground**; and the goat had a conspicuous horn between his eyes. He came up to the ram that had the two horns, which I had seen standing in front of the canal, and rushed at him in his mighty wrath. I saw him come beside the ram, and he was enraged at him, **and he struck the ram and shattered his two horns**, and the ram had no strength to withstand him. So he hurled him to the ground and trampled on him, and there was none to rescue the ram from his power. Then, the male goat magnified himself exceedingly. But as soon as he was mighty, **the large horn was broken, and in its place, there came up four conspicuous horns** toward the four winds of heaven."*

Daniel 8:1-8 (emphasis added)

The prophecy in Daniel chapter 8:1-8 lends much to understanding the "horns of the nations". The history in this passage takes place from the fall of Babylon in 539 BCE to the death of Alexander the Great in 323 BCE, a period of 216 years.

The ram with two horns depicts the Medo-Persian empire. The shorter horn represents the Medo Empire, while the longer horn represents the Persian Empire. These two joined forces to conquer the world, with Persia being the stronger of the two. Even more specifically, these two horns also represent the two great kings from that time, Cyrus the Great and Darius the Great. There were numerous battles and conquests during this period of time, captured in the statement, "I saw the ram butting westward, northward, and southward." The Persian empire pushed to be the largest empire the world had ever seen in its time, "…spanning a total of 5.5 million square kilometers (2.1 million square miles) from the Balkans and Egypt in the west to Central Asia and the Indus Valley in the east."[68]

Around the 7th century BC, the region of Persis in the southwestern portion of the Iranian plateau was settled by the Persians. From Persis, Cyrus rose and defeated the Median Empire as well as Lydia and the Neo-Babylonian Empire, marking the formal establishment of a new imperial polity under the Achaemenid dynasty.

In the modern era, the Achaemenid Empire has been recognized for its imposition of a successful model of centralized, bureaucratic administration; its multicultural policy; building complex infrastructure, such as road systems and an organized postal system; the use of official languages across its territories; and the development of civil services, including its possession of a large, professional army. Its advancements inspired the implementation of similar styles of governance by a variety of later empires.[69]

After a 200-year reign by the Persians, they were invaded by the male goat of Daniel 8:5 with the conspicuous horn between its eyes. This horn was none other than the famous Macedonian conqueror, Alexander the Great.

"Alexander the Great (Alexander III of Macedon) defeated the Persian armies at Granicus (334 BC), followed by Issus (333 BC), and lastly at Gaugamela (331 BC). Afterwards, he marched on Susa and Persepolis, which surrendered in early 330 BC. From Persepolis, Alexander headed north to Pasargadae, where he visited the tomb of Cyrus, the burial of the man whom he had heard of from the Cyropedia."[70]

With all the modernization done by the Persians through road building and improved trade routes, the invasion by Greece was swift and effective. This high-speed overthrow by Alexander is captured prophetically in Daniel 8:5, stating, *"A male goat was coming from the west over the surface of the whole earth without touching the ground."* The Persian empire fell in rapid succession to the powerful forces of Greece.

In 10 short years after the conquest of the then-civilized world by Greece, Alexander dies and leaves his empire to be divided among four of his generals. Just as Daniel saw in the vision, the large horn of the male goat was broken off, and four conspicuous horns rose in its place. A new era of wars begins, known as the Diadochi Wars, as these four generals struggle with each other to hold power.

The imagery associated with these extreme political changes in power is referred to as the pushing of horns. It is from comparing the Bible and history that this reference to horns becomes clear. The horns of Persia and Greece are not the only mention of horns. The fourth dreadful beast, also described in the book of Revelation, has seven heads and ten horns,

*"I kept looking in the night visions, and behold, **a fourth beast**, dreadful and terrifying and extremely strong; and it had large iron teeth. It devoured and crushed and trampled down the remainder with its feet, **and it was different from all the beasts that were before it, and it had ten horns**. While I was contemplating the horns, behold, another horn, a little one, came up among them, and three of the first horns were pulled out by the roots before it; and behold, this horn possessed eyes like the eyes of a man and a mouth uttering great boasts."*

Daniel 7:7-8 (emphasis added)

We will explore the fourth beast in a later discussion. The point is that the supernatural Horns, as revealed to us in the writing of Zechariah, the prophet, will continue to play a vital role in shaping the political landscape. They will prepare the world for the return of the Great Conqueror, the King of Kings, who will rule the nations with a scepter of iron.

The Conspicuous Horn Between the Eyes

The shaggy goat represents the kingdom of Greece, and the large horn that is between his eyes is the first king.

Daniel 8:21

The Biblical passage in the last section states that the male goat (Greece) had a "conspicuous horn between his eyes," and Alexander was represented by this horn. What is significant about the reference to "between the eyes"? Perhaps the answer lies in discovering what this metaphoric wordplay is pointing to.

The area of the forehead between the eyes is anatomically called the "*glabella*," and it is believed by some to have a spiritual significance.

In Hinduism, for example, participants place a small, red-colored dot, called a *bindi,* on the glabella (the forehead), indicating spiritual enlightenment.

"Traditionally, the area between the eyebrows (where the bindi is placed) is said to be the sixth chakra, Ajna, the seat of "concealed wisdom". The bindi is said to retain energy and strengthen concentration. The bindi also represents the third eye.

Ajna, meaning brow or third eye chakra, is the sixth primary chakra in the body according to Hindu tradition and signifies the unconscious mind, the direct link to Brahman (ultimate reality). The third eye is said to connect people to their intuition, give them the ability to communicate with the world, or help them receive messages from the past and the future."[71]

224

Is it possible that this "conspicuous horn" is the same, in function, as the third eye, influencing and enlightening its host? In ancient Egyptian symbolism, the imagery of a spiritual eye, also called the all-seeing-eye or the Eye of Horus, is used to explain spiritual enlightenment which provides perception beyond ordinary sight. There is another possible and more anatomical explanation.

"The third eye chakra is linked to the pineal gland which may inform a model of its envisioning. The pineal gland is a light-sensitive gland that produces the hormone melatonin, which regulates sleep and waking up and is also postulated to be the production site of the psychedelic dimethyltryptamine, the only known hallucinogen endogenous to the human body. Ajna's key issues involve balancing the higher and lower selves and trusting inner guidance."[72]

Whether you want to understand this scientifically (the pineal gland) or spiritually (a connecting point to the supernatural), it's plausible that the prophetic reference suggests that there was another force at work guiding Alexander in the conquests of the Greek empire.

The fact that Daniel's description of a "conspicuous horn between his eyes" is applied to this male goat representing Alexander, suggests that he was, at the very least, inspired by, if not actually empowered by, a spiritual force. This appears to be one of the Four Horns personally pushing him to believe he was a demi-god racing to conquer the world – and conquer he did!

The Greek empire conquered Babylon and all of Mesopotamia in a short decade under the military campaigns of Alexander. It was at this point that the mantle of the "spirit of Babylon" was passed on to

Greece. Greece becomes the dominate world power and takes its seat at the center of world trade. Its influence on language, religion, and culture would permeate the entire ancient world. The term "Hellenism" would be popularized during this time, which literally means "imitate Greeks."

Greece Divided – 323 BCE

The shaggy goat represents the kingdom of Greece, and the large horn that is between his eyes is the first king.

"The broken horn and the four horns that arose in its place **represent four kingdoms which will arise from his nation,** *although not with his power."*

Daniel 8:22

After Alexander's untimely death in Babylon at age 32, the new nation of Greece was divided among four of his generals, referred to as the Diadochi.

"The Diadochi, meaning "Successors," were the rival generals, families, and friends of Alexander the Great who fought for control over his empire after his death in 323 BC. The Wars of the Diadochi mark the beginning of the Hellenistic period from the Mediterranean Sea to the Indus River Valley.

The most notable Diadochi include Ptolemy, Antigonus, Cassander, and Seleucus as the last remaining at the end of the Wars of the Successors, ruling in Egypt, Asia-Minor, Macedon, and Persia respectively, all forging dynasties lasting several centuries."[73]

The two empires that cradled the land of Israel were the Seleucids to the north and the Ptolemies to the south. These are referred to as the King of the North and the King of the South in Daniel chapters 7 and 8. Out of the northern kingdom rose another horn, called the "small or little horn" in Daniel Chapter 8.

*"Out of one of them came forth a rather **small horn** which grew exceedingly great toward the south, toward the east, and toward the Beautiful Land. It grew up to the host of heaven and caused some of the host and some of the stars to fall to the earth, and it trampled them down. It even magnified itself to be equal with the Commander of the host, **and it removed the regular sacrifice from Him, and the place of His sanctuary was thrown down**. And on account of transgression, the host will be given over to the horn along with the regular sacrifice, and it will fling truth to the ground and perform its will and prosper."*

Daniel 8:9-13 (emphasis added)

Important to the subject of this book is the status of the land of Israel and the city of Jerusalem. The Greek ruler that most dramatically influences this period of time as it relates to the people of God, is the Seleucid King Antiochus IV Epiphanes. This Greek king eventually rises against the people of Yahweh and desecrates the Holy Temple in Jerusalem, declaring himself as god (Zeus).

Antiochus VI Epiphanes (or Epimanes?)

The Seleucid king Antiochus IV Epiphanes becomes an important figure in the prophecies of Daniel. Historically, he was the antagonistic ruler that triggered the Maccabean Revolt from 167-160 BCE, but there is possibly more to him than meets the eye.

A quick look at his name reveals an interesting thought. The Greek prefix *anti* – means opposed to, against, in place of, and *okhos* – means to have or to hold. The full name *antiokhos* renders a meaning of "to resist, to take hold against or in place of …[God]". Epiphanes means "god manifest." He was also known by his critics as Antiochus Epimanes (mad man), an interesting play on words.

The reveal is that the name *antiokhos* is similar in concept to *antikristos* or "antichrist," meaning the opposite of, or against – The Anointed One. The prophecy in Daniel 8:11 says of this little horn, *"It even magnified itself to be equal with the Commander of the host,"* and in verse 25, it says, *"He will even oppose the Prince of princes."* This little horn will exalt itself against the Anointed One. Both phrases are Old Testament references to Yeshua Messiah (Jesus Christ). I suggest then that Antiochus is a type of antichrist.

It is important now that we familiarize ourselves with the history of the period. It will help us identify patterns that will emerge later. If history is not your favorite subject, you may be in a little pain by now, but be patient. It will be worth the discovery.

Antiochus IV Epiphanes, originally named Mithradates, was born in 215 BCE and died in 163 BCE. His reign as one of the Seleucid emperors lasted from 175 to 163 BCE. He was the son of Antiochus III the Great (224–187 BCE) and the brother of Seleucus IV

Philopator. Antiochus IV's accession to the throne was a matter of contention, as some viewed him as a usurper.

Following the death of his brother Seleucus IV Philopator in 175 BCE, the legitimate heir should have been Seleucus's son, Demetrius I. However, Demetrius I was very young and held hostage in Rome at that time. Antiochus seized the opportunity to declare himself king, gaining the support of a significant portion of the Greek ruling class in Antioch.[74, 75]

Antiochus IV cultivated a reputation as an extravagant and generous ruler. He engaged in acts of generosity, such as distributing money to common people in the streets of Antioch, bestowing unexpected gifts upon strangers, contributing funds to the temple of Zeus in Athens and the altar at Delos, organizing grand military parades of his Western forces in Daphne (a suburb of Antioch), and hosting lavish banquets with the aristocracy, featuring the finest spices, clothing, and food.[76]

Upon ascending the throne, Antiochus IV took deliberate measures to maintain favorable relations with the Roman Republic. In 173 BC, he dispatched an embassy to Rome, carrying a portion of the outstanding indemnity owed from the Treaty of Apamea in 188 BC. During this embassy, they successfully secured a renewed treaty of friendship and alliance with Rome. This achievement was facilitated by the fact that Antiochus had come to power with the support of Eumenes II, who was Rome's principal ally in the region.[77]

Ruling the southern region of the Greek empire was King Ptolemy VI Philometor. There was often conflict between these two regional rulers, between the North and the South, and the land of Judea (Israel) was caught in the middle.

The Syrian Wars

The guardians of Southern King Ptolemy VI Philometor initiated a war against the Seleucids, believing that the kingdom was divided following Antiochus' murder of his nephew. However, Antiochus had been forewarned of the impending attack and had made thorough preparations. He had already assembled his forces and positioned them strategically.

As soon as the Egyptian forces vacated the major border city of Pelusium in the South, Antiochus IV and his Seleucid army launched an attack, defeating the Egyptians. This victory allowed the Seleucids to seize control of Pelusium, providing them with supplies and access to all of Egypt. Antiochus then proceeded to conquer most of Egypt, except for Alexandria, ultimately capturing King Ptolemy.[78]

This historical account aligns with the narrative presented in Daniel 8:10, which describes the small horn, now identified as Antiochus IV, as growing in power towards the South, the East, and the Beautiful Land, with the Beautiful Land referring to the land of Judea (Israel). The struggle for power and territorial expansion between the Seleucids and the Ptolemies played out in a series of conflicts known as the Syrian Wars. These wars were fought over the region then known as Coele-Syria, situated on the northern border of Israel, which served as one of the primary access points to the north for Egypt. While briefly mentioned in the biblical Books of the Maccabees, these wars had significant geopolitical implications for the region.[79]

During this period of conflict between the Seleucids and the

Ptolemies, the nation of Israel occupied a central position. This era is referred to as the Second Temple period of Judaism. The governance of Israel was entrusted to its High Priest, who functioned in a quasi-gubernatorial and high priestly capacity. In 175 BCE, the office of the High Priest was held by Joshua of the Oniad family of priests, who later adopted the Greek name Jason. Jason became the last of the Zadokite priests to hold this position, as they were the only remaining order authorized by the prophet Ezekiel 44:13-16 to assume the role of High Priest.[80]

Jason's tenure as High Priest occurred during a tumultuous period, and historical sources like the Book of 2 Maccabees cast him in a negative light due to his moderate Hellenistic tendencies, even though he may not have been as extreme as his successor. Antiochus apparently began auctioning off the High Priesthood to the highest bidder, allowing the individual who offered the most substantial annual tribute from the Temple in Jerusalem to the Seleucid government in Antioch to assume the position. Jason apparently outbid his brother for the role in 175 BCE, but a newcomer named Menelaus outbid Jason in 171 BCE, resulting in Jason's removal from the position.[81]

The New Culture vs the Old Ways

Under Jason's rule, he received approval to establish a Greek-style polis, or city, along with a gymnasium in or near Jerusalem, which was named Antioch or Antiochia. The residents of this new settlement were expected to raise their children in the Greek cultural tradition and acquire proficiency in the Greek language.

Similar Greek settlements were established throughout the empire. Jason was granted the authority to determine the eligibility of citizens and exert influence over the political affairs of this suburban area. Surprisingly, these alterations did not immediately provoke significant opposition from the majority of Jerusalem's population, and it appears that Jason continued to uphold the fundamental Jewish laws and principles during his leadership.[82]

Jason's tenure as High Priest came to an unexpected conclusion in 171 BCE. He dispatched Menelaus, who was the brother of Simon the Benjamite, on a mission to deliver funds to Antiochus IV in the Seleucid capital, Antioch. However, Menelaus seized this opportunity to outmaneuver Jason for the position of High Priest, effectively offering a higher bid for the office. Consequently, Antiochus IV ratified Menelaus as the new High Priest, marking the end of Jason's priesthood.[83]

According to the book of 2 Maccabees, while Antiochus was engaged in military operations in Egypt, a false rumor circulated suggesting that he had met his demise. Exploiting the chaos and uncertainty, Jason, the deposed High Priest, assembled a force of 1,000 soldiers and launched a surprise assault on the city of

Jerusalem. This unexpected attack prompted Menelaus, the High Priest who had been appointed by Antiochus, to flee Jerusalem in the midst of a riot.

However, when Antiochus returned from his Egyptian campaign in 168 BC, he was incensed by his defeat in the southern region. In retaliation, he besieged Jerusalem and reinstated Menelaus as High Priest. Furthermore, Antiochus carried out severe reprisals, resulting in the execution of numerous Jewish inhabitants.[84]

"When these happenings were reported to the king, he thought that Judea was in revolt. Raging like a wild animal, he set out from Egypt and took Jerusalem by storm. He ordered his soldiers to cut down without mercy those whom they met and to slay those who took refuge in their houses. There was a massacre of young and old, a killing of women and children, a slaughter of virgins and infants. In the space of three days, eighty thousand were lost, forty thousand meeting a violent death, and the same number being sold into slavery."

2 Maccabees 5:11–14[18]

Subsequent to reinstating Menelaus, Antiochus IV promulgated decrees intended to support the fervently pro-Greek faction of Jews, often referred to as "Hellenizers," in their struggle against the traditionalist Jewish community. His edicts included the prohibition of Jewish religious practices and customs, resulting in a significant transformation of the Temple in Jerusalem into a syncretic cult that amalgamated Greek and Jewish elements, including the veneration of Zeus. During this tumultuous period, Jerusalem suffered a second round of devastation. Antiochus further solidified his influence by establishing a fortified Greek citadel, known as the Acra, within Jerusalem. This citadel served as both a stronghold for Hellenized Jews and a military garrison for Greek forces. These events unfolded between 168 and 167 BC.[85]

The Abomination (which brings) Desolation – 168 BCE

Antiochus, by adopting the title "Epiphanes," signifying 'god manifest,' held a belief that he was a manifestation of Zeus himself. He displayed his devotion to this identity by making generous donations to Greek temples, including the renowned Temple of Zeus in Athens. This perception of being the ultimate deity granted him a sense of authority over all religious practices within his realm. Consequently, he embarked on a systematic campaign to transform the traditions of the Jewish people, rooted in the laws of Moses, in order to align them with Greek beliefs.[86]

Antiochus' initiatives for Hellenization might have encompassed the potential alteration of scriptures, such as introducing Greek cosmological concepts into the Hebrew Scriptures. Historical accounts report severe repercussions for individuals caught reading the Torah, including punishments and even death sentences. Sabbath observance was abolished, and circumcision was prohibited under the threat of capital punishment. Josephus' narrative illustrates this situation:

"Now Antiochus was not satisfied either with his unexpected taking the city, or with its pillage, or with the great slaughter he had made there; but being overcome with his violent passions, and remembering what he had suffered during the siege, he compelled the Jews to dissolve the laws of their country, and to keep their infants uncircumcised, and to sacrifice swine's flesh upon the altar; against which they all opposed themselves, and the most approved among them were put to death. Bacchides also, who was sent to keep the fortresses, having these wicked commands, joined to his own natural barbarity, indulged all sorts of extremist wickedness, tormented the worthiest of the inhabitants, man by man, and threatened their city every day with open destruction, till at length he provoked the poor sufferers by the extremity of his wicked doings to avenge themselves."[87]

In 168 or 169 BCE, Antiochus advanced upon Jerusalem, eliminating Jason, the last of the Zadokite High Priests, and desecrating the Temple by dedicating it to Zeus. He erected an image of Zeus in his own likeness upon the altar and offered a pig as a sacrificial offering within the Temple's sacred precincts. This event is remembered by the Jewish community as the "great desecration" or the "abomination of desolation," as foretold in Daniel 11:31 and 12:11. The Temple's revered treasures, including the golden candlesticks and the golden altar, were plundered. Copies of the Torah were annihilated alongside various structures. Additionally, he reconstructed the ancient city of David as a Seleucid stronghold, establishing dominance over the remainder of the city.[88]

This was a dark time in Jewish history. Pain and suffering were daily occurrences during this brutal persecution. The desecration of the Temple tore the hearts of the faithful among the people. The forcing of Greek culture on the Jewish people threatened to destroy any remaining true worship of Yahweh and even went as far as threatening the entire identity of the Jewish people. There would be one brave group of priests that would rise up and break off the stronghold of the mad ruler. They would become known as the Maccabees: the name means "Hammer."

The Maccabean Revolt

"...for they will cry to the LORD because of oppressors, and He will send them a Savior and a Champion, and He will deliver them."

Isaiah 19:20

The Maccabees were a group of Jewish rebel warriors who seized control of Judea during its incorporation into the Seleucid Empire. They went on to establish the Hasmonean dynasty, a ruling lineage that spanned from 167 BCE to 37 BCE. During a significant portion of this period, from around 110 to 63 BCE, Judea functioned as an independent kingdom. The Maccabees were known for their efforts to reassert the Jewish religion, expand Judea's territorial boundaries through conquest, and diminish the influence of Hellenism and Hellenistic Judaism.[89]

The term "Maccabee" is often used to refer to the entire Hasmonean dynasty, but it originally applied to Judas Maccabeus and his four brothers. "Maccabee" served as a personal epithet for Judah, and the later generations of the dynasty were not direct descendants of his. One explanation for the name's origins suggests it is derived from the Aramaic term "maqqəba," meaning "the hammer," in recognition of Judah's ferocity in battle.[90]

In the narrative of I Maccabees, the revolt against the Seleucid Empire was ignited by a rural Jewish priest, (according to Josephus and 1 Maccabees 7:14, of Aaronic lineage) named Mattathias the Hasmonean, hailing from Modiin. This uprising was sparked by his refusal to worship the Greek gods. Mattathias even went so far as to kill a Hellenistic Jew who intended to offer a sacrifice to an idol in his place.

Mattathias and his five sons subsequently retreated to the wilderness of Judah. Following Mattathias' passing, approximately one year later, in 166 BCE, his son Judah Maccabee led a band of Jewish insurgents to victory over the Seleucid dynasty, employing guerrilla warfare tactics. Initially, their efforts were directed against Hellenizing Jews, a significant presence at the time. The Maccabees dismantled pagan altars in villages, conducted circumcisions, and pushed Jews into a state of outlawry.[91]

The rebellion featured numerous battles, with the Maccabean forces gaining notoriety for their utilization of guerrilla tactics against the Seleucid army. After emerging victorious, the Maccabees entered Jerusalem triumphantly, purifying the Temple through ritual cleansing and reinstating traditional Jewish worship practices. Jonathan Maccabee was appointed as the high priest. Although a substantial Seleucid army was dispatched to quell the revolt, it withdrew to Syria following the death of Antiochus IV. Lysias, the commander of this army, was preoccupied with internal Seleucid affairs and agreed to a political settlement that restored religious freedom.[92]

The Jewish festival of Hanukkah commemorates the rededication of the Temple following Judah Maccabee's triumph over the Seleucids. According to rabbinic tradition, the victorious Maccabees could only find a small jug of uncontaminated oil sealed for the Menorah. Although this oil initially seemed sufficient for just one day, it miraculously lasted for eight days, allowing enough time to procure more oil.[93]

The Maccabees brought a counter-revolution to the oppression by the Greek ruler, Antiochus. They became a strong resistance against the movement to Hellenize the nation of Israel and subvert the Jewish people from the worship of Yahweh. The Maccabees became a righteous force intent on preserving their way of life and delivering their people from a dark, anti-God tyrant. With the rise of an Oppressor comes the appearance of a Deliverer, forcing the people to cry out and choose either the darkness or the light.

The Oppressor Analysis

It is important to break down this history into a snapshot. It will help us reveal a pattern. First, the pattern is as follows:

1. An Oppressor rises up (or is raised up) against Israel from the dominating world power, becoming **The Oppressor**.

2. This Oppressor sees himself as more than a man and attributes his authority to the gods of his day. He erects an image of himself to be worshiped – **Possessing a god Complex**.

3. He is against the worship of the true God, Yahweh, His Temple, and His people. He seeks to abolish the practice of Torah Law and persecutes and kills His people – he becomes **The Ultimate Antagonist** of his day.

4. He defiles the Holy Temple of Yahweh in an act of defiance. This intrusion will include acts considered an abomination in Yahweh's Torah or Law – he becomes **The Defiler**.

5. The people of Yahweh will be given into his hand for a season and it will end with the Oppressor being removed. To put it another way, his days are numbered, literally. He is given **Limited Reign**.

6. Last, it is very important to note that the Oppressor is only allowed to rise up for the purpose of judgment, this is Yahweh's judgment on His Land and on His people for their severe and chronic disobedience. The oppressor becomes an **Instrument of Judgement**.

***Then the sons of Israel did evil in the sight of the LORD** and* *served the Baals, and they forsook the LORD, the God of their fathers, who had brought them out of the land of Egypt, and followed other gods from among the gods of the peoples who were around them, and bowed themselves down to them; thus they provoked the LORD to anger. So they forsook the LORD and served Baal and the Ashtaroth.* **The anger of the LORD burned against Israel, and He gave them into the hands of plunderers who plundered them; and He sold them into the hands of their enemies around them, so that they could no longer stand before their enemies.**

Judges 2:11-14 (emphasis added)

Although we see plunders during earlier times of disobedience, this oppressor pattern begins with Nebuchadnezzar, king of Babylon. We could add an earlier Egyptian Pharaoh during the Exodus for fulfilling an oppressor role, which began as Israel was being formed as a people, but this counting of Oppressors starts when Israel became a nation, possessing their own land and a temple.

I remind you of the image that Nebuchadnezzar saw in his dream. The great image of gold, silver, bronze, and iron, representing the empires that would rise to power after Babylon. Nebuchadnezzar is the first, the head of gold. He becomes the first oppressor, yet Yahweh called him His servant (Jer 25:9). He was used to bring judgement upon a wicked and disobedient Israel. Does Nebuchadnezzar match the pattern?

1. **The Oppressor** - Nebuchadnezzar, was allowed to rise to power in the dominating world government, Babylon.

2. **Possessing a god Complex** - Nebuchadnezzar saw himself as more than a man and erected an image (of himself) for the world to worship (Dan 3).

3. **The Ultimate Antagonist** - Nebuchadnezzar is against the worship(ers) of Yahweh. He attacks the city of Jerusalem and takes the people captive.

4. **The Defiler** - Nebuchadnezzar defiles the Holy Temple. In a second attack He returns and burns the city and the Holy Temple (2 Chron 36:17-20). He plunders the sacred Temple and hauls the holy vessels back to Babylon, an act of defilement.

5. **Limited Reign** - The people of Yahweh are given into his hand for a numbered period of time, 70 years (Jer 29:10).

6. **Instrument of Judgement** - Nebuchadnezzar was allowed access to Israel as a form of judgment on the people (2 Chron 36:16-18).

This pattern is revealed whenever Yahweh's people forsake him and serve foreign gods. It is also important to note that Israel always defiles the Temple first, and then Yahweh allows the oppressor access to His Temple after He vacates it. The prophet Isaiah chronicles a time when Yahweh's presence left the Temple. In Isaiah 6, we see Yahweh sitting on a throne and the train of His robe filling the Temple, then in Ezekiel 10, the throne and the glory of Yahweh depart from the Temple in an entourage of cherubim and four living beings with whirling wheels.

"Then the glory of the LORD departed from the threshold of

the temple and stood over the cherubim. When the cherubim departed, they lifted their wings and rose up from the earth in my sight with the wheels beside them; and they stood still at the entrance of the east gate of the LORD'S house, and the glory of the God of Israel hovered over them."

Ezekiel 10:18-19 (emphasis added)

Is this same oppressor pattern revealed during the time period of the Greek empire? The only ruler that fits this pattern in every way, during this time period, is Antiochus IV Epiphanes.

1. **The Oppressor** - Antiochus IV Epiphanes becomes ruler of the dominant Greek power in the world, the Seleucid empire. His territory includes governing control of Judea. He believes his authority was given to him by Zeus, the highest deity in the Greek pantheon. His title, *Epiphanes,* meaning "god manifest", reveals that he considered himself a manifestation of Zeus.

This idea is also echoed in the New Testament writer's description of the man of lawlessness who saw himself as God, sitting in the temple of God.

*"...apostasy comes first, and the **man of lawlessness** is revealed, the **son of destruction**, who opposes and exalts himself above every so-called god or object of worship, so that **he takes his seat in the temple of God, displaying himself as being God.**"*

2 Thessalonians 2:3-4 (emphasis added)

Seeing that this was written by the Apostle Paul almost 200 years after Antiochus IV Epiphanes, this passage is alluding to a future anti-messiah (antichrist) figure who will also function as an oppressor of God's people and once again defile a rebuilt Temple.

So far in history, this is the second time an oppressor like this has manifested since the founding of the nation of Israel (or the third time if you count the Pharoah of the Exodus, although this was prior to Israel being established). According to an accurate reading of the Bible and history, there will be at least two more to come (which we will discuss later).

2. **Possessing a god Complex** - According to history, as we have discussed, Antiochus eventually erected a statue of Zeus in the Temple in Jerusalem. Because he sees himself as a manifestation of Zeus on earth, this can also be viewed as an image of himself. This is how, as The Oppressor, he "exalts himself above every so-called god or object of worship."

3. **The Ultimate Antagonist** – Antiochus becomes enraged at the Jews. He is determined to abolish their Biblical practices and convert them to his Greek culture. He persecutes the people of the true God by tormenting and killing many of them.

4. **The Defiler** – As we learned, Antiochus defiles the temple with the statue of a foreign god (aka, himself). In a greater act of defiance, he sacrificed a pig (an unclean animal) in the Temple and offered its blood on the Holy Altar, disrupting the "regular sacrifice". He also forced the priests to eat swine's flesh, another act of defilement.

5. **Limited Reign** - Antiochus is eventually stopped by the

Maccabees. Daniel prophesies that his reign of terror is limited to 2,300 days.

*"**How long will the vision about the regular sacrifice apply**, while the transgression causes horror, so as to allow both the holy place and the host to be trampled?" He said to me, "For 2,300 evenings and mornings, then the holy place will be properly restored."*

Daniel 8:13-14 (emphasis added)

6. **Instrument of Judgement** – It is clear in the book of Daniel that this "small horn" was given this authority from heaven because of the transgression of the people of God.

*"And **on account of transgression,** the host will be given over to the horn along with the regular sacrifice, and it will fling truth to the ground and perform its will and prosper."*

Daniel 8:12 (emphasis added)

Instruments (of judgment) are clearly wielded by a force greater than themselves. Yahweh determines their purpose and boundaries. He is ultimately in control of these situations.

Yahweh uses additional instruments to orchestrate the outcome in the days of judgment. Antiochus is considered a "horn," which connects us to the horn imagery seen by the prophet Zechariah during the time of the return of the Jews from Babylonian captivity, which was also a time of judgment. I want to revisit this passage and see the function of the Horns and Craftsmen.

"Then I lifted up my eyes and looked, and behold, there were

*four horns. So I said to the angel who was speaking with me, "What are these?" And he answered me, "**These are the horns which have scattered Judah, Israel, and Jerusalem**." Then the LORD showed me **four craftsmen**. I said, "What are these coming to do?" And he said, "These are the horns which have scattered Judah so that no man lifts up his head; but **these craftsmen have come to terrify them, to throw down the horns of the nations** who have lifted up their horns against the land of Judah in order to scatter it."*

Zechariah 1:18-21 (emphasis added)

So, when the Horns scatter Judah and Jerusalem as a form of judgment, the Craftsmen are enlisted to guide the process and limit the damage inflicted. It can be seen as a cosmic chess match, where the function of certain pieces keeps the opponents' pieces from advancing too far or can even eliminate their pieces entirely; all the while, each is protecting their kings. This is the essence of biblical geopolitics, or you could call this ***Theo-politics***.

As we move forward through history, we will see that Israel will turn back to Yahweh, although not entirely, and again, they will forsake Him. They will forget His ways, trample His laws, and defile His Holy Temple. They will kill His messengers and forsake the covenant they have with Him, and as it is written, "until there was no remedy" (2 Chr 36:16). What Israel needed was someone to rescue them from this downward spiral of disobedience leading to destruction, what they needed was a strong Deliverer who could turn the hearts of the people back to Yahweh!

The next empire will hold the key to Israel's freedom, but it will come to them in a mostly unrecognized way. The coming empire is Rome, a strong and powerful kingdom, as strong as iron, one might say. They came to power in what is known as the Iron Age. Would the nation of Israel receive the new Divine offer, a new covenant built on better promises, or would they reject their coming Deliverer, an Anointed One, called Messiah?

The Yasha

Since the Exodus of Israel from Egypt and through the nation's history in the promised land, Israel's faithfulness to Yahweh would wax and wane. They would repeatedly fall away from Yahweh and serve the pagan gods of The Nations. Practices that would include sacrificing their own children for these foreign deities and spilling innocent blood on the land. This act alone would invoke the wrath of Yahweh upon His people. In the early years as a nation, the Book of Judges records this statement,

"Then the sons of Israel did evil in the sight of the LORD and served the Baals, and they forsook the LORD, the God of their fathers, who had brought them out of the land of Egypt, and followed other gods from among the gods of the peoples who were around them, and bowed themselves down to them..."

Judges 2:11-12

These acts of unfaithfulness would anger the God of Israel. As a father disciplines his children, God, as their Father, would bring correction to the people in the form of plunderers, allowing Israel's enemies to rise up and oppress the people. In response, they would cry out to Yahweh for help.

As any father would, Yahweh often had compassion on His oppressed children and sent "deliverers" to bring relief and restore the covenant relationship between them. These were intended to be lessons, albeit some hard learned.

"When the LORD raised up judges for them, the LORD was with the judge and delivered them from the hand of their enemies all the

days of the judge; for the LORD was moved to pity by their groaning because of those who oppressed and afflicted them."

Judges 2:18

And consequently,

*"When the sons of Israel cried to the LORD, **the LORD raised up a deliverer for the sons of Israel to deliver them**, Othniel the son of Kenaz, Caleb's younger brother. **The Spirit of the LORD came upon him**, and he judged Israel."*

Judges 3:9-10 (emphasis added)

The Hebrew root word for "deliverer" is *Yasha* (Strong's H3467 - yāša'), meaning to deliver, avenge, or bring salvation. There were twelve Judges or Deliverers during this time in Israel's history. The Hebrew word for "Judge" is *shaphat* (Strong's H8202), which means to judge or govern. These were the first to bring order to Israel under a system of theocracy in which Yahweh was the Ruler or King, and the Judges were the human extension of His Divine governance.

The Judges were called *anointed ones* because they were empowered by the Holy Spirit. Historically, the spiritual leaders of Israel referred to these deliverers as messiahs (anointed ones).

"...for they will cry to the LORD because of oppressors, and He will send them a Savior and a Champion, and He will deliver them."

Isaiah 19:20

The cycle of sent Oppressors and the sending of Deliverers can be understood by the analogy of the Horns and the Craftsmen. I remind you that Zechariah 1:18-21 states that Yahweh would send the Four Horns to scatter Judah, Israel, and Jerusalem, and the Four Craftsmen were sent to throw down these scattering Horns. The Deliverers and the Craftsmen are intrinsically tied to each other, or to put it another way, the Craftsmen create a strategy for Israel's deliverance and use Deliverers to accomplish it.

So far in the cycle, we have the Oppressor, the Pharaoh of Egypt during the Exodus, and the Deliverer, Moses, the anointed one. Next, we see the Oppressor, Nebuchadnezzar, The Babylonian king, and the Deliverer, Cyrus, the Great, the anointed one. Later, the Oppressor Antiochus IV Epiphanies, and the Deliverer, Judah Maccabee, the Zadokite priest and anointed one.

This repeating pattern was intended to point believers in Yahweh to an ultimate Deliverer. As Moses, one of Israel's great deliverers, said,

"The LORD your God will raise up for you a prophet like me from among you, from your countrymen; you shall listen to him."
Deuteronomy 18:15

And the prophet Isaiah writes,

"And He [Yahweh] saw that there was no man,
And was astonished that there was no one to intercede;
Then His own arm brought <u>salvation</u> to Him,
And His righteousness upheld Him.
He put on righteousness like a breastplate,
*And a helmet of <u>**salvation**</u> on His head;*
And He put on garments of vengeance for clothing.
And wrapped Himself with zeal as a mantle."

Isaiah 59:16-17 (emphasis and underline added)

The word "salvation" in the emphasized passage is the same word, *Yasha* or deliverance. His own arm would bring deliverance as Yahweh put the helmet of salvation on His own head. The second word, "salvation," is a different Hebrew word, *Yeshua*, also taken from the root word *Yasha* with an additional meaning derived from *shua,* "to cry out" or proclaim deliverance (Strong's H7768). The Anointed One (Messiah) who was prophesied to come would be a deliverer and a redeemer. We find the final fulfillment of these roles in Yeshua, The Messiah (Jesus, The Christ). He is the final Savior and He is also the arm of Yahweh!

> *"Behold, God is my salvation [Yeshua],*
> *I will trust and not be afraid;*
> *For the LORD [Yahweh] GOD is my strength and song,*
> ***And He has become my salvation [Yeshua]."***

> *Isaiah 12:2* (emphasis added)

Yeshua, The Messiah, was destined to come at the appointed time. It is Yahweh's final answer to the complicated cycle of Oppressor/Deliverer. The question is, would Israel recognize their Deliverer when He came? The Messiah would be revealed under the oppression of the next empire, Rome.

Rome is the final "iron" empire in Nebuchadnezzar's image to rule the gentile nations. It was prophesied by Daniel that Rome would be divided into two governing powers (two legs) and then be broken up (feet of part iron and part clay) and its influence scattered throughout the world until the time of the last manifestation of the power of Rome (the ten toes) is revealed.

Chapter 9 – The Great Roman Empire – 146 BCE

"After this, I kept looking in the night visions, and behold, a fourth beast, dreadful and terrifying and extremely strong, and it had large iron teeth. It devoured and crushed and trampled down the remainder with its feet; it was different from all the beasts that were before it."

Daniel 7:7

The Greek peninsula fell under the dominion of the Roman Republic following the Battle of Corinth in 146 BC, which also resulted in the incorporation of Macedonia as a Roman province. Concurrently, southern Greece came under Roman influence, although certain significant Greek city-states maintained partial autonomy and were spared direct Roman taxation.

The definitive Roman occupation of the Greek world was solidified after the Battle of Actium in 31 BC. In this pivotal engagement, Augustus emerged victorious over Cleopatra VII, the Greek Ptolemaic queen of Egypt, and the Roman general Mark Antony. Subsequently, Augustus seized Alexandria in 30 BC, marking the conquest of the last major city in Hellenistic Egypt.[94]

From a geopolitical perspective, the Roman acquisition of Greece unfolded as a transitional takeover through a series of smaller conflicts spanning decades, contrasting starkly with the swift and vast military conquests undertaken by Alexander the Great.

Israel, known as Judea at this time, became a Roman tributary. Judea was governed by a Roman procurator tasked with overseeing its political, military, and fiscal matters. The restructuring of its governmental framework was overseen by Gabinius, the Roman governor of Syria, from 57 to 55 BCE. Gabinius divided the region into five synhedroi, or administrative districts, with the clear intent of superseding the longstanding system of toparchies—administrative districts comprising central towns and their surrounding rural areas. This system had endured since the reign of Solomon and had been successively governed by the Assyrians, Babylonians, Persians, Ptolemies, Seleucids, and others.[95]

Life in Greece continued relatively unchanged under the Roman Empire, and Roman culture was heavily influenced by Greek traditions. As Horace, the Roman poet, said, *graecia capta ferum victorem cepit* ("Captive Greece captured her rude conqueror"). The works of Homer served as inspiration for Virgil's Aeneid, and authors like Seneca the Younger adopted Greek literary styles. While some Roman aristocrats held a dismissive view of Greek culture, many embraced Greek literature and philosophy.

The Greek language enjoyed favor among the educated elite in Rome, exemplified by figures like Scipio Africanus, who delved into philosophy and admired Greek culture and scientific advancements.[96]

The 400 Silent Years

We are also coming to the end of what was considered the 400 silent years between the Old and New Testaments of the Bible, where no prophetic visions were given, and there were no notable prophets sent by Yahweh. The prophecies of Daniel did, however, describe in some detail what would take place during this time.

In Daniel 9 he receives a message from the angel Gabriel that started a prophetic clock. It is popularly called the Seventy Weeks of Daniel (weeks of years, not days), a period of 490 years, with the last week (seven years) to be separate from the first period and accomplished during the "end of time".

The events described throughout the book of Daniel cover a timeline that ultimately continues until what is also called the "end of days" or the "last days," being dubbed the "end times" by many prophecy teachers. The last chapter of Daniel states, *"But as for you, Daniel, conceal these words and seal up the book until the **end of time**,"* leaving us the conclude that Daniel's visions extended through this entire future.

Because Daniel's prophecies cover such a vast time frame, we find that some of these prophecies are dual in nature; they are repeating patterns of events that occurred early on in the timeline and are revealed and repeated again in the end times. This way of teaching is Yahweh's preferred method, as stated in Isaiah,

> *"Remember the former things long past,*
> *For I am God, and there is no other;*
> *I am God, and there is no one like Me,*

How do you declare the end from the beginning except by repeating it over and over in types and shadows? It is also infallible proof that Yahweh is orchestrating all things, and everything is under His domain. It reminds us that we must apply this logic to what we read in Daniel and even the other prophetic writings. We must ask the question - will it happen again?

1. A great beast (horned) empire rises up and rules over the nations - will it happen again?

2. Israel is protected from the nations until they are disobedient and rebel against Yahweh and His laws and reject His presence in their midst; the Temple – will it happen again?

3. An Oppressor is sent to scatter His people and close the doors to His House – will it happen again?

4. Yahweh raises up a deliverer, who will eventually restore His people, His land, and His house, the Temple – will it happen again?

5. The heavenly court sits in judgment of the nations – will it happen again?

The last days of Daniel reveal a final reckoning, a period that closes the door on human government and opens an age of theocracy.

This has always been the plan from the beginning: God is seated as the Supreme Sovereign, and humans (His children) would be enlisted into this theocratic kingdom to help govern it, but they must first be qualified.

They must be tried and tested, found to have a good (regenerated) heart and strong moral character forged in the furnaces of affliction. They will be led by the greatest of leaders, Yeshua Messiah, and learn to follow Him by walking as He did long before they would be capable of leading. We are also given Daniel as an example, a great biblical figure, who revealed these truths to us. Daniel served under at least five kings and two empires, yet he himself was a leader, by Divine wisdom, a servant-leader in his own right.

Israel Under Roman Rule

During this period, Israel transitioned from the rule of the High Priestly line of the Hasmoneans (the Maccabees) to the Roman-appointed and non-religious Herodian Dynasty.

Israel was governed under Hasmonaean rule from 140 BCE to 37 BCE. The Hasmoneans were the descendants of the Maccabee family. The name is derived from the name of their ancestor, Hasmoneus (Hasmon), or Asamonaios.[97]

The reorganization of Israel in 57 BCE by Gabinius allowed Rome to assert more authority over the region. Julias Ceasar restored certain territories to Judea and appointed Hyrcanus II, the son of Alexander Yannai, the Hasmonean King who ruled from 103-76 BCE.

Hyrcanus, as the high priest of Judea, faced challenges in administering the affairs of the region and collecting taxes effectively, rendering him a relatively weak figure. This weakness created an opportunity for Antipater, an Idumaean official under the Hasmoneans, to enter the political arena and assume significant power.

With the authority delegated by the Romans, Antipater gradually took control of nearly all state matters, a role that technically belonged to Hyrcanus as the high priest. Antipater's strategic move to appoint his sons, Herod over Galilee and Phasael over Jerusalem, set the stage for the emergence of the Herodian dynasty.

In 43 B.C.E., Antipater was poisoned, leaving the fate of Palestine [Judea] uncertain. Despite the challenges, Herod and Phasael managed to maintain their grip on power, even after Mark Antony assumed control over all of Asia in 42 B.C.E. Despite objections from their fellow countrymen, who sent embassies to Antony to voice their concerns, Herod and Phasael each acquired the title of tetrarch. There was a brief Parthian invasion in 40 BCE that led to the Hasmonaean, Antigonus II Mattathias, being inserted as the new ruler of the region, briefly replacing Herod and Phasael.

By 37 B.C.E., Herod had effectively subdued most of the region. With the support of Sossius, the Roman governor of Syria, at the behest of Antony, Herod received aid that enabled him to capture Jerusalem. This led to the capture and execution of Antigonus II Mattathias, the last Hasmonaean king, marking the end of the Hasmonean rule and the independence of Israel. The Herodian dynasty would go on to play a significant role in the region's history.[98]

Yeshua, the Messiah - 2 BCE to 32 CE

The rise of the Herodian dynasty set the political stage for the coming of Yeshua Messiah. The Herodian Tetrarchs governed the land of Judea, which was under Roman rule. The Jewish high priests still had religious authority along with the Sanhedrin court system.

The religious groups or schools of thought consisted mainly of the Sadducees, the Pharisees, and an isolated group called the Essences.[99]

A primary distinction between Pharisees and Sadducees was their disagreement about the resurrection of the dead and an afterlife. Sadducees were upper-class wealthy men, mostly from Jerusalem, who made up the Jewish aristocracy. Pharisees came from all economic classes but were distinguished by their rigid adherence to specific behavior prescriptions arising from their interpretation of the ambiguities in the Torah, with an emphasis on the so-called Oral Torah.

The Essene movement likely originated as a distinct group among Jews during Jonathan Apphus' (one of the sons of Mattathias) time, driven by disputes over Jewish law and the belief that Jonathan's high priesthood was illegitimate. Most scholars think the Essenes seceded from the Zadokite priests. They saw themselves as the genuine remnant of Israel, upholding the true covenant with God, and attributed their interpretation of the Torah to their early leader, the Teacher of Righteousness, possibly a legitimate high priest. Embracing a conservative approach to Jewish law, they observed a strict hierarchy favoring priests (the Sons of Zadok) [Ezekiel 44:10-16] over laypeople, emphasized ritual purity, and held a dualistic worldview.[100]

According to Jewish writers Josephus and Philo, the Essenes ritually immersed in water every morning (a practice similar to the use of the mikveh for daily immersion found among some contemporary Hasidim), they ate together after prayer, devoted themselves to charity and benevolence, forbade the expression of anger, studied the books of the elders, preserved secrets, maintained an accurate calendar based on Jubilee cycles, and were very mindful of the names of the angels kept in their sacred writings.

The Essenes have gained fame in modern times as a result of the discovery of an extensive group of religious documents known as the Dead Sea Scrolls, which are commonly believed to be the Essenes' library. The scrolls were found at Qumran, an archaeological site situated along the northwestern shore of the Dead Sea, believed to have been the dwelling place of an Essene community.

These documents preserve multiple copies of parts of the Hebrew Bible along with deuterocanonical and sectarian manuscripts, including writings such as the Community Rule, the Damascus Document, and the War Scroll, which provide valuable insights into the communal life, ideology, and theology of the Essenes.

One biblical figure that was tasked with heralding the arrival of Messiah was John (the Baptist) whose father was a Zadok priest named Zechariah. He was *"a voice of one crying in the wilderness, prepare the way of the LORD,"* and most likely an Essene. Yeshua Himself declared that John was the figurative Elijah who was to come (Mal 4:6; Matt 11:14).

As the son of a legitimate Zadok priest, it is speculated that he could have qualified as an unofficial choice for High Priest that year. In any event, it was John who officiated the baptismal (mikvah) ceremony that revealed Yeshua to the world as the coming Messiah, confirmed by a voice from heaven stating, *"This is My beloved Son in whom I am well-pleased"* (Matt. 3:17).

There is much to say about Yeshua, the Messiah. Many books have been written, and many lessons and sermons taught. His arrival split time in half, BCE, and CE. His life impacted the world with a presence that revealed a Divine destiny.

The miracles He performed and the truths He spoke were recorded for future generations to remember and learn. Yeshua was revealed to the world as the great Deliverer and Redeemer, the only begotten Son of God. Yet His most important act was discovered through His sacrificial death and displayed by His victory over the sentence of death, His resurrection.

In Matthew 28:6, the angel announced, *"He has risen, just as He said,"* accomplishing what no other person, no other deliverer in history could. Yeshua rose triumphant over the power of the grave, breaking the curse of Adam. He now offers freedom to all who will follow Him and believe His truths.

*"There was the true Light which, coming into the world, enlightens every man. He was in the world, and the world was made through Him, and the world did not know Him. **He came to His own, and those who were His own did not receive Him**. But as many as received Him, **to them He gave the right to become***

As a descendant of Abraham in His humanity, Yeshua came to His own genetic family first. His message was to promote a new kingdom that honored Yahweh foremost. This kingdom was not bound by the Roman occupation and was built on a greater High Priestly order. Yeshua offered immediate mediation between the believer and His Father, Yahweh. His message was not deliverance from Rome but salvation from a darker, even more insidious force, the Lord of Death, taught by Paul as *"the god of this world,"* or Satan.

Yeshua taught that the real enemy lies within the heart of each man and woman. This enemy is spurned on by a fallen human nature and fueled by dark principalities and powers. He reminded us that we all have the potential to harm or destroy ourselves, and the people around us, through our own words and actions. He showed us that we didn't need to conquer Rome; we needed to conquer the ruler within us. Yeshua had the authority to overcome these principalities, and by conquering death, He could help us do the same.

This was not the deliverer that a Jewish person under Roman occupation was looking for. Many believed that if only they were freed from Roman oppression, they would find salvation. Like others before them, they wanted to change their circumstances but not necessarily their lifestyle, or their hearts. Yeshua challenged them to look deeper and take personal responsibility, and because of this message, He was rejected by most of His own, the Jewish people.

The religious leaders in Israel wanted to continue in their broken traditions, even though Temple worship was missing the most important element, the Ark of the Covenant, also known as the Ark of Presence, Yahweh's presence. It had been missing since the Babylonian exile, and therefore, the Temple was officially unoccupied by The Holy One.

The covenant relationship Yahweh had desired was often reduced to a system of legal interpretations of Torah Law, arguing about who was right(eous) and which group was given "the right." This became a downward spiral that darkened the nation and drove them into apostasy.

The Fig Tree Parable

"And He began telling this parable: "A man had a fig tree which had been planted in his vineyard, and he came looking for fruit on it and did not find any. And he said to the vineyard keeper, **'Behold, for three years, I have come looking for fruit on this fig tree without finding any. Cut it down!** *Why does it even use up the ground?' And he answered and said to him, 'Let it alone, sir, for this year too, until I dig around it and put in fertilizer; and if it bears fruit next year, fine; but if not, cut it down.'"*

Luke 13:6-9 (emphasis added)

In the final days of the Messiah's third year of ministry, the fig tree served as a powerful symbol representing the fate of the nation of Israel. As the winter of A.D. 31 concluded, the crucial 3-year deadline for the prophetic tree was approaching quickly. In the spring of the following year was Yeshua's crucifixion. Over the preceding three years, Israel had been presented with many opportunities to turn their hearts to Messiah. Yet many failed to accept His message or truly recognize who He was.

The parable paints a vivid metaphorical picture, casting Israel as a meticulously tended fig tree that, despite all care, was found barren. The profound meaning becomes evident when the command was given to "cut it down," a foreshadowing of Jerusalem's destruction in 70 CE. The years of civil strife and the relentless Roman onslaught continued to erode the cohesiveness of the nation of Israel. As an unproductive fig tree, the lack of growth and fruitlessness left little hope for its survival.

The order to cut down the unfruitful tree was the final nail in the coffin for the nation of Israel. The Jewish leaders officially rejected their Messiah and sealed their fate by demanding His crucifixion.

In 70 CE, the final events unfolded just like the cutting down of the fig tree. The Roman army besieged Jerusalem, tore down the stones of the temple, and burned the city, marking a complete end of temple worship.

The Fig Tree Prophecy

"As they were passing by in the morning, they saw the fig tree withered from the roots up. Being reminded, Peter said to Him, 'Rabbi, look, the fig tree which You cursed has withered.'"

Mark 11:20-21

The fig tree reappears in another profound prophecy concerning Israel found in the gospel of Mark chapter 11. The narrative unfolds with the Messiah's triumphant entry into Jerusalem, where the crowd welcomes him with shouts of *"Hosanna; Blessed is He that comes in the name of the Lord"* (verse 9), a quote from Psalm 118:26, emphasizing Yeshua's triumphal entrance into the city in His Father's Name.

Upon entering the Temple, reminiscent of a priest inspecting a leprous house (verse 11), Yeshua's actions take a symbolic turn. The following day, enroute to Jerusalem, he encounters a fig tree lush with leaves but devoid of fruit. In response, he curses the fig tree (verse 14) before going on to cleanse the Temple, where He proceeds to overturn the merchants' tables and drive out the money changers. Accusing the leaders of turning the Temple into a "den of thieves," he exposes the corruption that had infiltrated the sacred space.

As evening falls, the Messiah and his disciples depart from Jerusalem (verse 17). The next morning, Peter observes this same fig tree, which by now was withered and dead, remembering that Yeshua had cursed the tree. (verses 20-21)

This narrative presents a second witness to the fig tree symbology of Israel. The image of the withered tree poignantly captures the spiritual state and destiny of Israel, providing, once again, a profound statement on the consequences of spiritual barrenness and corruption within the nation.

The Roman Oppressor

After the rejection of their Messiah, the door began to swing closed on Israel's second temple era, and their identity as a nation would soon dissolve. In 70 CE, it was slammed shut with the siege of Jerusalem by the Roman army led by general and future emperor Titus (Caesar) Vespasianus. Jerusalem was the center of the Jewish rebel resistance in the Roman providence of Judea. Following a five-month siege, the Romans destroyed the city and the Second Jewish Temple.

In April 70 CE, three days before Passover, the Roman army started besieging Jerusalem. The city had been taken over by several rebel factions following a period of massive unrest and the collapse of a short-lived provisional government. Within three weeks, the Roman army broke through the first two walls of the city, but a stubborn rebel standoff prevented them from penetrating the thickest and third wall. According to Josephus, a contemporary historian and the main source of the war, the city was ravaged by murder, famine, and cannibalism.

On Tisha B'Av, 70 CE (August 30), Roman forces overwhelmed the defenders and set fire to the Temple. Resistance continued for another month, but eventually, the upper and lower parts of the city were taken as well, and the city was burned to the ground. Titus spared only the three towers of the Herodian citadel as a testimony to the city's former might.

The siege had a major toll on human life, with many people being killed and enslaved and large parts of the city destroyed. This victory gave the Flavian dynasty the legitimacy to claim control over the empire. A triumph march was held in Rome to celebrate the conquest of Jerusalem, and two triumphal arches were built to commemorate the conquest. The treasures looted from the Temple were put on display.

The destruction of Jerusalem and the Second Temple marked a major turning point in Jewish history. The loss of the mother city and Temple necessitated a reshaping of Jewish culture to ensure its survival. Judaism's Temple-based sects, including the priesthood and the Sadducees, diminished in importance. A new form of Judaism that became known as Rabbinic Judaism developed out of the Pharisaic school and eventually became the mainstream form of the religion.[101]

The siege of Jerusalem in 70 CE carries an eerie echo from a time past. It was 657 years earlier, in 587 BCE, that Jerusalem was under siege by the Babylonians. On the very same day, Tisha B'Av, which is the 9th day of the Hebrew month of Av, Jerusalem fell to Nebuchadnezzar, and the first temple was destroyed. The precise recurrence of these dates sent a strong message to the nation: this was a judgment from the Hand of Yahweh.

Leading this charge was another Oppressor, Titus Vespasianus, son of emperor Vespasian. So ruthless was the conquering of Jerusalem and the second Temple that the historian Josephus states,

"Now as soon as the army had no more people to slay or to plunder because there remained none to be the objects of their fury (for they would not have spared any, had there remained any other work to be done), [Titus] Caesar gave orders that they should now demolish the entire city and Temple…"[102]

Not One Stone Left Upon Another!

The Romans ignited a destructive fire in the Temple's sanctuary, the amassed silver and gold intended for safekeeping liquefied, streaming down the walls between the stones. Roman soldiers tore apart the stones to retrieve the precious metals, fulfilling the prophecy foretold by Yeshua 40 years earlier in Matthew 24:2, where *"not one stone here will be left upon another, which will not be torn down."*

Initially, the Romans prohibited Jewish entry into Jerusalem, and six decades later, following another unsuccessful revolt against the Romans, the Jews faced exile from Judea. This marked the onset of the second Jewish exile, surpassing the duration of the first. Over the next 1,900 years, the Jewish people experienced widespread dispersion and enduring persecution globally.

Despite centuries of separation, Jerusalem remained the cherished aspiration in every Jewish heart, serving as the ancient capital and spiritual homeland. Through successive generations, during the annual Passover meal, Jews worldwide concluded their Seder with the fervent declaration, "L'Shana Haba'ah B'Yerushalayim!" (Next year in Jerusalem!)

Titus and the Oppressor model

An examination of Titus reveals the oppressor pattern we've seen previously in history. To remind us, the list starts with **The Oppressor**. Titus had the authority to subjugate the people of God. He commanded the Roman armies under the leadership of his father, Vespasian, emperor of Rome.

Titus eventually became emperor after the death of his father in 79 CE. He is the first Roman emperor to receive a succession of rulership from a father to his son. This is significant in view of an antichrist figure. Nebuchadnezzar and Antiochus also both received kingship from their fathers. I believe this to be a dark imitation of Yeshua receiving the Kingdom from His Father.

Titus **possesses a god complex**. According to the historian Suetonius, the practice of the imperial cult was revived by Titus, but apparently, it met with some difficulty since Vespasian was not deified until six months after his death. To honor and glorify the Flavian dynasty further, foundations were laid for what would later become the Temple of Vespasian and Titus, which was finished by Domitian (Vespasian's other son).[103]

Titus becomes **the ultimate antagonist** toward Israel. He successfully brought an end to Yahweh temple worship and began what is known today as the second exile of the Jewish people.

In an act of defiance, Titus and his men **defiled what is sacred,** looting the Temple at Jerusalem and hauling off the sacred temple furnishings. The spoils of war were put on full display in a victory march, including some of the Jewish captives from Jerusalem. He was received as a hero, and standing still today in Rome is the Arch of Titus commemorating the destruction of Jerusalem and its Temple in 70 CE.

This is again known as the prophetic "abomination that brings desolation." After Daniel prophesied this, it was first fulfilled by Antiochus in 167 CE and was repeated by Titus, and the second desolation was greater than the first. The Titus destruction is the event that Yeshua spoke of,

"Therefore when you see the ABOMINATION OF DESOLATION which was spoken of through Daniel the prophet, standing in the holy place (let the reader understand), then those who are in Judea must flee to the mountains."

Matthew 24:15-17

These words were spoken almost 200 years after Antiochus Epiphanes defiled the first Temple. Titus defiled the second Temple 40 years after this statement by Yeshua was made. Yet the prophecy fits both events because this is a double…no triple prophecy.

The actual seed of this prophecy was first planted by Nebuchadnezzar (in the early years of Daniel), and it will happen again in the last days when the third temple is built. We must remember that divine patterns repeat themselves; what has happened before will happen again (Ecc. 1:9).

His time is predetermined. The amount of time given for the destruction of Jerusalem and the exile of the nation of Israel will be covered in a little more detail later on. It has to do with a little mystery called "the times of the Gentiles." Two prophecies that were given by

Yeshua state,

*"Jerusalem, Jerusalem, who kills the prophets and stones those who are sent to her! How often I wanted to gather your children together, the way a hen gathers her chicks under her wings, and you were unwilling. **Behold, your house is being left to you desolate! For I say to you, from now on, you will not see Me until you say, 'BLESSED IS HE WHO COMES IN THE NAME OF THE LORD!'"***

Matthew 23:37-39 (emphasis added)

And this,

*"...for there will be great distress upon the land and wrath to this people; and they will fall by the edge of the sword, and will be led captive into all the nations, and **Jerusalem will be trampled under foot by the Gentiles until the times of the Gentiles are fulfilled.**"*

Luke 21:23-24 (emphasis added)

Although Israel miraculously became a nation again in 1948, the city of Jerusalem was not recaptured until the Six-Day War in 1967. Even now, the Temple Mount is not entirely under Israel's jurisdiction.

According to the AJC Global Voice, "After Israel took control of the Temple Mount, it granted the Islamic Waqf responsibility for the administration of the site. The Islamic Waqf was first established by Muslim military leader Saladin in 1187 CE, following his recapture of Jerusalem from the Crusaders."[104]

The Islamic Waqf is a joint Palestinian-Jordanian religious body.

He was used as an instrument of judgment. As we already discussed in both the Fig Tree parable and the Fig Tree prophecy, the rejection of the Messiah carried a heavy weight. In a parable quoted earlier, Yeshua reveals this same destruction,

> *"And He began to tell the people this parable: "A man planted a vineyard and rented it out to vine-growers and went on a journey for a long time. At harvest time, he sent a slave to the vine growers so that they would give him some of the produce of the vineyard, but the vine growers beat him and sent him away empty-handed. And he proceeded to send another slave, and they beat him also and, treated him shamefully, and sent him away empty-handed. And he proceeded to send a third, and this one also they wounded and cast out.*
>
> *The owner of the vineyard said, 'What shall I do? **I will send my beloved son; perhaps they will respect him.**' But when the vine growers saw him, they reasoned with one another, saying, 'This is the heir; let us kill him so that the inheritance will be ours.' **So they threw him out of the vineyard and killed him.***
>
> *What, then, will the owner of the vineyard do to them? **He will come and destroy these vine-growers and will give the vineyard to others**." When they heard it, they said, 'May it never be!'"*

> Luke 20:9-16 (emphasis and underline added)

This seals his role of Titus Vespasianus as an oppressor. Salvation would now come through the final Deliverer, Yeshua, The Messiah. A new kingdom-age of grace was growing stronger every day. The priestly role of temple service and atonement for the people was transferred to the High Priest of a greater Altar, a heavenly Temple. Yeshua is now the light of the world, the hope for all nations.

Chapter 10 – The Four Apocalyptic Horsemen – 70 CE

"For thus says the Lord GOD, "How much more when I send My four severe judgments against Jerusalem: sword, famine, wild beasts and plague to cut off man and beast from it!"

Ezekiel 14:21

The fall of Jerusalem was an apocalyptic event in its day. Israel would cease to be a Jewish nation for almost 2000 years. The land of Israel was occupied by the Roman empire until the 4th century CE, followed by the Byzantine period occupation, until the rise of the Muslim Califates starting in 650 CE.

Around 691-692 CE, the Dome of the Rock was built on the temple mount. Rather than a mosque, it is a shrine that enshrines the Foundation Stone. The Al-Aqsa Mosque was also built under Umayyad rule during the late 7th or early 8th century on the southern end of the temple compound.[105]

The nations would continue to occupy the region and the city of Jerusalem until the 20th century.

The term "apocalyptic" is applied here for destruction on a catastrophic scale. It is my belief that the Four Horsemen rode leading up to the great scattering of the Jewish people in the first century CE, also known as the second exile. This included the desolation of the Temple of Yahweh and the national identity of the Jewish people.

My hypothesis is that not only was this outcome prophesied, as we have discussed previously, but it was an orchestrated plan by heaven. The plan was a consequence, a judgment of the heavenly court, brought to pass because of gross and egregious failure on the part of the covenant people.

Let me first say that no one wants to consider openly that heaven was responsible for such destruction and death. It seems contrary to the very nature of Yahweh to be involved in these types of actions. The difficult reality is that the scriptures are filled with warnings of horrific judgment upon the disobedient and that every one of these atrocities is spelled out in detail, starting with the writings of Moses (Deu 28:15-68). We could also mention the great flood of Genesis here as a horrific judgment.

With that fact being established, the question is, "How would such punishment be carried out?" By necessity alone, there would have to be, at the very least, agents of change involved. We have seen in other historic examples that God uses the armies of the nations to exact His judgments. The truth is these human empires, and their armies do not act alone. Yahweh does not leave these planned outcomes to chance. Each step is guided by supernatural forces or principalities (spirit-realm ruling authorities)

We have previously learned that the Four Horsemen are the elite forces of geopolitical change, along with the Four Horns and the Four Craftsmen. We have seen the Four Horns at work through the Oppressors that were sent from the nations to oppress Israel. Under each oppression, a Deliverer was sent by the design of the craftsmen to offer a way of escape and to mitigate the damage. But when those efforts failed to result in a true repentance of the people, the Four

Horsemen were sent in.

The last time we saw the Horsemen ride was during the return of the exiles from Babylon. The Horsemen forced the fall of Babylon and the rise of the Persian empire. When the horsemen ride, they cause massive geopolitical change. Sometimes, this change favors Israel; other times, the intention is the opposite.

The War Horse

Let's review the events surrounding the fall of Jerusalem. We start with the White Horse. This rider is synonymous with these ideas:

To advance military conquest, white equals finality, signals the rise of a new empire or the fall of another, a shift of power in a region, exacting judgment (of nations), the rider is sent (by the Lord of Hosts), he will be victorious (he wears a victor's crown), their involvement in these missions is covert (they come from behind the myrtle trees, from between the two bronze mountains).

The mission of the White Horse in 70 CE was:

- To lead a final military conquest. He was sent to quash the Jewish revolt with the help of the Roman Army and put a final end to a Jewish national presence in the region. This required a complete destruction of the center of Yahweh worship, the Holy Temple, and to take away Jewish sovereignty.

- To fulfill the words of the prophets that described the destruction of the Temple, the city of Jerusalem, and the scattering of the people in a second exile.

- To achieve such a thorough destruction that the nation would not rise again until the appointed time at the end. The final breaking of the Jewish forces was accomplished sixty years later after the Bar Kokhba revolt in 132 CE was quashed.

The Horse of Chaos

Next, we examine the ideas surrounding the Red Horse. His main objective is to take peace from the earth. This goal is accomplished by stirring up ideological turmoil. The ideas are:

To incite ideological warfare through religious opposition and hatred, philosophical differences, and class warfare, to polarize people by their ethnicities, to fuel conflict by the use of "isms" (communism, socialism, atheism, Darwinism, feminism, pantheism… to name a few modern examples)

These types of deep-seated beliefs lead to serious conflicts. When Yeshua was asked about peace, he said, *"Do not think that I came to bring peace on the earth; I did not come to bring peace, but a sword."* (Matthew 10:34). He then quotes from a prophecy concerning the fall of the nation of Israel, from the book of Micah,

> *"The day when you post your watchmen,*
> *Your punishment will come.*
> *Then, their confusion will occur.*
> *Do not trust in a neighbor;*
> *Do not have confidence in a friend.*
> *From her who lies in your bosom*
> *Guard your lips.*
> *For son treats father contemptuously,*
> *Daughter rises up against her mother,*
> *Daughter-in-law against her mother-in-law;*
> ***A man's enemies are the men of his own household."***

> *Micah 7:4-6* (emphasis added)

The truths that Yeshua would bring into the world were far more volatile than discussions about political differences or national identity, more far-reaching than disagreements about cultural practices or ethnic allegiances. His message would shake a person down to their core and radically change their identity to become citizens of a new kingdom, a new family, and create an eternal alliance that separated people from all the other "isms."

With deep beliefs comes a strong hatred for those who oppose them; the actions of the Red Horse give rise to this type of warfare. This was not the case for believers in Yeshua. These new believers were taught to love their enemies and to do good to those who hate them, not to conduct acts of violence but to "turn the other cheek." This new attitude flew in the face of the Red Horse tactics. Therefore, the Red Horse rider is only effective on non-believers. Yeshua states,

"These things I have spoken to you, so that in Me you may have peace. In the world, you have tribulation, but take courage; I have overcome the world."

John 16:33

The mission of the Red Horse in 70 CE:

- To incite Rome against the Jewish people by intensifying the conflict between the monotheistic beliefs of the Jewish people and the polytheistic beliefs of the Romans. Jerusalem and the Jewish temple were the targets of that hatred. In the final siege, the Roman soldiers spilled the blood of many Jewish people near the sacred Altar and on the steps leading into the Temple. Sixty years later, the Romans built a temple to Jupiter

on top of the ruins of the Temple Mount, most likely inciting
the Bar Kokhba revolt.

- To incite a civil war between the Jewish people. Resulting in
internal factions between devote followers of Yahweh and the
people who were willing to forsake the Torah of Yahweh by
giving in to the changing culture and embrace worshipping
pagan Greco-Roman deities; this often led to bloodshed and
instability in the region.

- To use that instability to further Rome's intervention, resulting
in the loss of confidence in Judea's ability to self-govern.
These conflicts would eventually set the stage for the nation's
fall.

The Dark Horse

A third strong factor in geopolitics is the economic component. In order to subjugate a people, the aggressor must disrupt the flow of commerce and interrupt the food and water supply. It is easier to defeat a weakened enemy. A good military leader will seek to control these economic factors. The Black Horse rider is seen with a pair of scales in his hand (Rev 6:5). In this passage, the wheat and barley are measured and rationed. His actions are going to cause agricultural damage or rationing that affects the food supply and those who benefit from that commerce.

This same type of condition is described in the book of Genesis. There was a great famine in the days of Jacob, son of Isaac. The details of the story reveal that God orchestrated a series of events that brought Jacob's son, Joseph, into the courts of the Egyptian pharaoh, the world power of the day. In time, God gave the pharaoh a dream, which was interpreted by Joseph. This dream revealed a plan that seven years of plenty and seven years of famine would affect the whole region.

It was eventually realized that God had sent Joseph to Egypt to mitigate the disaster by giving him the wisdom to store grain during the years of plenty and sell it during the subsequent famine. God also gave Joseph favor with the pharaoh, and he was elevated to the Viceroy of Egypt.

The result of this divine intervention was a shift in the balance of power in the world. The wealth of Egypt rose dramatically, and in the end, the people sold all their lands to Pharaoh in trade for food. This is a historic example of how economic factors change the balance of power. I suggest that the Black Horse was riding in those winds of change.

Identifying the Black Horse will require looking for the following types of changes in a geopolitical crisis:

- An economic crisis that is caused by famine, shortages in food and water supplies, disruptions in the flow of commerce and trade, and imposes economic sanctions.
- These actions are often a consequence of Divine judgment.
- It can include any action that results in increasing or reducing power in a region through commerce.

The mission of the Black Horse was seen most obviously during the siege of Jerusalem in 70 CE. The purpose of a siege is to block the flow of goods and services from a city, which leads to an economic crisis. The result is often starvation and despair for those besieged. The siege of Jerusalem weakened the Jewish resistance, leading to a Roman victory.

As in the story of Joseph, the effects of the Black Horse are not limited to a single city or region. In the last days, his apocalyptic riding will have a global effect.

The Death Horse

This fourth and last rider is the most insidious of them all. It is hard to imagine why this rider is allowed to exist at all. The truth is that humanity invited him into the world. God never intended for death to enter our world, but we all have the choice, *"the wages of sin is death."*

Death is present with all four Horsemen. What makes the last Rider different is the way death comes. This grim reaper incites the "fear of death" through acts of terror. The only thing worse than death is the fear of death. Does Yahweh offer an escape from this hideous assault? Yes! The mission of Yeshua, the Deliverer, is described in Hebrews 2:10,

"Therefore, since the children share in flesh and blood, He Himself likewise also partook of the same, that through death He might render powerless him who had the power of death, that is, the devil, **and might free those who through fear of death were subject to slavery all their lives.***"*

(emphasis added)

We are more than conquerors through Yeshua! *"...if the Son makes you free, you will be free indeed."* John 8:36

The mission of the Pale Horse is to fan the flames of the fear of death in the world. The ways he accomplishes this are:

- Through terror events like disease, plague, epidemics, and pandemics.

-   As a result of slow, demoralizing waves of death by famine (mass starvation, mass genocide).

-   By extreme acts of violence, e.g., suicide bombers, mass shootings, serial killings, and torture. I will include Roman crucifixions in this list. This form of torture/death was carried out publicly to incite fear into the minds of the subjugated masses. We can similarly include burning victims at the stake, lynching, and public beheading.

It is interesting to note that the description in Rev. 6:8 includes the use of wild beasts to produce this death. In an earlier example, we discussed the Black Plague that occurred in the 1300's CE, truly a terror event. The plague was believed to be carried by fleas, who infested sewer rats, which spread the disease in the streets of European cities, resulting in the death of somewhere between 75 to 200 million people, according to some estimates.

Wild Beasts of the Earth

More modern day illnesses have been discovered to have resulted from a series of emergent viruses called SARS (severe acute respiratory syndrome) viruses. These are viruses that originate with animals and cross over to infect humans, e.g., the swine flu, the avian flu, and the bat flu, to name a few. These types of viruses are labeled as diseases of zoonotic origin.

"A zoonosis (/zoʊˈɒnəsɪs, ˌzoʊəˈnoʊsɪs/; plural zoonoses) or zoonotic disease is an infectious disease of humans caused by a pathogen (an infectious agent, such as a bacterium, virus, parasite or prion) that can jump from a non-human (usually a vertebrate) to a human and vice versa. The term is from Greek: ζῷον zoon "animal" and νόσος nosos "sickness".[106]

"Major modern diseases such as Ebola virus disease and salmonellosis are zoonoses. HIV was a zoonotic disease transmitted to humans in the early part of the 20th century, though it has now evolved into a separate human-only disease. Most strains of influenza that infect humans are human diseases, although many strains of bird flu and swine flu are zoonoses; these viruses occasionally recombine with human strains of the flu and can cause pandemics such as the 1918 Spanish flu or the 2009 swine flu."[107]

"Between 60 and 75 percent of emerging infectious diseases in humans come from other animals. Many zoonoses — rabies, Lyme, anthrax, mad cow disease, SARS, Ebola, West Nile, Zika — loom large in public consciousness; others are less familiar: Q fever, orf, Rift Valley fever, Kyasanur Forest disease. More than a few, including influenza, AIDS, and the bubonic plague, have caused some of the deadliest outbreaks in recorded history."[108]

The discovery of the microscopic world led to a new realm of science. Although human health has been a science for millennia, the understanding of bacteria and viruses has paved the way to breakthroughs in medicine and biosciences. Coupled with the leaps and bounds made in technology, viruses, in particular, have aided in genetic research.

Gain-of-Function Research

"Unbeknownst to humanity since the dawn of recorded history, viral infections have left their mark. The ancient Greeks and Romans chronicled plagues with mysterious origins, attributing infections to sins, divine punishment, imbalances of "vital humors," or the concept of "miasma" linked to foul odors. In the sixteenth century, Girolamo Fracastoro and Agostino Bassi proposed that infectious agents might be responsible for spreading diseases, with Bassi focusing on diseases afflicting silkworms.

The seventeenth century brought a revolutionary advancement with the invention of the microscope by Hook and Van Leeuwenhoek. This development unveiled a previously unknown microscopic realm teeming with tiny organisms.

In England, Edward Jenner demonstrated a groundbreaking concept by showing that smallpox, a feared disease, could be prevented through inoculation with a substance causing pockmarks in cows and dairymaids. This marked the inception of vaccination.

Louis Pasteur's experiments in the nineteenth century illuminated the microbial nature of diseases. He, along with colleagues like Pierre Roux, Jacob Henle, and Robert Koch, established that germs were the culprits behind bacterial diseases such as anthrax and tuberculosis. Pasteur and Roux further pioneered the development of a rabies vaccine by passing infectious material through rabbits. By the century's end, it became widely accepted that the majority of infectious diseases were caused by germs.

Simultaneously, in the realm of plant science, researchers identified a substance capable of passing through a fine filter that proved infectious to tobacco plants. Termed a "virus," derived from the Latin word for poison, these entities were also linked to leukemia and other chicken cancers. The twentieth century witnessed the discovery of bacteriophages—viruses attacking bacteria—and their utilization in launching studies in molecular biology, as well as unraveling the intricacies of DNA and RNA structures."[109]

Emerging from these discoveries is a controversial fact that bacteria and viruses have been researched for their use as biological weapons. This has been labeled as "dual-use technology." Dual-use items refer to goods, software and technology that can be used for both civilian and military applications. The military's need for this information is for one purpose: weaponization, both offensive and defensive. Included under this dual-use category is what is called gain-of-function research.

"Gain-of-function research (GoF research or GoFR) is medical research that genetically alters an organism in a way that may enhance the biological functions of gene products. This may include an altered pathogenesis, transmissibility, or host range, i.e., the types of hosts that a microorganism can infect. This research is intended to reveal targets to better predict emerging infectious diseases and to develop vaccines and therapeutics.

For example, influenza B can infect only humans and harbor seals. Introducing a mutation that would allow influenza B to infect rabbits in a controlled laboratory situation would be considered a gain-of-function experiment, as the virus did not previously have that function. That type of experiment could then help reveal which parts of the virus's genome correspond to the species that it can infect, enabling the creation of antiviral medicines which block this function."[110]

Most of the military side of dual function is held in classified secrecy. What is known has been seen through various wars by foreign powers, especially in the past 100 years.

"During the past century, more than 500 million people died of infectious diseases. Several tens of thousands of these deaths were due to the deliberate release of pathogens or toxins, mostly by the Japanese during their attacks on China during the Second World War. Two international treaties outlawed biological weapons in 1925 and 1972, but they have largely failed to stop countries from conducting offensive weapons research and large-scale production of biological weapons. And as our knowledge of the biology of disease-causing agents—viruses, bacteria, and toxins—increases, it is legitimate to fear that modified pathogens could constitute devastating agents for biological warfare.

The German army was the first to use weapons of mass destruction, both biological and chemical, during the First World War, although their attacks with biological weapons were on a rather small scale and were not particularly successful: covert operations using both anthrax and glanders attempted to infect animals directly or to contaminate animal feed in several of their enemy countries. After the war, with no lasting peace established, as well as false and alarming intelligence reports, various European countries instigated their own biological warfare programmes, long before the onset of the Second World War."[111]

"The US biological warfare programmes projects started in 1941 on a small scale but increased during the war to include more than 5,000 people by 1945. The main effort focused on developing capabilities to counter a Japanese attack with biological weapons, but documents indicate that the US government also discussed the offensive use of anti-crop weapons. Soon after the war, the US military started open-air tests, exposing test animals, human volunteers, and unsuspecting civilians to both pathogenic and non-pathogenic microbes."[112]

"A release of bacteria from naval vessels off the coasts of Virginia and San Francisco infected many people, including about 800,000 people in the Bay area alone. Bacterial aerosols were released at more than 200 sites, including bus stations and airports. The most infamous test was the 1966 contamination of the New York metro system with Bacillus globigii— a non-infectious bacterium used to simulate the release of anthrax—to study the spread of the pathogen in a big city.

President Nixon decided to abandon offensive biological weapons research and signed the Biological and Toxin Weapons Convention (BTWC) in 1972, an improvement on the 1925 Geneva Protocol."[113]

The point of this brief cursor through recent history and simplified education on virology is to inform the reader of a world of microbiology that, after being discovered, has been weaponized. It is my hypothesis that this is where the Pale Horse and Rider function.

This information was not understood by mankind when the book of Revelation was written nor during the time of the writings of the prophet Zechariah. The explanation of this insidious grim reaper can now be better understood through the advances of modern science. The use of microbiology by the spirit realm was always an understood technology and is now revealed to us by the Pale Horse and its rider.

The Pale Horse in 70 CE

The Pale Horse is observed in the massive death toll that occurred during the Jewish-Roman war.

The complete slaughter of men, women, and children was a sign of death's presence.

"Josephus wrote that 1.1 million people, the majority of them Jewish, were killed during the siege – a death toll he attributes to the celebration of Passover. Josephus goes on to report that after the Romans killed the armed and elderly people, 97,000 were enslaved. Josephus records that many people were sold into slavery, and that of the inhabitants of Jerusalem, 40,000 individuals survived, and the emperor let them go wherever they chose. Before and during the siege, according to Josephus' account, there were multiple waves of desertions from the city."[114]

"The partisans were no longer in a position to help; everywhere was slaughter and flight. Most of the victims were peaceful citizens, weak and unarmed, butchered wherever they were caught. Round the Altar, the heaps of corpses grew higher and higher, while down the Sanctuary steps poured a river of blood, and the bodies of those killed at the top slithered to the bottom."[115]

The Pale Horse spreads terror.

The siege of Jerusalem produced panic resulting from starvation and fear of brutality. According to Josephus, some people in the city resorted to eating their own children and other dead corpses out of depravity and desperation. This curse for disobedience was prophesied in the book of Deuteronomy,

"…and you will be an example of terror to all the kingdoms of the earth."

"The LORD will bring a nation against you from afar, from the end of the earth, as the eagle swoops down…"

"It shall besiege you in all your towns until your high and fortified walls in which you trusted come down throughout your land…"

"Then you shall eat the offspring of your own body, the flesh of your sons and of your daughters whom the LORD your God has given you, during the siege and the distress by which your enemy will oppress you…"

- *Deuteronomy 28:25,49-53*

The Pale Horse brings sickness and disease,

*"If you are not careful to observe all the words of this law which are written in this book, to fear this honored and awesome name, the LORD your God, then the LORD will bring **extraordinary plagues on you and your descendants, even severe and lasting plagues, and miserable and chronic sicknesses.** He will bring back on you all the diseases of Egypt of which you were afraid, and they will cling to you. Also, every sickness and every plague which, not written in the book of this law, the LORD will bring on you until you are destroyed. **Then you shall be left few in number**, whereas you were as numerous as the stars of heaven, because you did not obey the LORD your God"*

- *Deuteronomy 28:58-62* (emphasis added)

What is difficult to understand is the fact that Yahweh would "bring" these extraordinary plagues and diseases to any people. During the course of human history, it inevitably becomes necessary, by Yahweh, to remove people from this world, like excising a cancerous tumor from the body, but how they are removed is key.

Here is a divine truth. Actions are always met with consequences either in this life or the next, and judgment is unavoidable. The response to the convergence of consequence and judgment on a mass scale is given to the Pale Horseman, not only for this situation, but the Pale Horse will continue to ride again and again. The "innocent victims", who in wartime are labeled as collateral damage, will be sorted out in the end.

This would be a good place to insert some perspective. To mere men, death is a finality, a cessation of life in this world. By death, our work is left unfinished, and we are separated from loved ones. Our future beyond this world seems uncertain; some are even convinced that upon death, we cease to exist or are gone forever.

The reality, according to the Bible, is that death is a transition from one existence to another. We leave our corporeal bodies and enter an entirely new spiritual domain.

From God's perspective, we are just taken out of the game, so to speak. We will have our day in court, and a new future will be determined. Death is not as permanent as we believe. Now, if our day in court doesn't end well, there is what the Bible calls the second death. We should be much more concerned about that death and the One who has the power over it. In the words of Yeshua,

"Do not fear those who kill the body but are unable to kill the

soul, but rather fear Him who is able to destroy both soul and body in hell."

- Matthew 10:28

In this life, we must face something worse than death - the fear of death. Fear is our greatest enemy, hidden deep within our soul. It is like a cancer that grows, taking out our vital organs. It robs us of our mental clarity and paralyzes us emotionally. The fear of death keeps us prisoners in our own mortal bodies. To be successful in this life, we must conquer the fear of death. When we no longer fear dying, it is only then that we can truly live.

Yeshua came and conquered death, and He offered us eternal life. When we accept and follow Him, we no longer have to fear death because Our Deliverer has freed us from death's grip. Yeshua says that the believer in Him,

"...does not come into judgment, but has passed out of death into life"

- (John 5:24).

The Pale Horse has no real power over the believer in Yeshua!

Chapter 11 – The Culmination of the Metal Empires

There is an importance to the totality of the image revealed by Daniel in the distinction of its individual parts. First, the metal empires represent the timeline of human history in direct contrast to the spiritual journey of God's people in both the Old and New Testaments. There is an "us and them" theme that runs through the bible narrative.

The nations were formed and allowed to exist to give context to God's purpose. The distinctions of the great image reveal more of that context. For example, there is a reason Babylon is considered the "head" of this image.

Babylon was not the first empire to exist in the ancient world. The pre-flood civilization of Sumer, or the post-flood civilization of Akkad, existed long before the ancient Babylon of Hammurabi and the later Neo-Babylonian empire of Nebuchadnezzar. We must consider that the essence of Babylon first emerged in the early post-flood Genesis stories of Babel and Nimrod. The theme is a rebellious city-state that opposes the authority of the world's Creator God. This is the theme that continues throughout the metal empires.

Babylon is the "head of gold," with the emphasis on the term "head." The empires are intended to function as a human body would, the head is for thinking and speaking, the arms are for gathering, the thigh region for progenerating, the legs for mobility, and the feet for stomping or crushing. The head contains the brain, the organ that processes thought. Ideas are formed and executed by the brain. How does this apply to Babylon?

Babylon possesses the nature and function of a powerful city-state authority. As we discussed in an earlier chapter, there are six key characteristics to consider, which are language, location, religion or ideology, commerce, a formidable leader, and a military.

Hammurabi was one of the first great leaders to bring form to Babylon through his codex of laws and its legal system by establishing Babylon as a key center for commerce and culture and magnifying its religious pantheon of deities and practices.

The eyes are located in the head, and they are windows to the soul, revealing the spirit of Babylon. Eyes are also reflective of spiritual awareness or seeing into the spirit realm. The "gateway to the gods" doctrine of Babel is repeated over and over again throughout successive civilizations through their occult practices.

Ancient Babylon, reminiscent of Babel, was forceful in projecting these ideologies onto its population through legal enforcement. Babylon represents the emergence of a police state and the progressive ideas of authoritarian rule.

A city is the centralization of this type of power, but that power must be wielded like a sword in the hands of a warrior, showing us the critical purpose of a city-state in building an empire. Babel/Babylon stands as a mother of all others.

The influence of Babylon is perceived through the mouth in this head. The spirit of Babylon becomes a voice echoing through the world, the song of a siren, to entice the world to join its revolution, the great anarchy.

The spirit of Babylon lives beyond historical Babylon. The next metal empire, Medo-Persia, is represented by the arms that gathered the world and unified the nations under one empirical umbrella. Two arms, two nations working hand-in-hand, the Medes and the Persians. They possessed an aura of tolerance of other religions and fostered a multicultural policy. They built a complex infrastructure, such as road systems and an organized postal system, the use of official languages across its territories, and the development of civil services, including its possession of a large, professional army. Its advancements inspired the implementation of similar styles of governance by a variety of later empires.

The waist and thighs represent Greece, the third great empire. They quickly followed the trade routes created by the previous civilizations to conquer the ever-expanding empire. They were progenitors, as seen by the Hellenization of the world. Greek culture was a gathering of thought and philosophy, a solidifying of the Olympian pantheon of gods and goddesses, portraying their rulers themselves as demigods on a divine mission to conquer our globe. The Greek culture ultimately inspired the Roman culture, and both remain as influences in the modern world today. The spirit of Babylon moves into the final system.

The fourth and final beast is seen as the legs of iron, the Roman empire. The long legs and feet represent the continuing duration of Rome's power and influence. Just as the legs are two, the Roman Empire split into two centers of power, east and west or Rome and Byzantium, which was later renamed Nova Roma, or 'New Rome.'

by Emperor Constantine the Great in 330 CE. It was later called Constantinople, and it is modern-day Istanbul in Turkey.

The final iteration of the Roman empire, as seen in the feet of part iron and part clay, these will stomp down and crush the remainder of the beasts (Dan 7:7). This is the function of the feet: to subjugate the entire world through dominance and sorcery, it describes the spirit of our modern age.

We have other names for this ecumenism, like global initiatives, international agencies and policies, the merging of business into multi-national corporations, the sharing of technology, and peace-keeping efforts through international treaties and alliances. The world is rushing together quickly on multiple fronts. The beast is crushing all opposition to this new world order.

The last Roman influence is seen with the iron-like strength of the Roman republic, with its Senate and legal system, and the clay-like element of "we the people", but the two do not truly mix. "We the people" is an illusion never completely achieved (or sustained); it is still the Roman, Ceasar-like rule that is at work behind the scenes and in the shadows.

The Roman Empire eventually conquered most of what is now Europe. The official Roman Empire transitioned into the Roman Catholic Church in the 5th century CE, which acted as a church-state, possessing what was left of the authority and power of the Roman Empire in the West. The Roman church held power in the region until finally losing dominance in the 17th century through the conquests of Napoleon.

In the Middle Ages, the kingdoms and monarchies eventually gave way to a feudal system ruled by wealthy landowners, which eventually emerged as various forms of democracies or democratic republics. I know I just crunched a large chunk of history here for the sake of time. More exhaustive work can be done in another book examining this period. My goal is to bring us up to the 19th-20th centuries.

The USA is the latest emergence of an extended Rome. Besides the similarity in the forms of government, we do not need to look far to see that the architecture of Washington DC and the buildings in our state capitols are similar to Vatican City and an iteration of ancient Roman architecture. Our forefathers wanted to emulate Rome, both ancient and modern Rome. Even our national symbol, the Eagle with wings unfurled, is strikingly similar to the Roman eagle.

The last iteration of Rome is being discovered through biblical prophecy. It is seen in the great image as the ten toes. The tips of the feet are the last and furthest extension of the image of the body. At this point in the image, the metal iron is mixed with clay, loosely representing republic-style democracies with Ceazar-style rule. The ten toes will eventually be identified, but that is outside the scope of this work.

We are now seeing that the forms of democracy that exist in the 21st century are just shells of governance, with a dark underbelly of the beast hidden in shadow administrations and governments. These obscure national power centers are coalescing to form a tyrannical totalitarian global cabal.

The spirit behind this evil beast was revealed in Germany with the rise of Hitler and the Third Reich. It is currently being emboldened again through the CCP, the Chinese Communist Party. All the nations of the world have become infatuated with "the spirit of the age." They are all drinking the intoxicating wine from the cup of Babylon!

We will come back to the rise of the beast, but we first need to add a little more context. We need to answer the question: how did we get here?

Two Women, Two Cities, and Two Destinies

"How the faithful city has become a harlot,
She who was full of justice!
Righteousness once lodged in her,
But now murderers."

Isaiah 1:21

When God chose to assign gender to a city, He chose a woman. The idea goes back to the beginning when man was created. God formed man out of the dirt, but the woman was *banah* (in Hebrew) or "built" from a man (Gen 2:21). It is the same word used to describe building a city; both are fashioned from (or by) men. The word *banah* is also used in a figurative sense to describe the role of a women in building a family, often referred to as "building a house." Women play a critical role in God's plan for building up generations of households. Likewise, a city is a critical environment where families grow and develop. These similarities in function go hand in hand and speak to the use of this gender identification for cities.

A woman can be righteous, pure, and virtuous, or she can be immoral, seductive or enticing, and destructive to building a family. The same can be said for cities. For example, Jerusalem is likened to a faithful woman. The Apostle Paul draws an analogy between Jerusalem and Sarah, wife of Abraham, who himself is called the father of many nations; Paul states that Sarah figuratively represents Jerusalem from above, who is *"the mother of us all."* (Gal 4:25 KJV)

The extra-biblical book of 1 Esdras contains a story from the time period of the return of the Jewish exiles from Babylon under the leadership of Zerubbabel. The story goes something like this.

When Zerubbabel was a young man, he and two of his companions were part of the bodyguard of Darius, the king of Persia. They decided to try and garnish favor before the great king by asking and answering an important question. The question was – what is the one thing that is strongest on earth? Their plan was to present their answers to the king in person.

The day came when they were given an audience before the king, and each presented his written statement. The first wrote, "Wine is the strongest." The second wrote. "The king is the strongest." The third, Zerubbabel, wrote, "Women are the strongest, but Truth is the victor over all things."

The king summoned the nobles of Persia and Media, the satraps, the generals, all the governors and prefects. They called upon the young men to explain their statements. The first said, "Gentlemen, how is wine the strongest? It leads astray the minds of all who drink it. It makes equal the mind of the king and the orphan, of the slave and the free, of the poor and the rich. It turns every thought to feasting and mirth and forgets all sorrow and debt. It makes all hearts feel rich, it forgets kings and satraps, and it makes everyone talk unrestrained.

When men drink, they forget to be friendly with friends and brothers, and before long, they draw their swords. And when they recover from the wine, they do not remember what they have done. Gentlemen, is not wine the strongest since it forces men to do such things?" When he said this, he stopped speaking.

Then the second, who asserted that the king was the strongest, began to speak: "Gentlemen, are not men strong, who rule over land and sea and all that is in them? But the king is stronger; he is their lord and master, and whatever he says to them, they obey. If he tells them to make war, they do it. If he sends them out against the enemy, they go. They kill and are killed and dare not disobey the king's command. Likewise, the farmers till the soil, and when they reap the harvest, they are compelled to pay taxes to the king. All his people and his armies obey him while he reclines, eats and drinks, and sleeps. Gentlemen, why is not the king the strongest since he is to be obeyed in this fashion?" And he stopped speaking.

Then Zerubbabel began to speak, "Gentlemen, is not the king great, and are not men many, and is not wine strong? Who then is their master, or who is their lord? Is it not women?

Women gave birth to the king and to everyone that rules over the sea and land. Women brought up the very men who plant vineyards, from which comes wine. Women make clothes; they bring men glory; men cannot exist without women. If men gather gold and silver or any other beautiful thing and then see a woman, lovely in appearance and beauty, they let all those things go, and gape at her, and with open mouths stare at her, and all prefer her to gold or silver or any other beautiful thing. A man leaves his own father, who brought him up, and his own country and cleaves to his wife, and with his wife, he ends his days.

Hence, you must realize by now that women rule over you! Do you not labor and toil and bring everything home and give it to women? Many men have lost their minds because of women and have become slaves because of them. Many have perished, stumbled, or sinned because of women.

And now, do you still not believe me? "Is not the king great in his power? Do not all lands fear to lay a hand on him? Yet I have seen him with Apame, the king's concubine, the daughter of the illustrious Bartacus; she would sit at the king's right hand and take the crown from the king's head, put it on her own, and slap the king with her left hand. At this, the king would gaze at her with mouth agape. If she smiles at him, he laughs; if she loses her temper with him, he flatters her so that she may be reconciled to him. Gentlemen, why are not women strong since they do such things?"

Then the king and the nobles looked at one another, and then Zerubbabel began to speak about Truth:

"Gentlemen, are not women strong? The earth is vast, and heaven is high, and the sun is swift in its course, for it makes the circuit of the heavens and returns to its place in one day. Is God not great? Who does these things? But Truth is also great and stronger than all things. The whole earth calls upon Truth, and heaven blesses her *(a little context inserted here: Truth was often personified as a woman in ancient cultures)*. All God's works quake and tremble, and with him, there is nothing unrighteous. Wine is unrighteous; the king is unrighteous; women are unrighteous. All the sons of men are unrighteous; all their works are unrighteous; in all such things, there is no truth in them, and in their unrighteousness, they will perish. But Truth endures forever. It lives on and prevails forever and ever. With her, Truth, there is no partiality or preference, but she does what is righteous instead of anything that is unrighteous or wicked. All men approve of her deeds, and there is nothing unrighteous in her judgment. To her belongs the strength, and the kingship, and the power, and the majesty of all the ages. Blessed be the God of Truth!" and He ceased speaking; then all the people shouted and said, "Great is Truth, and strongest of all!"

Thus, we have both a virtuous woman of truth, and a dark seductress who wields the greatest power over mankind.

Babylon is described as the latter, the dark seductress, the great harlot; she operates with the spirit of a harlot. She prostitutes herself for wealth and material gain, but what she truly desires is power. She seduces the world around her to partake in her indiscretions, her rebellion against the Father of spirits.

"Come here, I will show you the judgment of the great harlot who sits on many waters, with whom the kings of the earth committed acts of immorality, and those who dwell on the earth were made drunk with the wine of her immorality."

... and on her forehead a name was written, a mystery, "BABYLON THE GREAT, THE MOTHER OF HARLOTS AND OF THE ABOMINATIONS OF THE EARTH."

Revelation 17:1-2,5

In Revelation chapter 12, you see a virtuous woman who represents truth and righteousness, both of these are also descriptors of the city of Jerusalem. In contrast, in chapter 17, you see a great harlot, the city of Babylon. Two women, two cities, and two different destinies!

I need to ask the question, which city do you live in?

In the chapters following the introduction to the great prostitute city of Babylon, God pleads,

"Come out of her, my people, so that you will not participate in her sins and receive of her plagues."

Revelation 18:4,9

Woe, woe, woe to that great city Babylon; her destruction will come strong and swift!

What city do we want to live in? In Hebrews 11 it says of Abraham,

*"By faith Abraham, when he was called, obeyed by going out to a place which he was to receive for an inheritance; and he went out, not knowing where he was going. By faith he lived as an alien in the land of promise, as in a foreign land, dwelling in tents with Isaac and Jacob, fellow heirs of the same promise; **for he was looking for the city which has foundations, whose architect and builder is God.**"*

Hebrews 11:8-10 (emphasis added)

The book of Revelation ends with the Bride of Christ descending from heaven as a beautiful, luminescent holy city, majestic in all her glory. She is called the new Jerusalem; the kings of the earth will enter her gates and bring their glory into it. In this immortal city, every tear will be wiped from their eyes, and there will be no more death!

Jezebel, the Seductress

*"But I have this against you, that **you tolerate the woman Jezebel, who calls herself a prophetess**, and she teaches and leads My bond-servants astray so that they commit acts of immorality and eat things sacrificed to idols. I gave her time to repent, and she does not want to repent of her immorality. **Behold, I will throw her on a bed of sickness, and those who commit adultery with her into great tribulation**, unless they repent of her deeds. **And I will kill her children with pestilence,** and all the churches will know that I am He who searches the minds and hearts;"*

Revelation 2:20-23 (emphasis added)

What is this - Jezebel is in the church?

The church of Yeshua is supposed to be a virtuous bride, a woman of purity and truth. Yet Yeshua declares in the letter written to the church in Thyatira, one of the seven letters to the churches recorded in John's vision, that Jezebel has returned, and she is alive in the church. But wait a minute, Jezebel had been dead for almost 900 years at the time of that writing… ah, but the spirit of Jezebel lives on.

We might be tempted to stop here and assign the information to a simple metaphoric comparison. What I am suggesting is that the entity that inhabited the ninth-century BCE queen is the same spirit that was troubling the first-century CE churches. It is the ancient, power-hungry seductress, the spirit of Babylon.

Who or what was the spirit that operated in Babylon? For this, we must once again explore the pantheon of ancient Babylon for answers. Emerging from Sumerian culture was a female deity known as *Inanna*, she is known by the Akkadian Empire, the Babylonians, and the Assyrians as *Ishtar*. Her primary title was "the Queen of Heaven."[116]

A later iteration of *Inanna/Ishtar* emerges as *Astarte or Asherah* in Phoenicia.

This Goddess, Inanna/Ishtar/Astarte/Asherah, was known as the goddess of love, beauty, sexual desire, fertility, war, justice, and political power. She is essentially the controller of all aspects of human life.

This female deity, *Astarte*, was worshiped in the Phoenician city-state of Tyre. She was the consort of the Phoenician god *Melqart,* also known by the title *Baal* or "master." In 900 BCE, the king of Tyre had a daughter named Jezebel.

"It came about, as though it had been a trivial thing for him [king Ahab] to walk in the sins of Jeroboam the son of Nebat, that he [Ahab] married Jezebel the daughter of Ethbaal king of the Sidonians, and went to serve Baal and worshiped him. So he erected an altar for Baal in the house of Baal which he built in Samaria. Ahab also made the Asherah."

1 Kings 16:31-33 (brackets added for clarity)

Jezebel is introduced into the biblical narrative as a Phoenician princess, the daughter of Ithobaal I, king of Tyre, she was also a priestess of Astarte/Asherah. Her political marriage to Ahab, king of Israel, was the culmination of the friendly relations existing between Israel and Phoenicia at the time. Jezebel and her husband introduced Baal and Asherah worship into Israel's Yahweh culture. She trained 450 prophets to serve Baal and 400 additional prophets to serve Asherah. The prophets of Yahweh were persecuted and went into hiding during her reign as Queen.

This upset of national worship practices and this spiritual upheaval led to a showdown between Jezebel's prophets of Baal, and Elijah, the prophet of Yahweh. Elijah calls down the fire of Yahweh from heaven to prove who the true God was. Jezebel and her prophets were exposed as imposters. In the end, Jezebel is killed from being pushed out of a window by Jehu, as prophesied, and the dogs eat her carcass as a predicted judgment upon her.

So, when Jezebel is introduced in Revelation as having entered the church, this was more than just a sexual scandal in the church; her presence there was meant to disrupt the worship of Yahweh/Yeshua and replace it with pagan influences. This was a veiled attempt to corrupt the largest and most prominent organization of Christianity in the world, the "General (Catholic) Church".

Yet there is more to this. We must now look at *when* this happened. I believe the answer lies in understanding the letters to the seven churches and the not-so-obvious reference to the timeline. As we have discussed, prophecy is often, and almost always, multi-layered. There were, in fact, seven churches in the first century in those same regions and they each received these seven messages. Additionally, each of these seven messages can also apply to all the churches, collectively. They can also be used instructively to point out various obstacles in the personal lives of each believer. There are multiple purposes for the giving of these seven letters.

But there is another application to observe. Each letter represents a successive period in time, a timeline, that the churches of Yeshua would live through. Each church age would be challenged to overcome specific issues. For example, the first church age of Ephesus was challenged with not losing their first love.

Over time, love wore thin, and a strong admonition was necessary. In successive generations, believers in Yeshua would need to be reminded of this core attribute, especially as persecution grew. That letter also stated that they hated the deeds of the Nicolaitans, a heretical teaching of certain disruptors of the faith.

The next church age was marked by increased persecution, most likely referring to a time of dark Roman oppression in the 2nd and 3rd centuries. By the next church age, Pergamum, the Nicolaitans were spreading heretical doctrines inside the churches. They were also plagued with multiple other doctrinal struggles leading up to the church councils of Nicaea and Ephesus. Each progressive church age can be noted by historical events when they are viewed in context with the seven letters.

It is a fascinating study, but I will not attempt to expound on the minutia of all the connections to church history here. Rather, I would like to concentrate on a few specific periods on the timeline that are relevant to our topic.

The references will begin with the historical period of the church of Thyatira. I refer back to the quote at the beginning of this section, Jezebel is in the church at this point - and when did this happen?

The Thyatira age began around the sixth century CE when the

Papal system needed to settle political disputes. In Italy, the pope, as the largest landowner and most prestigious figure in Italy, began by default to take on much of the ruling authority that the Byzantines were unable to exercise in the areas surrounding the city of Rome.

"As Byzantine power weakened, though, the papacy assumed an ever-larger role in protecting Rome from the Lombards, but lacking direct control over sizable military assets, the Pope relied mainly on diplomacy to achieve as much. From the 9th century to the 12th century, the precise nature of the relationship between the popes and emperors – and between the Papal States and the Empire – is disputed. It was unclear whether the Papal States were a separate realm with the pope as their sovereign ruler, merely a part of the Frankish Empire over which the popes had administrative control, as suggested in the late-9th-century treatise Libellus de imperatoria potestate in urbe Roma, or whether the Holy Roman emperors were vicars of the pope (as a sort of archemperor) ruling Christendom."[117]

The political foundation was set for the rise of a powerful church-state to rule over the nations, with Rome in the west and Constantinople in the east. During this period, a more sinister force was at work and growing in the Church. Wherever there is an amassing of political power and authority, you will find the spirit of Babylon lurking. This is that same ancient goddess, Inanna/Ishtar/Astarte/Asherah and now Jezebel. She slipped into the church pews as Mary, mother of Jesus, but more than in the pews, she became the debated subject of the great church councils.

"The theological development of devotion to Mary begins with Justin Martyr (100–165), who articulated Mary's role in salvation history as the Second Eve. This was followed up by Irenæus, whom Herbert Thurston calls 'the first theologian of the Virgin Mother.'

The Catholic Church's magisterium has identified four teachings about Mary as dogmas of faith. These include belief in her virginal conception of Jesus, taught by the First Council of Nicaea in 325. The Council of Ephesus in 431 applied to her the description "Mother of God" (Theotokos). The perpetual virginity of Mary was taught by the ecumenical Second Council of Constantinople in 553, which described her as "ever virgin" and was also expressed by the Lateran synod of October 649; the doctrine of the Immaculate Conception states that from the first moment of her existence, Mary was without original sin. This doctrine was proclaimed a dogma ex-cathedra by Pope Pius IX in 1854. The dogma of the Assumption of Mary, defined by Pope Pius XII in 1950, states that, at the end of her earthly life, her body did not suffer corruption but was assumed into heaven and became a heavenly body."[118]

In time, the veneration of Mary moved to theology in the Roman Catholic Church. Veneration and devotional practices have often preceded formal theological declarations by the Magisterium.

"Marian veneration was theologically sanctioned with the adoption of the title Theotokos at the Council of Ephesus in 431 CE. The earliest known churches dedicated to Mary were built shortly after that date, among these the Church of the Seat of Mary (Kathisma) near Mar Elias Monastery, between Jerusalem and Bethlehem. The first Marian churches in Rome date from the 5th and 6th centuries: Santa Maria in Trastevere, Santa Maria Antiqua and Santa Maria Maggiore. However, the very earliest church dedicated to the Virgin Mary still dates to the late 4th century in Syria, where an inscription dedicating it to the Theotokos (Mother of God) was found among the ruins."[119]

"The veneration of the Blessed Virgin takes place in various ways. Marian prayers and hymns usually begin with veneration (honor) of her, followed by petitions. The number of Marian titles continued to grow as of the 3rd century, and many titles existed by the 5th century, growing especially during the Middle Ages."[120]

The theological or doctrinal support of Mary as an essential part of worship was not the only factor that led to Mariology. There are a number of "supernatural" events or apparitions that have contributed to the phenomena. This created a groundswell of interest and support for the doctrines. Mary is seen as an intermediate to Christ and an advocate of the people. As such, she assumed an effective role in salvatory doctrines over time.

"Growth of Roman Catholic veneration of Mary and Mariology has often come not from official declarations, but from Marian writings of the saints, popular devotion, and at times reported Marian apparitions. The Holy See approves only a select few as worthy of belief, the most recent being the 2008 approval of certain apparitions from 1665."[121]

"The Catechism of the Catholic Church, in paragraphs 721–726, claims that Mary is the first dwelling-place of God in salvation history. As such, she is the masterwork of God and the start of God bringing mankind into communion with Jesus. In Mary's womb, Jesus is the manifestation of God's wonders, the fulfillment of God's plan of loving goodness, and the definitive theophany. As such, Mary is typified by the Burning Bush in the Book of Exodus and by wisdom in the Book of Proverbs."[122]

As veneration became the theology of the church, the natural role of Mary as the mother of Jesus became an ethereal force that, in many ways, upstages the work and person of Yeshua Messiah himself. This is the exact nature of Jezebel!

I want to be clear here, I am in no way trying to disrespect or disregard Mary, the actual mother of Yeshua. She was to be counted as blessed by all generations according to The Magnificat recorded in Luke 1:46-56,

"And Mary said:
'My soul exalts the Lord,
And my spirit has rejoiced in God my Savior.
For He has had regard for the humble state of His bondslave;
For behold, from this time on all generations will count me blessed.
For the Mighty One has done great things for me;
And holy is His name.'"

Luke 1:46-49

It is not what I am suggesting here. This is not about Mary the human mother of Yeshua, this is about a spirit, an entity that assumed the role of Mary in doctrine and theology. This spirit has no interest in helping the suffering souls of humanity. Like Queen Jezebel, this is about usurping the Kingdom of God on Earth.

Queen Jezebel, the wife of Ahab, usurped the throne and steered the nation of Israel into Idolatry, creating a separation from the true worship of Yahweh. She replaced the prophets of Yahweh with her own prophets, introduced practices that led the people away from Yahweh's commandments and replaced Yahweh's temple worship with the worship of Baal and Asherah.

The significance of undermining temple worship should not be underestimated. When the temple is defiled by unholy practices or neglect, the holiness of God demands that He remove Himself from His seat of authority among the people of that nation; He is effectively usurped then by another spirit. This is the ultimate goal of the spirit of Jezebel.

In the case of Jezebel entering the church, she redirected the worship due to Yahweh through Yeshua (the only true way, truth, and life), the only divinely given advocate between us and the Father, by placing herself in the middle as the object of worship, claiming to be a mediator for those who are suffering.

Posing as the mother of Yeshua, she now heard prayers and offered to deliver these petitions to her Son and this mediation claimed to offer greater effectiveness in prayer. A famous prayer of petition to Mary is called "The Hail Mary." This entity directly positioned itself to be petitioned as a mediator. In contrast, Yeshua taught us to pray to the Father in His name, through Him, not through anyone else, as seen in 1 Timothy 2:5, John 14:6; 16:23

*"For there is one God, and **one mediator also between God and men, the man Christ Jesus**, who gave Himself as a ransom for all, the testimony given at the proper time."*

1 Timothy 2:5-6 (emphasis added)

The Babylon spirit and the final city of Babylon in the book of Revelation is called "a mystery, Babylon the Great, Mother of Harlots and of the Abominations of the Earth." This is Jezebel's real identity and her true motive.

What was Yeshua's response to Jezebel moving into the church?

*"I gave her time to repent, and she does not want to repent of her immorality. **Behold, I will throw her on a bed of sickness, and those who commit adultery with her into great tribulation**, unless they repent of her deeds. **And I will kill her children with pestilence**, and all the churches will know that I am He who searches the minds and hearts; and I will give to each one of you according to your deeds."*

Revelation 2:21-23 (emphasis added)

In ride the Four Horsemen! The War Horse (white) and the Death Horse (pale) seem to have been sent to disrupt the influence of Papal control.

In a unique work written by William H. McNiell, one of America's senior historians, who served as a professor of history at the University of Chicago forty years, titled "Plagues and Peoples" gives us a clue to key events between the time period of 1490 – 1570 CE.

"Both syphilis and typhus appeared in Europe during the long series of Italian wars, 1494 – 1559. The first of them broke out in epidemic fashion in the army that the French king, Charles VIII, led against Naples in 1494. When the French withdrew, King Charles discharged his soldiers, who thereupon spread the disease far and wide to all adjacent lands. Syphilis was regarded as a new disease not merely in Europe but in India, where it appeared in 1498 with DaGama's sailors, and in China and Japan as well, where it arrived in 1505.

Symptoms were often peculiarly horrible so that the disease attracted a great deal of attention wherever it appeared.

Some competent experts continue to believe that syphilis came to Europe from America and was, therefore, exactly what contemporaries thought it was – a new disease against which Eurasian populations had no established immunities. The timing of the first outbreak of syphilis in Europe and the place where it occurred certainly seems to fit what one would expect if the disease had been imported from America by Columbus' returning sailors. This theory, once it had been promulgated in 1539, became almost universally accepted among Europe's learned.

However conspicuous and distressful syphilis may have been for those who contracted it, its demographic impact does not seem to have been very great. Royal houses often suffered, and the political decline of Valois France (1559 – 1589) and of Ottoman Turkey (after 1566) may have been related to the prevalence of syphilis in the respective reigning families of the two states. Many aristocrats suffered similarly. But the inability of royal and aristocratic families to give birth to healthy children merely accelerated social mobility, making more room at the top of society than there would otherwise have been.

Lower down the social scale, syphilis had less devastating effects, for the fact seems to be that European populations continued to increase throughout the sixteenth century when the disease was at its height."[123]

The scripture describes this period of the Church with a scathing rebuke.

*"Behold, I will throw her on **a bed of sickness**, and those who **commit adultery** with her into great tribulation, unless they repent of her deeds."*

Revelation 2:22 (emphasis added)

The judgment upon those who entertained the influences of Jezebel was a "bed of sickness," a disease resulting from "committing adultery," in essence, a sexually transmitted disease. The passage goes on to say, "I will kill her children with pestilence." The article states that the royal and aristocratic families were burdened with unhealthy children as a result of the spread of syphilis. It is not a stretch to conclude that the royalty and aristocratic families in the papal hierarchy were also plagued with this disease. The idea of affected children can also be understood figuratively as those royalties and aristocracies that made political alliances with the "mother of all harlots"; hence, they became her children.

The Italian Wars, which led to the spread of disease, are where we can see the two horsemen riding. These conditions affected the balance of power in Europe and other parts of the world. It was a pronounced judgment from heaven upon the leaders of Christianity, or should we say the church-state(s), for bringing foreign or pagan doctrines into the church.

The Greater Disruptor

Between the wars and disease, this disruption in political power was timed with the life span and work of Martin Luther, a German priest. Luther was the seminal figure of the Protestant Reformation, and his theological beliefs formed the basis of Lutheranism.

"Luther was ordained to the priesthood in 1507. He came to reject several teachings and practices of the Roman Catholic Church; in particular, he disputed the view on indulgences. Luther proposed an academic discussion of the practice and efficacy of indulgences in his Ninety-five Theses of 1517. His refusal to renounce all of his writings at the demand of Pope Leo X in 1520 and the Holy Roman Emperor Charles V at the Diet of Worms in 1521 resulted in his excommunication by the Pope and condemnation as an outlaw by the Holy Roman Emperor. Luther died in 1546 with Pope Leo X's excommunication still in effect."[124]

The *Ninety-five Theses* became a launching pad for other reforms in Christian doctrine that were to emerge over the next 400 years. In general, these reforms brought to light fundamental biblical principles that had been distorted or even lost over the centuries. My goal is not to list, expound on, or debate these doctrinal topics but to point out that reformation was accomplished because of a vast new audience who were given access to the Bible. To explore that idea, we must understand another well-timed invention, the mechanical printing press, and the rise of literacy in the then-modern world.

"News Flash, Stop the Press!"

…or should we say, "Start the press!" In Germany, around 1440, the goldsmith Johannes Gutenberg invented the movable-type printing press, which started the Printing Revolution.

"Modelled on the design of existing screw presses, a single Renaissance movable-type printing press could produce up to 3,600 pages per workday, compared to forty by hand-printing and a few by hand-copying. Gutenberg's newly devised hand mould made possible the precise and rapid creation of metal movable type in large quantities. His two inventions, the hand mould and the movable-type printing press, together drastically reduced the cost of printing books and other documents in Europe, particularly for shorter print runs."[125]

The first major book printed in Europe using mass-produced metal moveable type was the Gutenberg Bible. It marked the start of the "Gutenberg Revolution" and the age of printed books in the West.

"Preparation of the Bible probably began soon after 1450 [CE], and the first finished copies were available in 1454 or 1455. It is not known exactly how long the Bible took to print. The first precisely datable printing is Gutenberg's 31-line Indulgence, which certainly existed by 22 October 1454."[126]

According to the dates reviewed here, The Bible was put into the hands of the common people just prior to Martin Luther's challenge to the Catholic leaders. These two events were timed precisely with the Italian wars and disease that spread through Europe, weakening the hold that papal power had over the people. This "new information", or access to it, caused a large and growing population to question the accuracy and integrity of the Roman Catholic Church.

The next horse, the Red Horse, rode during The Enlightenment in religious ideology known as Protestantism. The stronghold Jezebel had over the people was slowly being broken, and it took the Horsemen to accomplish it. It is hard to imagine or even suggest that these events and their precise timing were some great coincidences or somehow a coordinated effort by men. I believe they were driven by the supernatural forces of Heaven.

Whatever you may believe about the protestant reforms, Protestantism did entirely change the world. It marked the beginning of the decline of the Catholic Church as the supreme spiritual authority in Christendom, and it gave rise to many other groups of bible-believing followers of Yeshua. It was this impetus that led to the search for a new world where religious practices were not dominated by papal or state authorities like the Church of England.

To be clear, Jezebel did not leave the church; the people left Jezebel. The final word to the church of Thyatira was,

"He who overcomes, and he who keeps My deeds until the end, TO HIM I WILL GIVE AUTHORITY OVER THE NATIONS; AND HE SHALL RULE THEM WITH A ROD OF IRON, AS THE VESSELS OF THE POTTER ARE BROKEN TO PIECES, as I also have received authority from My Father;"

Revelation 2:26-27

According to the prophecy, the people who would overcome political Christian systems that were seeking to dominate the world would be granted a seat on the throne of Messiah when He returns to rule the nations. This will be true authority not mingled with the seductions and sins of Jezebel.

According to the book of Revelation, the spirit of Jezebel is still a key component of the last governmental system called "the beast," she rides on the beast.

"...and I saw a woman sitting on a scarlet beast, full of blasphemous names, having seven heads and ten horns."

Revelation 17:3

She (the supernatural entity) will only be defeated once and for all by the power and authority of Yeshua when He returns on His war horse and the saints with Him.

Jezebel's earthly human counterpart will be judged with a fitting judgment. According to the prophecy, she(he) will be eaten like the dogs that ate Queen Jezebel of the ancient past.

*"And the ten horns which you saw, and the beast, these will hate the harlot and will make her desolate and naked, **and will eat her flesh** and will burn her up with fire. For God has put it in their hearts to execute His purpose by having a common purpose, and by giving their kingdom to the beast, until the words of God will be fulfilled."*

Revelation 17:16-17 (emphasis added)

Babylon is a pagan religious system and also a city, a center of political power. The idea of comparing her to a harlot is seen in the definition of prostitution. A prostitute is a woman who sells her body for both material gain and influential advantage – power. When applied to a city, the advantages are wealth and political power.

It is interesting to note that the seat of power for the Catholic Church became the independent, international city-state (legally, a landlocked independent country) of Vatican City on February 11, 1929, by the Lateran Treaty between the Holy See and Italy.[127] This treaty ultimately elevates the Roman Catholic Church to the status of a city.

The Book with Seven Seals

The mysterious book, locked with seven seals as described in John's revelation, holds the key to the destiny of Babylon. Over the centuries, there has been much speculation as to what will be found when its pages are opened. What we need to know is that the destiny of Babylon is not found on its pages but is contained in the seven seals located on the outside of the book.

The subject of the seals is the judgment of the nations. It dates back to the foundation of Babel and finishes with the fall of the last Babylon. It feeds into the greater narrative of defeating the adversaries of Yahweh's creation and pronouncing eternal judgment upon them.

Recorded in the pages of this salient book is the destiny of mankind. Until the seals are broken, the book cannot be opened. John records this,

*"I saw in the right hand of Him who sat on the throne a book written inside and on the back, sealed up with seven seals. And I saw a strong angel proclaiming with a loud voice, **"Who is worthy to open the book and to break its seals?"** And no one in heaven or on the earth or under the earth was able to open the book or to look into it. **Then I began to weep greatly because no one was found worthy to open the book or to look into it**; and one of the elders said to me, **"Stop weeping; behold, the Lion that is from the tribe of Judah, the Root of David, has overcome so as to open the book and its seven seals."***

*"Worthy are You to take the book **and to break its seals**; for You*

were slain, and purchased for God with Your blood men from every
tribe and tongue and people and nation.
You have made them to be a kingdom and priests to our God; and
they will reign upon the earth.*"*

Revelation 5:1-5, 9-10 (emphasis added)

The destiny of mankind is to be gloriously transformed into beings of light, shedding our mortality, then to be joined to Yeshua as His Bride, ruling and reigning as kings and priests at His side for eternity. Contained in the pages of the book is the completion of that story and Yeshua is the only one worthy to open it and make it come true.

All the way back in the garden, Yahweh blessed Adam and said,

"God blessed them; and God said to them, "Be fruitful and multiply, and fill the earth, and **subdue it; and rule over** *the fish of the sea and over the birds of the sky and over every living thing that moves on the earth.""*

Genesis 1:28 (emphasis added)

The charge was to take dominion of the creation and rule over it. Adam gave that right away to the serpent entity, and Yeshua legally bought it back. The kingdoms that the adversary used man to build, the cities, the city-states, the empires, and their religious systems, need to be toppled until only one kingdom remains.

"In the days of those kings **the God of heaven will set up a kingdom which will never be destroyed,** *and that kingdom will not be left for another people;* **it will crush and put an end to all these kingdoms,** *but it will itself endure forever. Inasmuch as you saw that*

a stone was cut out of the mountain without hands and that it **crushed the iron, the bronze, the clay, the silver and the gold**, *the great God has made known to the king what will take place in the future;"*

Daniel 2:44-45 (emphasis added)

As we have learned, The Stone, the *eben* (Father and Son as one), Yeshua, is the only one worthy to open the book and its seven seals and unleash the destiny of mankind. Yeshua is the Stone that will crush all the governments of the nations. He will use His Four Horsemen to accomplish this.

The Four Horsemen are revealed in the opening of the first four seals. So, in essence the one who sends the Four Horsemen is Yeshua, He opens the seals.

There is excitement and anticipation as we have waited almost two thousand years for the opening of the Book, but this is a bittersweet. The opening of the seals first brings conflicts and wars. It brings famine and disease, and much death. It begins a great march that ends in the fall of the nations and governments of this world. This is called the judgement of the nations, and it is necessary.

The opening of the seals are also signs for those who have eyes to see and ears to hear, those who are spiritually in-tune with heaven's plans. It also creates a timeline which we can watch unfold, a countdown for the return of Yeshua to the Earth. When the events of the Four Horsemen begin, there is no going back, the clock is now ticking.

Yeshua compares it to a woman who goes into labor, there is great joy and anticipation for the child that is coming but first will come pain and hard labor. When the labor begins, it must be followed through to the end.

*"You will be hearing of wars and rumors of wars. See that you are not frightened, for those things must take place, but that is not yet the end. For nation will rise against nation, and kingdom against kingdom, and in various places there will be famines and earthquakes. **But all these things are merely the beginning of birth pangs.**"*

Matthew 24:6-8 (emphasis added)

The mission of every believer in Yeshua is to share His message with those around you. We are to speak of His shelter from the storm, our invitation to become a part of His Kingdom, and His eminent return to receive us to Himself.

*"This gospel of the kingdom shall be preached in the whole world as a testimony to all the nations, **and then the end will come.**"*

Matthew 24:14 (emphasis added)

The end will come! The end of human governance by wicked rulers, the end of corrupt agendas to enslave mankind into a rigged system that serves the elite, the few, those who wish to dominate the rest. The end of pain and suffering caused by each of our own fallen natures and selfish ambitions.

We must strive to remember that the end leads to a new beginning, different from anything we know.

…But for now, it is the beginning of the end.

Chapter 12 - The Final Ride of the Four Horsemen, the Assembling of the Nations

" 'Therefore wait for Me' declares the LORD,
'For the day when I rise up as a witness.
Indeed, My decision is to gather nations,
To assemble kingdoms,
To pour out on them My indignation,
All My burning anger;
For all the earth will be devoured
By the fire of My zeal.' "

Zephaniah 3:8 (emphasis added)

The question to ask is when does, or did, the "final" gathering of nations begin? …and what do the Four Horsemen have to do with it?

Centralizing power must begin with taking power away from individual people or governments or at least convincing them that joining together would be better than remaining independent. There would, by necessity, need to be "a cause" for the independent countries to rally around. Conflict or war provides the necessary motivation. If someone goes to war with your neighbor, you would be wise to ally with one or the other, and probably the one you were most convinced would win. International politics is much the same way; you may not like your neighbor…but what is the alternative?

The first step in gathering all the nations together would be to break independent national allegiances. This is the job of the White Horseman. He is the war horse, but the conflict would need to be on a global scale, a world war. What would catapult the modern world into war? Could it be the success of the United States of America?

The United States Constitution and its system of justice, its guaranteed personal and religious freedoms, and its entrepreneurially driven markets and financial successes made the US extremely attractive to other nations of the world. The rise in consumption and wealth in the United States has driven nations to want to participate in trade negotiations. Changes in foreign governmental policies, therefore, became necessary in order to contract with US companies in commerce and trade agreements.

Capitalism became an ideology of the new world, and also gave birth to joining the world markets together. International commerce was not a new idea. For centuries merchants had traded by land and sea, but the pathway to forming multi-national companies had gained new potential. With new technologies like railroads, gas combustion engines, and air travel, import and export became much easier and allowed for the quick expansion of markets.

The formation of large industrial operations gave unprecedented power and wealth to these corporations, sometimes even rivaling that of their own governments. This did not bode well with all the people of the nations. A counter-revolution rose up against capitalism and the free market system. These other nations were reluctant to trust in a new global system.

Workers who were employed by these large industrial complexes were becoming restless. They viewed with skepticism these new Oligarchs who built their businesses on the backs of the common people. An ideology arose that fueled this distrust into a revolution called Marxism.

The Countermove, Marxism

For the White Horse to start its mission, the Red Horse of ideological conflict needed to ride in to foster "the cause." The opposing ideology was Socialist Communism. Communism was birthed out of the Russian Revolutions of 1905 and 1917, but the ideology emerged fifty years earlier out of Prussia (Germany). Its brainchild was a Jewish philosopher named Karl Marx.

"Marx became interested in the recently deceased German philosopher Georg Wilhelm Friedrich Hegel, whose ideas were then widely debated among European philosophical circles. During a convalescence in Stralau, he joined the Doctor's Club (Doktorklub), a student group which discussed Hegelian ideas, and through them, became involved with a group of radical thinkers known as the Young Hegelians in 1837.

Like Marx, the Young Hegelians were critical of Hegel's metaphysical assumptions but adopted his dialectical method to criticize established society, politics and religion from a left-wing perspective.

Marx was considering an academic career, but this path was barred by the government's growing opposition to classical liberalism and the Young Hegelians.

On 28 August 1844, Marx met the German socialist Friedrich Engels at the Café de la Régence, beginning a lifelong friendship. Engels showed Marx his recently published "The Condition of the Working Class in England," in 1844, convincing Marx that the working class [known as the proletariat] would be the agent and instrument of the final revolution in history.

In collaboration with Engels, Marx also set about writing a book which is often seen as his best treatment of the concept of historical materialism, called The German Ideology. Like so many other early writings of his, German Ideology would not be published in Marx's lifetime and would be published only in 1932.

These books laid the foundation for Marx and Engels's most famous work, a political pamphlet that has since come to be commonly known as The Communist Manifesto. While residing in Brussels in 1846, Marx continued his association with the secret radical organization, League of the Just. Both Marx and Engels participated in drawing up the program and organizational principles of the new Communist League.

Proceeding on from this, the Manifesto presents the argument for why the Communist League, as opposed to other socialist and liberal political parties and groups at the time, was truly acting in the interests of the proletariat [the working class] to overthrow capitalist society and to replace it with socialism."[128]

"The Marx–Engels Institute was established in 1919 by the government of Soviet Russia as a branch of the Communist Academy, intended as an academic research facility to conduct historical studies and to collect documents deemed relevant to the new socialist regime."

"The Marx–Engels institute was later attached to the governing Central Committee of the Communist Party of the Soviet Union and served as a research center and publishing house for officially published works of Marxist thought. From 1956 to 1991, the institute was named the Institute of Marxism–Leninism (IML)."[129]

Communism/Socialism was a reaction to the growing wealth and power of the industrial revolution. With the expansion of railroads and the invention of automobiles, large industries like the steel and oil industries were amassing great wealth and influence. Every new technology and invention brought new potential for extracting the wealth of the common people, the "retail customer".

Marx saw this as an unfair advantage that enslaved workers to the wealthy class. His new message was "workers revolt". Rather than seeing this new influx of goods and services as beneficial to the world, it was viewed as a threat. Yet, there was a darker agenda to Marx's ideology. Marx was an avowed atheist. In a book titled "The Devil and Karl Marx" written by Paul Kengor, Paul states:

"Marx portrayed himself as chosen for hell, or chose hell for himself; in still other cases, he, in the role of the master of hell, consigned others to it.

"Thus Heaven, I've forfeited. I know it full well," wrote Marx in an 1837 poem, one of many explored in the pages ahead. "My soul, once true to God, is chosen for Hell." That certainly seemed the perverse destiny for Marx's ideology. That statement also seems at least partly autobiographical, given that Marx, once a believer, once a Christian, had once been true to God. In another poem, Marx wrote, "The hellish vapors rise and fill the brain, Till I go mad and my heart is utterly changed. See the sword – the Prince of Darkness sold it to me." Here, too, seems an ironic metaphor for the bloody sword of communist ideology, surely favored if not wielded by the Prince of Darkness. And it, too, seems partly autobiographical, given how Marx's own heart had been utterly changed."[130]

Another quote from Kengor's book cites author Stephane Courtois' *The Black Book of Communism,* in which he states:

"Communism committed a multitude of crimes not only against individual human beings but also against world civilizations and national cultures.

In 1999, *The Black Book of Communism* endeavored to attempt the impossible task of tabulating a Marxist-Leninist death toll in the twentieth century. It came up with a figure approaching 100 million. Here is the breakdown:

- USSR: 20 million deaths

- China: 65 million deaths

- Vietnam: 1 million deaths

- North Korea: 2 million deaths

- Cambodia: 2 million deaths

- Eastern Europe: 1 million deaths

- Latin America: 150,000 deaths

- Africa: 1.7 million deaths

- Afghanistan: 1.5 million deaths

- The international communist movement and Communist parties not in power: about 10,000 deaths."[130]

Remember, the Red Horse was given a "great sword" to take peace from the earth. This is clearly seen in the number of deaths/murders wherever this hideous ideology is implemented. Mentioned in this list are the atrocities of communist China starting under the dictatorship of Mao Zedong.

In a book by Michael Pillsbury, "The Hundred-Year Marathon," he makes a case for the long game China has been playing to achieve world domination.

"As President Xi Jinping took office in March 2013, China watchers in America did not yet know what to make of him. China's hawks admired him, but the prevailing sentiment among Western observers was that Xi, a rather harmless-looking man of sixty with thick black hair and a genial smile, was a Gorbachev-like reformer intent on displacing China's old guard and finally realizing these observers' long-held conviction that China would become the free market–style democracy of their dreams. But Xi soon demonstrated that he had a dream of his own—one of a resurgent China that would reclaim its rightful place atop the global hierarchy. This has been a Communist Party ambition since Mao took power in 1949, the date commonly understood by China's leaders as the beginning of the Hundred-Year Marathon."[131]

One can make the case that a hundred-year marathon of the Nations actually began in 1917 when The Bolshevik revolution toppled Russia's government and established the first communist government. Marxist-Leninist philosophy was translated and introduced in China as early as 1900,

"Marxist philosophy was initially imported into China between 1900 and 1930, in translations from German, Russian, and Japanese. The Chinese translator of the Origin of Species, Ma Junwu, was also the first one to introduce Marxism into China. For Ma, evolutionism and Marxism are the secrets of social development. This was before the formal dialectical materialism of the Chinese Communist Party, in which many independent radical intellectuals embraced Marxism. Many of them later joined the Party."[132]

The clash of these two strong ideologies, Marxism/Communism and Capitalism/Democracy, came to a boiling point in 1917, during WWI. The Russian Revolution marked the beginning of the end of the war for Russia. The Russian army was now in a state of chaos, forcing its new leader, Vladimir Lenin, to sign a peace treaty with Germany in March 1918 and eventually with Poland in March 1921.[133]

The First Seal is Broken

*"**Then I saw when the Lamb broke one of the seven seals**, and I heard one of the four living creatures saying as with a voice of thunder, 'Come.' I looked, **and behold, a white horse**, and he who sat on it had a bow; and a crown was given to him, and he went out conquering and to conquer."*

Revelation 6:1-2 (emphasis added)

The final mission of the White Horse was to crush all the independent nations and gather them together under one global governance. I believe this is the breaking of the first seal. This purpose is understood in the scripture quoted earlier,

"My decision is to gather nations, To assemble kingdoms."

Zephaniah 3:8

This is Yahweh's decision, not a man's. In another place, He says,

"I will gather all the nations
And bring them down to the valley of Jehoshaphat.
Then I will enter into judgment with them there
On behalf of My people and My inheritance, Israel,
Whom they have scattered among the nations;
And they have divided up My land."

Joel 3:2

The gathering of the nations is for the purpose of final judgment, and the crushing of independence from Yahweh because the nations of the world stand in rebellion to Yahweh's land and his people and the given destiny of mankind. It was also prophesied in Daniel 7,

*"...the four winds of heaven [**the Four Horsemen**] were stirring up the great sea. And four great beasts were coming up from the sea, different from one another."*

*"The fourth beast [the final beast] will be a fourth kingdom on the earth, which will be different from all the other kingdoms **and will devour the whole earth and tread it down and crush it**."*

Daniel 7:2-3, 23 (emphasis added, brackets added for clarity)

The four winds of heaven are the ones who stir up the people of the nations and their governments; as I have discussed, these four winds are the Four Horsemen.

The world was marching to the beat of its own music, rushing headlong into building a unified society through trade and commerce that satisfies their hunger for material gain, prosperity, dominance, and complete sovereignty from God, and declaring in a sense, "we want to live as gods."

Even mainstream Christianity is living the Laodicean dream (Rev 3:17), to be rich and increased with goods, having need of nothing, yet Yeshua said they are wretched, miserable, poor, blind, and naked!

The Four Horsemen are influencing an outcome to a condition already existing among the nations, which is their selfish drive toward an unattainable Utopia.

Time was up, is up, but it would prove to be one hundred plus year march to completion. It would take two (or three) world wars wrangled in ideological conflict, and a future series of economic collapses to crush the independence of the nations, and a series of amazing technological advances coming upon the world in rapid succession.

These jolts from one change upon another are forced upon the people, by the terror of disease, rumors of biological warfare, the fear of pandemics and lockdowns, and ruthless acts of chaotic violence. Add to that list the numerous economic crisis and crashes of the last century. The masses are systematically thrown into chaos, weakened, and made ready for more change. Emerging from the final chaos will be a New World Order, which I describe as the world giving birth to an ancient dark entity, whose original purpose from the beginning was world domination.

This is an Anti-Christ, an imposter of Messiah, seeking to take-over the world with a kingdom of darkness. This is the ancient entity we saw in the Garden of Eden: Satan and the fallen ones, and their evil offspring.

We, as believers in the True Messiah, have been watching as these dark forces have infiltrated every form of government. They seek to seduce the world into alignment with their nefarious agenda, but they will only be allowed to go so far.

The woman of Revelation 12 is pregnant with a manchild that will bring true hope and change. She holds our destiny, and her Child will rule the world. Yeshua compares to these last events to a woman in labor.

> *"For <u>nation will rise against nation</u>, and <u>kingdom against kingdom</u>, and in various places there will be famines and earthquakes. **But all these things are merely the beginning of birth pangs.**"*
>
> *Matthew 24:7-8* (emphasis and underline added)

Whether we like it or not, the "times of the gentiles [the nations]" are coming to an end, while at the same time the nation of Israel and the city of Jerusalem are being restored (not without conflict). The White Horseman is charged with making both objectives a reality. The second of these two goals began with the release of the land of Palestine (Israel) from Ottoman control through war and to encourage the nations to allow for the restoration of the Jewish people back to their homeland.

Achieving these two objectives was going to take a longer process, not a short war. Like a woman ready to give birth, the "birth pangs" would signal the beginning of that process. There are a number of steps necessary to rearrange the geopolitics of the world and gather the nations together under one governing power, but the beginning is noteworthy.

I believe 1912 - 1917 marks the beginning of the breaking of the first seal on the great scroll in Revelation. The apex event was the First World War (WWI).

One of the outcomes of WWI was the fall of the Ottoman Empire. The Ottoman Empire held control over the land of Israel or Palestine for 401 years. Toward the end of the war, on January 10, 1920, the victorious allied powers formed an international cooperation called the League of Nations. This unified and allied organization would begin the official effort to unite the nations as discussed in the Encyclopedia Brittanica article, League of Nations.

"The central, basic idea of the movement was that aggressive war is a crime not only against the immediate victim but against the whole human community. Its creation was an event of decisive importance in the history of international relations. The League was formally disbanded on April 19, 1946; its powers and functions had been transferred to the nascent United Nations."[134]

So now, two objectives were achieved: the pathway for Israel to become a nation again and the beginning of a unified world governance. This is the breaking of the first seal!

"Another 19th-century development which had influenced the plan makers was the growth of international bureaus, such as the Universal Postal Union, the International Institute of Agriculture, and numerous others, set up to deal with particular fields of work in which international cooperation was plainly essential. They had no political function or influence, but within their very narrow limits they worked efficiently. It was concluded that wider fields of social and economic life, in which each passing year made international cooperation more and more necessary, might, with advantage, be entrusted to similar international administrative institutions.

Such ideas were strengthened by the fact that, during the war, joint Allied commissions controlling trade, shipping, and procurement of raw materials had gradually developed into powerful and effective administrative bodies. Planners questioned whether these entities, admitting first the neutrals and later the enemy states into their councils, could become worldwide centers of cooperation in their respective fields."[135]

The interesting aspect of these international agencies is that decisions were, and still are, being made by unelected officials which shields them from accountability to the common people of the world. They operate behind the scenes, far removed from democratic processes.

Current groups like the World Economic Forum (WEF), the World Health Organization (WHO), and the World Trade Organization (WTO) are examples of thought leaders and international policymakers that affect all of our lives yet have no accountability to any of us. We are left to assume that they have our best interests at heart and, of course, no ulterior motives. The reality is that these types of groups each play a role in an agenda of world domination under a centralized world governance that will prove to be disastrous in many ways.

The Rise of the Nation of Israel

A long-awaited prophetic event emerges on the world scene. The world authorities moved to create a Jewish nation, or better said, allow them to return to their original homeland. A series of events took place that led to a pathway of independence.

"Immediately following their declaration of war on the Ottoman Empire in November 1914, the British War Cabinet began to consider the future of Palestine; within two months, a memorandum was circulated to the Cabinet by a Zionist Cabinet member, Herbert Samuel, proposing the support of Zionist ambitions in order to enlist the support of Jews in the wider war."[136]

Through a decision by the League of Nations, Brittian was given a mandate to provide administration for the territories of Palestine and Transjordan. The British mandate for Palestine inspired the issuing of the Balfour Declaration.

"The Balfour Declaration was a public statement issued by the British Government in 1917 during the First World War announcing its support for the establishment of a "national home for the Jewish people" in Palestine, then an Ottoman region with a small minority Jewish population. The declaration was contained in a letter dated 2 November 1917 from the United Kingdom's Foreign Secretary Arthur Balfour to Lord Rothschild, a leader of the British Jewish community, for transmission to the Zionist Federation of Great Britain and Ireland. The text of the declaration was published in the press on 9 November 1917."[137]

The Balfour Declaration opened the door and began a thirty-year

Zionist march to Israel's statehood. After 2000 years, the Jewish people were given a national identity and began resettling in their own land. It culminated with the establishment of Israel as an independent nation on May 14th, 1948.

What About China, You Ask?

After the fall of its last dynasty, China has gone through a number of transformations along the way, bringing it to its last identity as a communist ruled country.

"In 1912, after over two thousand years of imperial rule, a republic was established to replace the monarchy. The Qing dynasty that preceded the republic experienced instability throughout the 19th century and suffered from both internal rebellion and foreign imperialism. A program of institutional reform proved too little and too late. Only the lack of an alternative regime prolonged the monarchy's existence until 1912."[138]

China experimented with a republic democracy for a few decades as other ruling nations in the world attempted to influence its progressive new leadership. One nation that attempted to take advantage of China's fragile new government was Japan.

"A republic was formally established on 1 January 1912 following the Xinhai Revolution, which itself began with the Wuchang uprising on 10 October 1911, successfully overthrowing the Qing dynasty and ending over two thousand years of imperial rule in China. From its founding until 1949, the republic was based in mainland China. Central authority waxed and waned in response to warlordism (1915–1928), a Japanese invasion (1937–1945), and a full-scale civil war (1927–1949), with central authority strongest during the Nanjing Decade (1927–1937), when most of China came under the control of the authoritarian, one-party military dictatorship of the Kuomintang (KMT)."[139]

China is officially known today as the People's Republic of China and its ruling government is the CCP, Chinese Communist Party.

Japan has emerged as a constitutional monarchy with a parliamentary government. Prime Minister Yoshihiko Noda, leader of the Democratic Party of Japan, derives his authority to govern from the [Japan's] constitution.[140]

Taiwan Remains a Democratic Republic

Another Democratic ally in the Pacific region is Taiwan. The history of Taiwan is interesting. Taiwan was taken as part of the conquests of Japan before WWII. China retook Taiwan after the war, but it became home to China's ousted government in 1949.

"In 1945, at the end of World War II, the Empire of Japan surrendered control of Taiwan and its island groups to the Allies, and Taiwan was placed under the Republic of China's administrative control. The communist takeover of mainland China in 1949, after the Chinese Civil War, left the ruling Kuomintang [KMT] with control over only Taiwan, Penghu, Kinmen, Matsu, and other minor islands. With the loss of the mainland, the ROC [Republic of China] government retreated to Taiwan, and the KMT declared Taipei the provisional capital. Meanwhile, the CCP [Chinese Communist Party] took over all of mainland China and founded the People's Republic of China (PRC) in Beijing."[141]

China is currently considering taking control of Taiwan again and pulling it into its communist grasp. There is continuing tension between the United States and China over Taiwan. "Taiwan is a key U.S. partner in the Indo-Pacific. Though the United States does not have diplomatic relations with Taiwan, we have a robust unofficial relationship."[142]

The Global Shift of 1917

I would like to explain the critical nature and prophetic implications of the timing of this global shift. There are important global changes in several key areas that occurred in the world from 1912-1918, events that changed the course of history. Like the moving of pieces on a game board, national governments and long-vested power structures at national levels began to crumble.

During this time, the world experienced the fall of China's last imperial dynasty, the collapse of Russia's Czar ruling class, Japan's meteoric rise to power, and the fall of the Ottoman Empire. There were major revolutions in Russia, Mexico, and China. These revolutions created completely new political and or military structures in their respective countries.

Much of Europe was drawn into the First World War, and eventually, the United States entered the war. The devastation after the First World War left Germany, Austria, Poland, Russia, and France in desperate ruin, with a death toll of over 8-10 million from both sides.

Here are some of the changes that occurred from 1912 to 1918 in world geopolitics, at a glance:[143, 144]

- **China's dynastic period ends**. The overthrow of the Qing Dynasty marked the end of over two thousand years of imperial rule in China. On **January 1, 1912,** following the Xinhai Revolution, the **Republic of China (ROC)** was established until the communist takeover of mainland China in 1949 by the CCP (Chinese Communist Party).

- **<u>Japan gains an international reputation</u>** with its victory in the **Russo-Japanese War** in 1905. Japan sought to further consolidate its position in China by presenting the **Twenty-One Demands** to Chinese President Yuan Shikai in **January 1915**.

- **<u>The Mexican Revolution – June 18, 1914</u>**. The Mexican Revolution was an extended sequence of armed regional conflicts in Mexico from 20 November 1910 to 1 December 1920. It has been called **"the defining event of modern Mexican history".** It resulted in the destruction of the Federal Army and its replacement by a revolutionary army, and the transformation of Mexican culture and government.

- **<u>The event that started WWI</u>** - **June 28th, 1914**, the assassination of Archduke Franz Ferdinand of Austria, triggering the July Crisis, a series of interrelated diplomatic and military escalations among the major powers of Europe, beginning **on July 28, 1914,**

- <u>World War I</u> officially began on **August 1st, 1914,**

  - **The German Empire declares war on the Russian Empire**, following Russia's military mobilization in support of Serbia; Germany also begins mobilization.

  - **France orders general mobilization** - August 23rd, 1914.

  - **Japan declares war on Germany** – September 1914.

- **Turkey and South Africa declare war on Germany** – September 1914.

- **Canada sends troops to Europe** - October of 1914.

- **Russia, France, and Britain declared war on the Ottoman Empire on November 5, 1914,** after Ottoman warships shelled a Russian Black Sea port. Ottoman Sultan Mehmed V proclaimed holy war in the 1914 Ottoman Jihad Proclamation.

- <u>**The Bolshevik Revolution**</u> topples the 370-year rule of Russian Czars and creates a new form of government, the communist Soviet Union on **November 7, 1917**.

The evidence of the White Horseman riding is found all over the world at this point. It is by far the largest series of conflicts the modern world has ever seen in size and scope. The crushing of nations becomes obvious as we look back on the outcomes of these battles. Crushing does not mean total annihilation; it means destroying the old systems while leaving their national identities intact - for a time. Future conflicts will challenge the identity of these national cultures and seek to unify the world under a new identity as global citizens of a new world order.

The Second Seal is Broken

*"**When He broke the second seal**, I heard the second living creature saying, 'Come.' And another, **a red horse**, went out; and to him who sat on it, it was granted to take peace from the earth, and that men would slay one another; and a great sword was given to him."*

Revelation 6:3-4 (emphasis added)

The fall of long-standing empirical dynasties opened the door for ideological shifts. This usually begins with the unrest of the people living under their auspices. We discovered that the "stirring of the waters," a phrase taken from Daniel chapter 7, describes the agitation of the common people. Agitation can lead to revolts, which can, in turn, lead to revolutions. We have already learned that the Four Winds are the Four Horsemen. The specific Horseman responsible for stirring up the ideological waters is the Red Horseman.

Each of the Horsemen works in conjunction with one another. Even though the White Horse is the war horse, the fuel for those conflicts comes from the Red Horseman. This is why the Red Horseman is seen possessing a great sword. His job is to take peace from the earth and to cause men to slay one another. This type of rage starts in the mind and goes deep into the heart of a man; this is where ideologies exist.

Deep in the core of a person are their true convictions and strongly held beliefs. When these beliefs are challenged, some men will resort to giving up their lives for their convictions. Other men are moved to create or demand change from the ones holding power over them; they revolt. Whether it is against a government leader or a business owner, a rich sovereign or even a demanding neighbor, men will revolt when pushed too far.

Listed below are critical ideological shifts that were taking place at the same time governments were falling.:

- **Communism/Socialism** spread throughout the world with the revolution of the Bolsheviks in Russia in 1917. Even democratic countries, like the United States, were experiencing the rise of splinter groups of Marxism and Communism.

- **Fascist Ideology rises in Germany and Italy** after WWI as an alternative to Democratic Republics and Communism, led by Adolf Hitler in Germany and Benito Mussolini in Italy. Japan was still ruled by an emperor until after WWII in 1947.

- Economic and political turmoil in the 1920s, including the Great Depression, led to the rise of **militarism, nationalism, statism, and totalitarianism**. This ideological shift eventually culminated in Japan joining the Axis alliance in WWII with Nazi Germany and Fascist Italy.

- **China enters into a feudal system of warlords** after the fall of their last dynasty, the Qing Dynasty, in 1905, which lasted for almost fifty years. The Republic of China was established in 1912 but struggled to maintain control of the country.

- In 1917-1920 WWI influenced **Suffrage Movement's** successes, eventually giving rise to the ideology of the modern feminist movement. On May 21, 1919, the House again passes what would become the 19th Amendment, popularly known as the Susan B. Anthony Amendment. The Senate would follow suit, and the 19th Amendment was finally passed on June 4, 1919. [145]

- I call this last category **radical social upheavals.** These are marked by strong and sudden shifts in social behavior, followed by the legalization of acts that were previously morally unacceptable, and unlawful. Although this is not new to human behavior, radical shifts are like stress fractures that reveal a deeper moral decline. These cracks became more noticeable in the West in the roaring 20s and into the 30s, brought on by war and the years of alcohol prohibition, organized crime became deeply rooted in our cities.

  The two major signs of moral fraying were the rise of homosexuality and an increase in abortions. These have had the greatest effect on the decline of Western society.

  I could go on to mention the free love movement of the 1970s, or the drug culture of the 80s, the rise of terrorism starting in the 80s and continuing, the rise of atheism and the occult, the rise of radical feminism (not to be confused with women's rights), the rise of racism in the last twenty years, and the current gender identity wars. In all these social upheavals, we have seen the breakdown of the basic family as a unit. It is my opinion that we are being divided systematically so we can be conquered.

The great sword of the Red Horseman is unleashed. The clash of these ideologies are bringing the world to the brink of a deep internal conflict. The second seal is now broken open and we will look at the signs of the breaking of the third seal.

The Third Seal is Broken

*"**When He broke the third seal**, I heard the third living creature saying, 'Come.' I looked, and behold, **a black horse**; and he who sat on it had a pair of scales in his hand. And I heard something like a voice in the center of the four living creatures saying, 'A quart of wheat for a denarius, and three quarts of barley for a denarius; and do not damage the oil and the wine.'"*

Revelation 6:5-6 (emphasis added)

The world was experiencing the second industrial revolution in the early twentieth century. Industry was growing at a rapid pace and the world was racing to create industry to meet the new demands. New mechanical inventions in gas combustion engines created the automobile industry. Flight was achieved by the Wright Brothers in 1903, and a new aviation industry was created. Inventions like the radio, television, and advances in the telephone connected the world a little tighter. New industries were created to supply the growth of these new infrastructures.

International trade was already well established by the textile industry in the 1800s, but the war effort created new international trade. Two notable world financial organizations were instituted:

- The **Federal Trade Commission (FTC)** was formed **in 1914**. Its mission is the enforcement of civil (non-criminal) antitrust laws and the promotion of consumer protection.

- The **Federal Reserve Bank** of the United States officially opened for business in November **of 1914**. This began the rise of larger international banking systems to rival the already instituted Central Banks of Europe by the Rothschilds.

It All Came Crashing Down

The economic boom of the early twentieth century would be brought to its knees as the Black Horseman would start to ride during WW1. In the ten years following the war there would be four major financial disasters. The United States, the leading economic power in the world at the time, would be crippled by growing pains and a series of unusual financial setbacks. It started with the crash of the Wall Street Stock Market on November 21st, 1916, followed by another crash on November 3rd, 1919. Ten years later the Market experienced two, back to back crashes, one on October 3rd, 1929, and the granddaddy of them all on April 17th, 1930. This was the beginning of The Great Depression of the 1930s. These four stock market crashes are among the top ten worst crashes in history, and most of the other crashes occurred in the early 1900s.[158]

The Black Horseman was given a pair of scales and told to ration the grains but not to hurt the oil and wine. A fulfillment of this prophecy was seen when the Dust Bowl phenomena occurred in the 1930's.

The combined effects of World War I and the disruption caused by the Russian Revolution decreased the supply of wheat and other commodity crops in the world. This led to increased agricultural prices and this new demand encouraged farmers to dramatically increase cultivation.

The agricultural methods farmers favored during this period created the conditions for large-scale erosion under the current environmental conditions.

For example, the widespread conversion of land by deep plowing and other soil preparation methods eliminated the native grasses necessary to hold the soil in place. These grasses would have helped retain moisture during dry periods.

Furthermore, cotton farmers left fields bare during the winter, when winds in the High Plains are highest, and burned the stubble as a means to control weeds before planting, thereby depriving the soil of organic nutrients and surface vegetation.

"After fairly favorable climatic conditions in the 1920s with good rainfall and relatively moderate winters, which permitted increased settlement and cultivation in the Great Plains, the region entered an unusually dry era in the summer of 1930.

The drought dried the topsoil, and over time, it became friable, reduced to a powdery consistency in some places. Without indigenous grasses in place, the plains' high winds picked up the topsoil and created massive dust storms.

Dust worked its way into even the most sealed homes, leaving a coating on food, skin, and furniture. That winter (1934–35), red snow fell on New England.

On April 14, 1935, known as "Black Sunday," 20 of the worst "black blizzards" occurred across the entire sweep of the Great Plains, from Canada south to Texas."[146]

Here the Black Horse rider was told to cause a rationing (given a pair of scales) of the grain crops in the agricultural heartland in one of the wealthiest nations in the world, creating a shortage of grains and corn.

"Do not damage the oil and the wine." This limitation was also given to the Black Horseman. It is interesting to note that the oil production was not damaged during this time. As a matter of fact,

"…during the Great Depression, massive oil discoveries in Texas, alongside falling global demand for energy, sent oil prices tumbling downwards. As was reported in 1931, that not only caused investors in oil firms to suffer huge losses but also contributed to deflation around the world."[147]

We see from this report that "not hurting the oil" actually contributed to the economic downturn; perhaps this was the desired outcome. It also eventually increased the production of oil from the newly found oil reserves, which would be critical to the world economy in years to come.

"Not hurting the wine" is a little more complicated. In 1917, the United States Congress passed the Eighteenth Amendment that established the prohibition of alcohol in the US, and it was ratified by the requisite number of states on January 16, 1919. This ban on alcohol hurt the alcohol industry, including wine manufacturing and imports. This ban was effectively lifted on December 5th, 1933, by the passing of the twenty-first amendment by Congress, conclusively ending the nation's ban on the manufacture and distribution of alcohol.[148]

The lifting of the ban coincides with the riding of the Black Horse during the Great Depression. It is possible then, to perceive the lifting of the ban as the rider successfully restoring the wine.

The opening of the fourth seal, the riding of the Pale Horseman, marks only the beginning of his reign of terror; the same is the case of the other riders. Each Horseman begins an approximately one-hundred-year march, depending on when you mark the fifty year jubilee cycles, somewhere between 1917 - 1925, and 1967 - 1975, and 2017 - 2025.

These Horsemen scenarios are not one-time events but the beginning of multiple escalating events to achieve their objectives. They are clearly marked by their signature effects according to their horse's colors.

I do realize that other prophecy teachers have not considered this approach to the timing of the Apocalyptic Horsemen, and many if not most, believe they have not begun riding yet. That said, the evidence for their missions beginning in 1917 is overwhelming. Also, it does not mean that each of the Horsemen won't have a signature event that culminates in the end, a last hurrah if you will; it is likely they will.

The Fourth Seal is Broken

*"**When the Lamb broke the fourth seal**, I heard the voice of the fourth living creature saying, 'Come.' I looked, and behold, **an ashen horse**; and he who sat on it had the name Death; and Hades was following with him. Authority was given to them over a fourth of the earth, to kill with sword and with famine and with pestilence and by the wild beasts of the earth."*

Revelation 6:7-8 (emphasis added)

A Pandora's box was opened in 1918, known as the Spanish Flu or the Great Influenza; it was the beginning of an era of influenza-type viral infections. These deadly viruses affect the ability of a person to breathe; they literally constrict the airway and deprive them of life-giving oxygen. The Spirit of God breathes life into man; this spirit of death chokes the life out of a man. The latest strain of this deadly virus killed over 3.4 million people worldwide[149] and caused the entire world to be put in lockdown; it was the SARS CoV-2 Virus, aka COVID-19.

Health officials began a labeling sequence that is still used today. It recognizes three broad virus groups, influenza A, B, and C. Influenza A is the most common type, and H1N1 is a type of influenza A. The designation "H1N1" indicates unique traits, which exhibit characteristics that identify the virus to the immune system and allow for attachment and replication of the virus. The "H" (hemagglutinin) and the "N" (neuraminidases) are both proteins that are found on the outer shell or envelope of the virus. Different viruses have different hemagglutinin and neuraminidase proteins. There are 16 (H1 to H16) known types of hemagglutinin and 9 (N1 to N9) known types of neuraminidase, which gives 144 different possible combinations of these proteins."[150]

The "flu" is an acute viral infection of the respiratory tract known as influenza, from Latin influentia, "to flow into," in medieval times intangible fluid given off by stars was believed to affect humans. La influenza comes from Italian, meaning "visitation" or "influence." The Italian influenza referred to any disease outbreak thought to be influenced by stars. In 1743, what Italians called an influenza di catarro ("epidemic of catarro") spread across Europe, and the disease came to be known in English as simply "influenza."[151]

"The 1918–1920 flu pandemic, also known as The Great Influenza epidemic or by the common misnomer The Spanish flu, was an exceptionally deadly global influenza pandemic caused by the H1N1 influenza A virus. The earliest documented case was in March 1918 in the state of Kansas in the United States, with further cases recorded in France, Germany, and the United Kingdom in April. Two years later, nearly a third of the global population, or an estimated 500 million people, had been infected in four successive waves. Estimates of deaths range from 17 million to 50 million, and possibly as high as 100 million, making it one of the deadliest pandemics in history."[152]

The pale or ashen horse and rider is named "Death". Although the sword and famine are associated with this rider, the unique characteristic is death by pestilence and "by the wild beasts of the earth". If you combine these two last ideas you stumble upon the modern term, Zoonosis. As explained earlier, this type of pestilence or plague was discovered to have come from viruses found in animals.

These viruses then mutate, either by natural means or in a laboratory as a product of human engineering, and then become a deadly outbreak. The vehicle they have chosen to use is influenza.

This brings us back to what is called Gain-of-Function research, which is still going on today. This research has been weaponized since WWI and even more prolific in WWII. After WWI, governments of the world created agencies to study and research the use of viruses as biological weapons, including Russia, the UK, Germany, Japan, and the United States. This research led to dual-use technology, meaning technologies shared by science and the military.

Gain-of-Function laboratory research has been explained to the public as a means to prevent mass outbreaks and to get ahead of "the science". The reality is that there has been the inevitable "lab leak" or the mishandling of highly contagious engineered viruses and the sale of such on the black market, resulting in dangerous technologies in the hands of rogue elements of the world who are bent on destruction.

An even worse scenario is the possibility that certain elites of the world have decided to use these and other methods to depopulate the earth. Some people may not be willing to accept the idea that there are people out there who think this way. It is my view that the Pale Horseman ultimately decides when, where, and how this type of death will visit the world. He will use human agents to achieve his goal, but God is and always has been in control!

Technologies of the Global Shift

A final category added to the list of causes of the global shift of the early twentieth century is the advances in technology that occurred during this time. Each of the following technologies made the world much more war-ready than any previous time in history. Each of these coincidentally occurred during this time.

- **The first powered flight was achieved by the Wright brothers Dec 17th, 1903,** in their Kitty Hawk Flyer.

- **The 1905 launch of the HMS Dreadnought** sparks an arms race. The late nineteenth and early twentieth centuries were periods of rapid technological innovation. **The automobile, radio, and television were invented in 1886, 1901, and 1927, respectively,** and would each go on to change the course of history. But it was the launch of the British warship HMS Dreadnought that brought together a series of new technologies that sparked the first arms race of the twentieth century. The ship, a feat of naval engineering, featured twelve-inch guns, submerged torpedo tubes, and steam turbine engines, which had never been brought together before. A coinciding arms race on land produced long-range weapons, chemical gas, and difficult-to-reverse military mobilizations. This frenzied militarization among the world's most powerful countries ultimately helped provide the kindling for World War I.[153]

- **The Signal Corps of the United States Army established an Aviation Section,** giving definite status to its air service for the first time **in July of 1914.**

Other events of importance

- **The Exploration of Antarctica,** dubbed "the last frontier," begins. December 5, 1914, The Imperial Trans-Antarctic Expedition begins its attempt to make the first land crossing of Antarctica. The Imperial Trans-Antarctic Expedition of 1914–1917 is considered to be the last major expedition of the Heroic Age of Antarctic Exploration. Conceived by Sir Ernest Shackleton, the expedition was an attempt to make the first land crossing of the Antarctic continent. After Roald Amundsen's South Pole expedition in 1911, this crossing remained, in Shackleton's words, the "one great main object of Antarctic journeyings." Shackleton's expedition failed to accomplish this objective but became recognized instead as an epic feat of endurance. Shackleton had served in the Antarctic on the Discovery expedition of 1901–1904 and had led the Nimrod expedition of 1907–1909.

- **The Panama Canal is officially opened**, August 1914. The Panama Canal transforms U.S. and Global Economy.

What happened in 1912 – 1918 was just the beginning of the birth pangs. During the Great Depression of the 1930s, two important things were growing in the West: Zionism and Fascism. In the Far East, China was experiencing the rise of Communism under Mao Tse-Tung, and Imperialist Japan was ready to conquer the world. The East (Japan) and the West (Germany and much of Europe) would clash on multiple fronts, pulling the US into the war, in what we now know as

WWII. This brings us to the opening of the fifth seal of the great book.

There has been much written about WWII and what led up to the rise of dictators like Adolph Hitler, Italy's Benito Mussolini, and Japan's Emperor, Hirohito. The world was ripe for change, and Germany was desperate for a strong leader that would pull them out of the aftermath of WWI. On the heels of the great European crisis rose a man who promised change, but that change came with a great price.

The theme was a new world order, the promise of a utopian age of socialism, where everyone would be treated fairly and equally, and an era where peace could finally be achieved. This was far from true, especially if you were not willing to conform to their ideological mold. The Arian race had no tolerance for those who did not agree with them, especially the Jews.

The Fifth Seal is Broken

*"**When the Lamb broke the fifth seal, I saw underneath the altar the souls of those who had been slain because of the word of God, and because of the testimony which they had maintained**; and they cried out with a loud voice, saying, 'How long, O Lord, holy and true, will You refrain from judging and avenging our blood on those who dwell on the earth?' And there was given to each of them a white robe; and they were told that they should rest for a little while longer, until the number of their fellow servants and their brethren who were to be killed even as they had been, would be completed also."*

Revelation 6:9-11 (emphasis added)

The backdrop for the breaking of the fifth seal was a world poised for another major global shift. The world was not ready for a fascist leader, and they would not tolerate a totalitarian governance - yet. Any form of strong dominance would have to operate outside the bounds of "we the people" democracies that existed in major countries. Germany would ultimately test the resolve of its citizens and the rest of the world.

The German government in the 1930s entered into an era of lies and propaganda. At a time when the rest of the world was reeling from the great depression, The Nazi regime was willing to subjugate its citizens by convincing them that the government's intentions were to help create equality for all, but history would prove that that message could not have been farther from the truth.

The reality was that Hitler used the economic crisis to reshape

German society. He built a war machine and planned to dominate the world. This spirit of domination and subjugation was seen in every aspect of Hitler's rise to power. This spirit was dark and demonic. It exposed the insidious under-belly of what will eventually become the final beast. What was revealed was not the creation of a utopian society of peace and equality, but it revealed a much darker agenda. A world where the few ruled over the many. A society where the smarter and wealthier, those willing to join the rebellion against God, their creator, would try to crush all knowledge of God in His world.

Hitler's hatred for God's chosen people was made evident in his plans for a new society; tolerance was not an option. The primary targets for murder were the Jewish people, but other segments of society were also murdered and killed for their beliefs. The Christian Church in 1930's Germany was split on the issue of Nazism.

"In 1933, a group called the German Christians (Deutsche Christen) began to promote the Nazification of German Protestantism through the creation of a pro-Nazi "Reich Church." The German Christians wanted Protestantism to conform to Nazi ideology, and they pushed for the implementation of the state "Aryan laws" within the churches. The German Christians claimed that Jews, as a "separate race," could not become members of an "Aryan" German Church through baptism.

The ideological and theological extremism of the German Christians provoked a backlash among more moderate Protestants, leading to the formation of the Confessing Church in May 1934."[154]

The Confessing Church leaders and other sympathizers like

Dietrich Bonhoeffer were targeted as dissidents, and many were arrested.

Dietrich Bonhoeffer was a German Protestant theologian who became part of the resistance in Germany. His work brought to light the widespread antisemitism that exposed the Nazi's dark agenda and was permeating the churches. He was eventually arrested and executed in the Flossenbürg concentration camp on April 9, 1945.

"The first deportations of Berlin Jews to the east occurred on October 15, 1941. A few days later, Bonhoeffer and Friedrich Perels, a Confessing Church lawyer, wrote a memo giving details of the deportations. The memo was sent to foreign contacts as well as trusted German military officials in the hope that it might move them to action. Bonhoeffer also became peripherally involved in "Operation Seven," a plan to get Jews out of Germany by giving them papers as foreign agents. After the Gestapo uncovered the "Operation Seven" funds that had been sent abroad for the emigrants, Bonhoeffer and his brother-in-law Hans von Dohnanyi were arrested in April 1943."[155]

Nazi Germany committed mass murder on an unprecedented scale. Before and especially during World War II, the Nazi German regime perpetrated the Holocaust and other mass atrocities. The death statistics lay bare the enormity of the Holocaust and other Nazi crimes. In total, six million Jewish men, women, and children were murdered by the Nazi German regime and its allies and collaborators. This figure does not include the estimated six million or more non-Jewish people that were also killed under the Nazi Regime.

The Nazi German regime created five killing centers specifically to murder Jewish people using poison gas. These killing centers were called Chełmno, Belzec, Sobibor, Treblinka, and Auschwitz-Birkenau. Approximately 2.7 million Jews were murdered at killing centers.

The Germans and their allies and collaborators carried out mass shooting operations and related massacres of Jews in more than 1,500 cities, towns, and villages across occupied Eastern Europe. About 2 million Jews were murdered in mass shooting operations and related massacres.

In ghettos, concentration camps, and labor camps created by the Germans and their allies and collaborators, Jews were murdered through deliberate privation, disease, brutal treatment, and arbitrary acts of violence. Between 800,000 and 1,000,000 Jews were murdered in ghettos, labor camps, and concentration camps.

The Germans and their allies and collaborators killed Jewish people in acts of violence and deprivation that took place outside of sites of detention (camps and ghettos). This includes Jews murdered in antisemitic riots, in individual executions, as partisans, and en route to and between sites of detention (on forced marches, trains, and ships). At least 250,000 Jews were murdered in other acts of violence outside of camps and ghettos.[156]

The world should not underestimate or forget the atrocities that occurred in Nazi Germany. I believe the bible records this horrific martyrdom revealed in the opening of the fifth seal,

*"... I saw **underneath the altar** the souls of those who had been*

*slain because of **the word of God,** and because of **the testimony which they had maintained**"*

Revelation 6:9 (emphasis added)

Many bible scholars have attributed this passage to the martyrdom of Christians in the last days. I believe a closer look at the details reveals a different group of people who became martyrs for their identity as Jews.

First, we find the souls of the martyrs are *"under the altar."* This reveals that these people are still in need of what is on the Altar; they have not been able to move past the Altar into the heavenly sanctuary. We know that there is only one true sacrifice on the heavenly Altar. It is the Lamb of God, Yeshua the Messiah.

The Jewish people (as a whole) have not yet accepted Yeshua as their Messiah, yet the mercy of God would not let their sacrifice go unnoticed. I am not suggesting that every Jewish person that was killed was a religious Jew. Even Christian martyrs start out as sinners saved by grace. Yet there is a place under the Altar for those who need to partake of the Altar. Those who have qualified as worthy by their confession, their testimony, as children of Abraham.

There are those Jews who hid their identity during WWII. I am certainly not here to shame them or anyone trying to avoid the Nazi regime's death camps. These souls under the Altar were slain "because of the Word of God." They believed in their identity, according to the Torah, as descendants of Abraham at a time when most of the Jewish people were exiled from their homeland and could have easily chosen to assimilate into the nations. Yet, they struggled to maintain their heritage in a world that often rejected them. Even many Christians viewed them with distain because their ancestors rejected Jesus. Yet, they "maintained" the testimony that they held as descendants of Abraham.

What I am suggesting is that God's anger does not last forever. David records this same sentiment in the Psalms.

> *"The LORD is compassionate and gracious,*
> *Slow to anger and abounding in lovingkindness.*
> *He will not always strive with us,*
> ***Nor will He keep His anger forever.***
> *He has not dealt with us according to our sins,*
> *Nor rewarded us according to our iniquities.*
> *For as high as the heavens are above the earth,*
> ***So great is His lovingkindness toward those who fear Him.***
> *As far as the east is from the west,*
> *So far has He removed our transgressions from us.*
> *Just as a father has compassion on his children,*
> ***So the LORD has compassion on those who fear Him."***

> *Psalms 103:8-13* (emphasis added)

He also spoke through the prophets that He would have compassion again and restore His people.

> ***"He does not retain His anger forever,***
> ***Because He delights in unchanging love.***
> *He will again have compassion on us;*
> *He will tread our iniquities under foot.*
> *Yes, You will cast all their sins*

Into the depths of the sea.

You will give truth to Jacob

And unchanging love to Abraham,

Which You swore to our forefathers

From the days of old."

Micah 7:18-20 (emphasis added)

And in another place,

"Thus says the LORD,

Who gives the sun for light by day

And the fixed order of the moon and the stars for light by night,

Who stirs up the sea so that its waves roar;

The LORD of hosts is His name:

"If this fixed order departs

From before Me," declares the LORD,

"Then the offspring of Israel also will cease

From being a nation before Me forever."

Jeremiah 31:35-36 (emphasis added)

This is only a sample of dozens of prophecies just like it where Yahweh reveals his plan to restore the people and nation of Israel. Yes, they do need to accept Yeshua in His way and in His time. Until then, some of them are "souls under the Altar."

The pathway to the restoration of Israel was already underway since the Balfour Declaration of 1917. The Holocaust was a difficult reminder that there was a new home for the Jewish people now.

Continuing to examine Revelation 6:10-11, We find another

identifying marker that points us to these martyrs being Jewish. They cry with a loud voice, saying, *"How long, O Lord, holy and true, will You refrain from judging and avenging our blood on those who dwell on the earth?"* This would not be the cry of true Christian martyrs.

The earliest records of Martyrs for Yeshua are recorded in the Book of Acts. The account of the first martyr starts with the stoning of Stephen in Acts chapter 7. Stephen's cry was not for vengeance on his persecutors, but for mercy.

*"They went on stoning Stephen as he called on the Lord and said, "Lord Jesus, receive my spirit!" Then falling on his knees, he cried out with a loud voice, **"Lord, do not hold this sin against them!"***

Acts 7:59-60 (emphasis added).

Stephen was responding in the spirit of Yeshua who Himself had a similar testimony.

The Gospels record some of Yeshua's final words as the Roman soldiers drive the nails into His hands and feet to a cross of wood,

*"When they came to the place called The Skull, there they crucified Him and the criminals, one on the right and the other on the left. But Jesus was saying, **"Father, forgive them; for they do not know what they are doing."***

Luke 23:33-34 (emphasis added)

This is the heart of Yeshua and His followers: to forgive them and not to lay the charge of their sins upon them. Why would they be crying out for vengeance as end time martyrs?

In contrast, the Torah reveals that a promise of vengeance would be uttered in the song of Moses and given to the physical descendants of Abraham.

"So Moses wrote this song the same day, and taught it to the sons of Israel."

"...I will render vengeance on My adversaries,

And I will repay those who hate Me.

Rejoice, O nations, with His people;

For He will avenge the blood of His servants,

And will render vengeance on His adversaries,

And will atone for His land and His people..."

Deuteronomy 31:22; 32:41,43 (emphasis added)

It is made clear in this passage that God intended for the descendants of Abraham to remember these words. Rightly so, the nations of the world have been persecuting the people of the nation of Israel since the exodus from Egypt and the book of Revelation ends with the battle of Armageddon, when the nations of the world try one last time to destroy God's people. We know how that ends!

Are you still not convinced? It states the "white robes were given to them." This reveals that they had not previously obtained "white robes." Every believer in Yeshua has already obtained a white robe when accepting the sacrifice of Yeshua as payment for their sins. The great multitude recorded in Revelation chapter 7 are already clothed in white robes. The angel told John that *"they have washed their robes in the blood of the Lamb. For this reason, they are before the Throne of God."*

In contrast, the souls under the Altar are not standing before the

Throne yet and they are "given" white robes after their deaths as martyrs. I am convinced that these are the Jewish martyrs from the Holocaust, they are told that,

*"they should rest for a little while longer, until the number of their fellow servants **and their brethren** who were to be killed even as they had been, would be completed also."*

Revelation 6:11 (emphasis added)

This also tracts with the idea that there will be other Jewish martyrs during the great tribulation. Perhaps, a time when the Church will be raptured from the earth and no longer here. Revelation 12:17 speaks of a group that is persecuted by the dragon in the last days who "keep the commandments of God and hold the testimony of Yeshua." Keeping the commandments of God is a clear reference to Torah-observant Jews, who also have received Yeshua as their Messiah. The dragon sets out to make war with them, suggesting there will be other Messianic Jewish martyrs.

The Sixth Seal

If this analysis is accurate so far, that would place us today, at the time of writing of this book, between the fifth and sixth seals. The Four Horsemen are still riding towards their respective mission goals. The birth pangs, now becoming contractions, are growing stronger and closer. With each news report, every day reveals a new cycle of events, like tremors, reverberating into the world. These tremors are becoming faster and faster, louder and louder, until the actual earthquake of the sixth seal will occur. We are literally watching prophecy unfold before our eyes.

The breaking of the sixth seal starts with a "great earthquake," but it seems that the events on Earth are preceded by a celestial event.

*"I looked **when He broke the sixth seal**, and **there was a great earthquake**; and **the sun became black** as sackcloth made of hair, and **the whole moon became like blood**; and **the stars of the sky fell to the earth**, as a fig tree casts its unripe figs when shaken by a great wind. **The sky was split apart like a scroll when it is rolled up, and every mountain and island were moved out of their places**.*

Revelation 6:12-14 (emphasis added

First the sky is split, then the earthquake happens. The result of the celestial event causes the sun to be blackened out and produces a red hue upon the moon, or perhaps this all happens during an event known as a *Blood Moon.*

Also, stars falling to the earth in a dramatic display can be explained as a cascade or shower of meteoric objects entering earth's atmosphere. This sounds like a comet or more likely an asteroid passing through the earth's atmosphere close enough to appear as the sky splitting and rolling up like a scroll, followed by smaller debris entering with it. If the object is large enough, the gravitational effect on Earth would cause the Earth to respond with seismic shifts or earthquakes. As the fault lines open in the oceans, great plumes of steam and gases would be released into the atmosphere blocking the sun for a period of time.

Small particles in orbit of the asteroid during the time it passes by would be cast down on the earth in an array of light and explosions. This is how I envision the opening of the sixth seal. It will be obvious to the whole world when it happens. It will also set in motion a crisis which would require a global response, a new world cooperation to manage the chaos. This event could likely begin the clock on a 7-year great tribulation and give reason for the final beast system to take control.

Such an event has been predicted by the late Dr. Thomas Horn, in his book titled The Wormwood Prophecy.[157] Horn suggests that an asteroid named Apophis, that was discovered by NASA, is headed toward us, and will pass by (or crash into) Earth in 2029. Horn states on page 26-27 of his book,

"…consider how is June 2004 astronomers at the Kitt Peak National Observatory detected a sizable asteroid heading in the direction of Earth. Subsequent efforts made later in 2004 by a team at the Siding Spring Survey in Australia identified the asteroid again. The next year, the team that discovered the asteroid named it Apophis (after the ancient Egyptian spirit of evil, darkness, and destruction, a malevolent force that cannot be stopped, according to the legend).

Immediately the possibility of a collision of the celestial body with our planet became the focus of calculation and preparation on behalf of prevention efforts across the world.

The enormous asteroid Apophis will reportedly pass disturbingly close to Earth on April 13, 2029, according to NASA's website. In fact, NASA admits Apophis in 2029 will be so close to Earth that it will "put some of our orbiting satellites in peril" and even be visible in the daytime sky."

This would fall in line with the idea that the Four Horsemen have already been riding and have broken the first four seals. The fifth seal was broken during WWII, with the Holocaust. We are watching and waiting for the breaking of the sixth seal!

As much as I would like to go on, to discuss this further would take us outside the scope of this work and will perhaps be the subject of a future work.

So far what we have discussed is the birth pangs of prophecy, the beginning of the end. The contractions are coming faster and harder. There will come a time, shortly I believe, when we will enter into what would figuratively be called "hard labor." Although the seals of the book have been opened as I see it, the Four Horsemen will also activate the "hard labor" event. We should be looking for their patterns just before the sixth seal cosmic event occurs.

Just as we know that labor pains bring something to birth. It's not a matter of if, but a matter of when, and that when, is on its way soon! I don't believe we are looking at decades before a great tribulation, but months, or maybe years. Hard labor is short and difficult, and it is the most painful part. Many theologians interpret it as a seven year period culminating in the return of Yeshua. During that time the world will change drastically, cities will fall, and two-thirds of the population will die (and/or vanish, i.e., the Rapture).

But the storm will eventually subside, and the sun will rise again, giving light to a brand new world.

> *Thus says the LORD,*
> *"Cursed is the man who trusts in mankind*
> *And makes flesh his strength,*
> *And whose heart turns away from the LORD.*
> *"For he will be like a bush in the desert*
> *And will not see when prosperity comes,*
> *But will live in stony wastes in the wilderness,*
> *A land of salt without inhabitant.*
>
> ***"Blessed is the man who trusts in the LORD***
> ***And whose trust is the LORD.***
> *"For he will be like a tree planted by the water,*
> *That extends its roots by a stream*
> *And will not fear when the heat comes;*
> *But its leaves will be green,*
> *And it will not be anxious in a year of drought*
> *Nor cease to yield fruit.*
>
> *Jeremiah 17:5-8* (emphasis added)

In Summary

As elusive as the four Horsemen are, there is much evidence placing them at the return of the Jewish people from Babylonian captivity as described by the prophet Zechariah. There are also many hidden references to their presence at various events in history. We have seen the numerous scriptural mentions of heavenly activity that mirror the same functions as the Horsemen. I believe this to be beyond coincidence.

As I have shown in this book, the Four Horsemen are the Four Winds and the Four Spirits, described in the Bible. This opens up much more insight into who they are, and what their purpose is. It is these same Four Winds that stir the great sea of people in the Daniel 7 prophecy and cause the metal empires to emerge, including the fourth and final beast empire that crushes all the others.

We have learned that they are Yahweh's elite military forces used to affect geopolitical changes on the earth. They answer the question of *how* Yahweh influences outcomes and directs the nations and their armies to carry out His purposes. As the supreme Commander-in-Chief, Yahweh has His own army and His policing forces: because righteousness in the world does not just happen, it must be managed and enforced, and even sometimes demanded by force!

We have seen that a necessary aspect of God's Law is a set of consequences for breaking those laws; these are called God's judgments. Some judgments are punishments and can be more immediate, while others are stored up and dealt with at a future time. These consequences are carried out by supernatural beings, who are sometimes called angels or heavenly hosts. Among these supernatural beings are the Four Horns, the Four Craftsmen, and the Four Horsemen.

We also learned that the Horsemen work through human agents to affect geopolitical changes. The colors of their horses reveal the aspects of their missions. They are sent to affect four key elements of human life, controlling world dominance through warfare, shifts in ideological beliefs, the balance of commerce and trade, and they use death and terror, or the fear of death itself. Once that becomes clear, it is easier to identify the presence of the Four Horsemen throughout human history.

When we compare history and the Bible, we are left to see a blend between the natural and supernatural worlds, explained like an intricate cosmic chess match. Bible prophecy explains that the rise and fall of the nations is at the heart of the matter. As the great Babylonian ruler said,

"But at the end of that period, I, Nebuchadnezzar, raised my eyes
toward heaven and my reason returned to me, and I blessed the
Most High and praised and honored Him who lives forever;
For His dominion is an everlasting dominion,
And His kingdom endures from generation to generation.
All the inhabitants of the earth are accounted as nothing,
But He does according to His will in the host of heaven
And among the inhabitants of earth;
And no one can ward off His hand
Or say to Him, 'What have You done?'"

Daniel 4:34-35

Yahweh will ultimately take back full control of the Earth. He will destroy those who destroy the Earth and will defeat the great city, Babylon, forever! His people will rule and reign with their Messiah, Yeshua, enthroned in the beautiful city of righteousness and truth, the Holy City of Jerusalem.

…but afterwards, will the Four Horsemen ride again?

References

1. *"Rearming for the Cold War, 1945-1960" | www.dau.edu. (n.d.). Retrieved February 18, 2024, from https://www.dau.edu/node/178541*

2. *Black Death - Causes, Symptoms & Impact | HISTORY. (n.d.). Retrieved February 18, 2024, from https://www.history.com/topics/middle-ages/black-death*

3. *Wind of Change (speech). (n.d.). Retrieved February 18, 2024, from https://dbpedia.org/page/Wind_of_Change_(speech)*

4. *Kamikaze of 1274 and 1281 | East Asia, Typhoons | Britannica. (n.d.). Retrieved February 18, 2024, from https://www.britannica.com/event/kamikaze-of-1274-and-1281*

5. *Geopolitics | Political Science, Global Relations & International Security | Britannica. (n.d.). Retrieved February 18, 2024, from https://www.britannica.com/topic/geopolitics.*

6. *Watcher (angel) - Wikipedia. (n.d.). Retrieved February 18, 2024, from https://en.wikipedia.org/wiki/Watcher_(angel)#cite_ref-30*

7. *Ibid*

8. *Gilbert, D. P. (2017). The Great Inception. Defender Publishing.*

9. *Heiser, M. S. (2015). The Unseen Realm: Recovering the Supernatural Worldview of the Bible. Lexham Press.*

10. *Gilbert, D. P. (2017). The Great Inception. Defender Publishing.*

11. *Tisha B'Av - Wikipedia. (n.d.). Retrieved February 18, 2024, from https://en.wikipedia.org/wiki/Tisha_B%27Av*

12. *Librado, P., Khan, N., Fages, A., Kusliy, M. A., Suchan, T., Tonasso-Calvière, L., Schiavinato, S., Alioglu, D., Fromentier, A., Perdereau, A., Aury, J. M., Gaunitz, C., Chauvey, L., Seguin-Orlando, A., der Sarkissian, C., Southon, J., Shapiro, B., Tishkin, A. A., Kovalev, A. A., ... Orlando, L. (2021). The origins and spread of domestic horses from the Western Eurasian steppes. Nature, 598(7882), 634–640. https://doi.org/10.1038/s41586-021-04018-9*

13. *Communist Party of the United States of America (CPUSA) | Britannica. (n.d.). Retrieved February 18, 2024, from https://www.britannica.com/topic/Communist-Party-of-the-United-States-of-America*

14. *The Black Book of Communism - Wikipedia. (n.d.). Retrieved February 18, 2024, from* https://en.wikipedia.org/wiki/The_Black_Book_of_Communism

15. *Dust Bowl - Wikipedia. (n.d.). Retrieved February 18, 2024, from* https://en.wikipedia.org/wiki/Dust_Bowl

16. *The Black Sunday Dust Storm of 14 April 1935. (n.d.). National Weather Service: Norman, Oklahoma Weather Forecast Office. Retrieved February 18, 2024, from* http://www.srh.noaa.gov/oun/?n=blacksunday

17. *Dust Bowl - Wikipedia. (n.d.). Retrieved February 18, 2024, from* https://en.wikipedia.org/wiki/Dust_Bowl

18. *World Oil Production | Nature. (n.d.). Retrieved February 18, 2024, from* https://www.nature.com/articles/132344d0

19. *Black Death - Causes, Symptoms & Impact | HISTORY. (n.d.). Retrieved February 18, 2024, from* https://www.history.com/topics/middle-ages/black-death

20. *Ibid*

21. *How the Black Death Spread Along the Silk Road | HISTORY. (n.d.). Retrieved February 18, 2024, from* https://www.history.com/news/silk-road-black-death

22. *History of 1918 Flu Pandemic | CDC Archive. (n.d.). Retrieved February 18, 2024, from* https://archive.cdc.gov/#/details?url=https://www.cdc.gov/flu/pandemic-resources/1918-commemoration/1918-pandemic-history.htm

23. *How 5 of History's Worst Pandemics Finally Ended | HISTORY. (n.d.). Retrieved February 18, 2024, from* https://www.history.com/news/pandemics-end-plague-cholera-black-death-smallpox

24. *The Urban Revolution on JSTOR. (n.d.). Retrieved February 18, 2024, from* https://www.jstor.org/stable/40102108

25. *History of cities - Wikipedia. (n.d.). Retrieved February 18, 2024, from* https://en.wikipedia.org/wiki/History_of_cities#cite_ref-12

26. *Ibid*

27. *Flood myth | Definition, Accounts, & Mythologies | Britannica. (n.d.). Retrieved February 18, 2024, from* https://www.britannica.com/topic/flood-myth

28. *The sixteen grandsons of Noah. (n.d.). Retrieved February 18, 2024, from* https://creation.com/the-sixteen-grandsons-of-noah

29. Schweid, Eliezer. (1985). *The land of Israel : national home or land of destiny*. 225.

30. Heiser, M. S. (2015). *The Unseen Realm: Recovering the Supernatural Worldview of the Bible* . Lexham Press.

31. *Ibid*

32. *Semiramis, Queen of Babylon*. (n.d.). Retrieved February 18, 2024, from https://www.ldolphin.org/semir.html

33. *Ancient chronology and the Old Testament: part 1*. (n.d.). Retrieved February 18, 2024, from https://creation.com/ot-ancient-chronology-1

34. *Babel | Etymology of the name Babel by etymonline*. (n.d.). Retrieved February 18, 2024, from https://www.etymonline.com/word/Babel

35. Gilbert, D. P. (2017). *The Great Inception*. Defender Publishing.

36. Johnson, K. Th. D. (2021). *Ancient Mysteries of the Essenes: the Ken Johnson Collection*. Defender Publishing.

37. *Second Temple - Wikipedia*. (n.d.). Retrieved February 18, 2024, from https://en.wikipedia.org/wiki/Second_Temple

38. *Foundation Stone - Wikipedia*. (n.d.). Retrieved February 18, 2024, from https://en.wikipedia.org/wiki/Foundation_Stone

39. *Midrash Tanchuma, Kedoshim 10:1*. (n.d.). Retrieved February 18, 2024, from https://www.sefaria.org/Midrash_Tanchuma%2C_Kedoshim.10.1?lang=bi

40. *Nun | The amazing name Nun: meaning and etymology*. (n.d.). Retrieved February 18, 2024, from https://www.abarim-publications.com/Meaning/Nun.html

41. *Eleazar | The amazing name Eleazar: meaning and etymology*. (n.d.). Retrieved February 18, 2024, from https://www.abarim-publications.com/Meaning/Eleazar.html

42. *Torah and Proto-Canaanite Hebrew Studies Class: 04/25/17*. (n.d.). Retrieved February 18, 2024, from https://shaunamanfredine.blogspot.com/2017_04_25_archive.html

43. Pinches, T. G. (1908). *The Old Testament: In the light of the Historical Records and Legends of Assyria and Babylonia*. Archived at The Way Back Machine, 324.

44. *Jebusites - Wikipedia*. (n.d.). Retrieved February 18, 2024, from https://en.wikipedia.org/wiki/Jebusites

45. *Ibid*

46. *Ibid*

47. *Babylon - Wikipedia. (n.d.). Retrieved February 18, 2024, from https://en.wikipedia.org/wiki/Babylon*

48. *List of Mesopotamian dynasties - Wikipedia. (n.d.). Retrieved February 18, 2024, from https://en.wikipedia.org/wiki/List_of_Mesopotamian_dynasties*

49. *Ken Johnson, Th. D. (2013). Ancient Book of Jasher: Vol. Chapter 8:1-4.*

50. *Babylon - Wikipedia. (n.d.). Retrieved February 18, 2024, from https://en.wikipedia.org/wiki/Babylon*

51. *Hammurabi - Wikipedia. (n.d.). Retrieved February 18, 2024, from https://en.wikipedia.org/wiki/Hammurabi*

52. *6 Early Human Civilizations | HISTORY. (n.d.). Retrieved February 18, 2024, from https://www.history.com/news/first-earliest-human-civilizations*

53. *Babylon - Wikipedia. (n.d.). Retrieved February 18, 2024, from https://en.wikipedia.org/wiki/Babylon*

54. *Battle of Carchemish - Wikipedia. (n.d.). Retrieved February 19, 2024, from https://en.wikipedia.org/wiki/Battle_of_Carchemish*

55. *Nebuchadnezzar Chronicle - Wikipedia. (n.d.). Retrieved February 18, 2024, from https://en.wikipedia.org/wiki/Nebuchadnezzar_Chronicle*

56. *Ibid*

57. *How the Black Death Spread Along the Silk Road | HISTORY. (n.d.). Retrieved February 18, 2024, from https://www.history.com/news/silk-road-black-death*

58. *Zoroastrianism - Wikipedia. (n.d.). Retrieved February 18, 2024, from https://en.wikipedia.org/wiki/Zoroastrianism*

59. *Elam - Wikipedia. (n.d.). Retrieved February 18, 2024, from https://en.wikipedia.org/wiki/Elam*

60. *Meet The Man Responsible For The Letter "J" - Dictionary.com. (n.d.). Retrieved May 10, 2024, from https://www.dictionary.com/e/j/*

61. *Nabonidus - Wikipedia. (n.d.). Retrieved February 18, 2024, from https://en.wikipedia.org/wiki/Nabonidus*

62. *Battle of Opis - Wikipedia. (n.d.). Retrieved February 18, 2024, from https://en.wikipedia.org/wiki/Battle_of_Opis*

63. *Alexander the Great - Wikipedia. (n.d.). Retrieved February 18, 2024, from https://en.wikipedia.org/wiki/Alexander_the_Great*

64. *Ibid*

65. *Alexander the Great as a God - World History Encyclopedia. (n.d.). Retrieved February 18, 2024, from https://www.worldhistory.org/article/925/alexander-the-great-as-a-god/*

66. *Ibid*

67. *Ibid*

68. *Ibid*

69. *Ibid*

70. *Ibid*

71. *Ajna - Wikipedia. (n.d.). Retrieved February 18, 2024, from https://en.wikipedia.org/wiki/Ajna*

72. *Ibid*

73. *Diadochi - Wikipedia. (n.d.). Retrieved February 18, 2024, from https://en.wikipedia.org/wiki/Diadochi*

74. *Antiochus IV Epiphanes - New World Encyclopedia. (n.d.). Retrieved February 18, 2024, from https://www.newworldencyclopedia.org/entry/Antiochus_IV_Epiphanes*

75. *Antiochus IV Epiphanes - Wikipedia. (n.d.). Retrieved February 18, 2024, from https://en.wikipedia.org/wiki/Antiochus_IV_Epiphanes*

76. *Ibid*

77. *Ibid*

78. *Ibid*

79. *Syrian Wars - Wikipedia. (n.d.). Retrieved February 18, 2024, from https://en.wikipedia.org/wiki/Syrian_Wars*

80. *Jason (High Priest) - Wikipedia. (n.d.). Retrieved February 18, 2024, from https://en.wikipedia.org/wiki/Jason_(High_Priest)*

81. *Ibid*

82. *Ibid*

83. *Ibid*

84. *Ibid*

85. *Antiochus IV Epiphanes - Wikipedia. (n.d.). Retrieved February 18, 2024, from https://en.wikipedia.org/wiki/Antiochus_IV_Epiphanes*

86. *Antiochus IV Epiphanes - New World Encyclopedia. (n.d.). Retrieved February 18, 2024, from https://www.newworldencyclopedia.org/entry/Antiochus_IV_Epiphanes*

87. *Ibid*

88. *Ibid*

89. *Maccabees - Wikipedia. (n.d.). Retrieved February 18, 2024, from https://en.wikipedia.org/wiki/Maccabees*

90. *Ibid*

91. *Ibid*

92. *Ibid*

93. *Ibid*

94. *Greece in the Roman era - Wikipedia. (n.d.). Retrieved February 18, 2024, from https://en.wikipedia.org/wiki/Greece_in_the_Roman_era*

95. *The Land of Israel Under Roman Rule | My Jewish Learning. (n.d.). Retrieved February 18, 2024, from https://www.myjewishlearning.com/article/palestine-under-roman-rule/*

96. *Greece in the Roman era - Wikipedia. (n.d.). Retrieved February 18, 2024, from https://en.wikipedia.org/wiki/Greece_in_the_Roman_era*

97. *The Antiquities of the Jews, by Flavius Josephus. (n.d.). Retrieved February 19, 2024, from https://www.gutenberg.org/files/2848/2848-h/2848-h.htm#link2HCH0006*

98. *The Land of Israel Under Roman Rule | My Jewish Learning. (n.d.). Retrieved February 18, 2024, from https://www.myjewishlearning.com/article/palestine-under-roman-rule/*

99. *Pharisees, Sadducees & Essenes. (n.d.). Retrieved February 19, 2024, from https://www.jewishvirtuallibrary.org/pharisees-sadducees-and-essenes*

100. *Essenes - Wikipedia. (n.d.). Retrieved February 19, 2024, from https://en.wikipedia.org/wiki/Essenes*

101. *Siege of Jerusalem (70 CE) - Wikipedia. (n.d.). Retrieved February 19, 2024, from https://en.wikipedia.org/wiki/Siege_of_Jerusalem_(70_CE)*

102. *Ibid*

103. *Ibid*

104. *What to Know About Jerusalem's Temple Mount and the Status Quo Agreement | AJC. (n.d.). Retrieved February 19, 2024, from https://www.ajc.org/news/what-to-know-about-jerusalems-temple-mount-and-the-status-quo-agreement*

105. *Jerusalem in the Qur'ān on JSTOR. (n.d.). Retrieved February 19, 2024, from https://www.jstor.org/stable/826193*

106. *Zoonosis - Wikipedia. (n.d.). Retrieved February 19, 2024, from https://en.wikipedia.org/wiki/Zoonosis*

107. *Ibid*

108. *How Humanity Unleashed a Flood of New Diseases - The New York Times. (n.d.). Retrieved February 19, 2024, from https://www.nytimes.com/2020/06/17/magazine/animal-disease-covid.html*

109. *Taylor, M. W. (2014). Introduction: A Short History of Virology. Viruses and Man: A History of Interactions, 1. https://doi.org/10.1007/978-3-319-07758-1_1*

110. *Gain-of-function research - Wikipedia. (n.d.). Retrieved February 19, 2024, from https://en.wikipedia.org/wiki/Gain-of-function_research*

111. *Cohen, A., Robenshtok, E., Rotman, E., & Sagi, R. (2003). The history of biological warfare. EMBO Reports, 4(Suppl 1), S47. https://doi.org/10.1038/SJ.EMBOR.EMBOR849*

112. *Ibid*

113. *Ibid*

114. *Siege of Jerusalem (70 CE) - Wikipedia. (n.d.). Retrieved February 19, 2024, from https://en.wikipedia.org/wiki/Siege_of_Jerusalem_(70_CE)*

115. *Ibid*

116. *Ancient Mesopotamian Gods and Goddesses - Inana/Ištar (goddess). (n.d.). Retrieved February 19, 2024, from https://oracc.museum.upenn.edu/amgg/listofdeities/inanaitar/*

117. *Papal States - Wikipedia. (n.d.). Retrieved February 19, 2024, from https://en.wikipedia.org/wiki/Papal_States*

118. *Veneration of Mary in the Catholic Church - Wikipedia. (n.d.). Retrieved February 19, 2024, from https://en.wikipedia.org/wiki/Veneration_of_Mary_in_the_Catholic_Church*

119. *Ibid*

120. *Ibid*

121. *Ibid*

122. *Ibid*

123. *McNeill, W. H. (1998). Plagues and Peoples (3rd Edition). Anchor Books, a division of Random House. Inc.*

124. *Martin Luther - Wikipedia. (n.d.). Retrieved February 19, 2024, from https://en.wikipedia.org/wiki/Martin_Luther*

125. *Printing press - Wikipedia. (n.d.). Retrieved February 19, 2024, from https://en.wikipedia.org/wiki/Printing_press*

126. *Gutenberg Bible - Wikipedia. (n.d.). Retrieved February 19, 2024, from* *https://en.wikipedia.org/wiki/Gutenberg_Bible*

127. *Vatican City - Wikipedia. (n.d.). Retrieved February 19, 2024, from* *https://en.wikipedia.org/wiki/Vatican_City*

128. *Karl Marx - Wikipedia. (n.d.). Retrieved February 19, 2024, from* *https://en.wikipedia.org/wiki/Karl_Marx*

129. *Marx–Engels–Lenin Institute - Wikipedia. (n.d.). Retrieved February 19, 2024, from* *https://en.wikipedia.org/wiki/Marx%E2%80%93Engels%E2%80%93Lenin_Institute*

130. *Kengor, P. (2020). The Devil and Karl Marx. TAN Books.*

131. *Pillsbury, M. (2015). The Hundred Year Marathon. eBook.*

132. *Chinese Marxist philosophy - Wikipedia. (n.d.). Retrieved February 19, 2024, from* *https://en.wikipedia.org/wiki/Chinese_Marxist_philosophy*

133. *Russo-Polish War | History, Facts, & Significance | Britannica. (n.d.). Retrieved February 19, 2024, from* *https://www.britannica.com/event/Russo-Polish-War-1919-1920*

134. *League of Nations - Wikipedia. (n.d.). Retrieved February 19, 2024, from* *https://en.wikipedia.org/wiki/League_of_Nations*

135. *Ibid*

136. *Balfour Declaration - Wikipedia. (n.d.). Retrieved February 19, 2024, from* *https://en.wikipedia.org/wiki/Balfour_Declaration*

137. *Ibid*

138. *Republic of China (1912–1949) - Wikipedia. (n.d.). Retrieved February 19, 2024, from* *https://en.wikipedia.org/wiki/Republic_of_China_(1912%E2%80%931949)*

139. *Ibid*

140. *Democracy in Japan | Chatham House – International Affairs Think Tank. (n.d.). Retrieved February 19, 2024, from* *https://www.chathamhouse.org/2022/09/democracy-japan*

141. *Republic of China (1912–1949) - Wikipedia. (n.d.). Retrieved February 19, 2024, from* *https://en.wikipedia.org/wiki/Republic_of_China_(1912%E2%80%931949)*

142. *U.S. Relations With Taiwan - United States Department of State. (n.d.). Retrieved February 19, 2024, from https://www.state.gov/u-s-relations-with-taiwan/*

143. *1914 - Wikipedia. (n.d.). Retrieved February 19, 2024, from https://en.wikipedia.org/wiki/1914*

144. *Timeline (1914 - 1921) | A World at War | Articles and Essays | Stars and Stripes: The American Soldiers' Newspaper of World War I, 1918-1919 | Digital Collections | Library of Congress. (n.d.). Library of Congress, Washington, D.C. 20540 USA.*

145. *19th Amendment: A Timeline of the Fight for All Women's Right to Vote | HISTORY. (n.d.). Retrieved February 19, 2024, from https://www.history.com/news/19th-amendment-women-vote-timeline*

146. *Dust Bowl - Wikipedia. (n.d.). Retrieved February 18, 2024, from https://en.wikipedia.org/wiki/Dust_Bowl*

147. *Oil gluts, Great Depression style. (n.d.). Retrieved February 19, 2024, from https://www.economist.com/news/2014/12/30/oil-gluts-great-depression-style*

148. *Prohibition in the United States - Wikipedia. (n.d.). Retrieved February 19, 2024, from https://en.wikipedia.org/wiki/Prohibition_in_the_United_States*

149. *The true death toll of COVID-19: estimating global excess mortality. (n.d.). Retrieved February 19, 2024, from https://www.who.int/data/stories/the-true-death-toll-of-covid-19-estimating-global-excess-mortality*

150. *Types of Influenza Viruses | CDC. (n.d.). Retrieved February 19, 2024, from https://www.cdc.gov/flu/about/viruses/types.htm*

151. *Influenza - Wikipedia. (n.d.). Retrieved February 19, 2024, from https://en.wikipedia.org/wiki/Influenza*

152. *Spanish flu - Wikipedia. (n.d.). Retrieved February 19, 2024, from https://en.wikipedia.org/wiki/Spanish_flu*

153. *Essential Events Between 1900 and 1945 | World101. (n.d.). Retrieved February 19, 2024, from https://world101.cfr.org/contemporary-history/world-war/essential-events-between-1900-and-1945*

154. *Dietrich Bonhoeffer | Holocaust Encyclopedia. (n.d.). Retrieved February 19, 2024, from https://encyclopedia.ushmm.org/content/en/article/dietrich-bonhoeffer*

155. *Ibid*

156. *Documenting Numbers of Victims of the Holocaust and Nazi Persecution | Holocaust Encyclopedia. (n.d.). Retrieved February 19, 2024, from https://encyclopedia.ushmm.org/content/en/article/documenting-numbers-of-victims-of-the-holocaust-and-nazi-persecution*

157. *Horn, T. (2019). The Wormwood Prophecy. Charisma House.*

158. *Bulls and Bears: Tales of the Zoo: The 10 worst stock market crashes in U.S. History. (n.d.). Retrieved May 10, 2024, from https://stocktaleslot.blogspot.com/2006/10/10-worst-stock-market-crashes-in-us.html*